D1080518

THE
EVERYTHING
Dog Breed Guides

A S THE OWNER of a particular type of dog—or someone who is thinking about adopting one—you probably have some questions about that dog breed that can't be answered anywhere else. In particular, you want to know what breed-specific health issues and behavioral traits might arise as you plan for the future with your beloved canine family member.

The **EVERYTHING** dog breed guides give you clear-cut answers to all your pressing questions. These authoritative books give you all you need to know about identifying common characteristics; choosing the right puppy or adult dog; coping with personality quirks; instilling obedience; and raising your pet in a healthy, positive environment.

The dog breed guides are an extension of the bestselling **EVERYTHING** series. These authoritative, family-friendly books are specially designed to be one-stop guides for anyone looking to explore a specific breed in depth.

EVERYTHING

YOU NEED TO KNOW ABOUT...

Golden Retrievers

Dear Reader,

Golden Retrievers have been part of our lives now for more than a decade and we will never be without them. They are soulful and willing companions capable of learning anything you take the time to teach them. Golden Retrievers have a wonderful sense of humor, a knack for bringing joy wherever they go, and are natural healers of the soul.

The Golden Retriever does not come without vices, but if you are willing to exercise and train them, they make the most wonderful companions. In our years of training and raising dogs as working companions and family pets we have never seen a more willing, more forgiving breed than the Golden Retriever.

We hope that you will find great information on the pages that follow to help you maximize the potential of your great dog. From family pet to search-and-rescue dog, Goldens are the ultimate versatile companion. As you begin your journey into the ownership of a Golden Retriever, we hope that you enjoy each moment you are together. You will never forget the love that this dog will bring to your life.

EVERYTHING

YOU NEED TO KNOW ABOUT...

Golden Retrievers

**GERILYN J. BIELAKIEWICZ AND
PAUL S. BIELAKIEWICZ**

David and Charles

Dedication:
To Sam, my wonder dog–you did it all with style!

A DAVID & CHARLES BOOK
Updates and amendments copyright © David & Charles Limited 2006
Copyright © 2004 F+W Publications Inc.

David & Charles is an F+W Publications Inc. company
4700 East Galbraith Road
Cincinnati, OH 45236

First published in the UK in 2006
First published in the USA as The Everything® Golden Retriever Book,
by Adams Media in 2004

All rights reserved. No part of this publication may be reproduced,
stored in a retrieval system, or transmitted, in any form or by any
means, electronic or mechanical, by photocopying, recording
or otherwise, without prior permission in writing
from the publisher.

A catalogue record for this book is available from the British Library.

ISBN-13: 978-0-7153-2494-3 paperback
ISBN-10: 0-7153-2494-2 paperback

Printed in Great Britain by CPI Bath
for David & Charles
Brunel House   Newton Abbot   Devon

Visit our website at www.davidandcharles.co.uk

David & Charles books are available from all good bookshops;
alternatively you can contact our Orderline on 0870 9908222 or
write to us at FREEPOST EX2 110, D&C Direct, Newton Abbot,
TQ12 4ZZ (no stamp required UK only).

Everything You Need to Know About Golden Retrievers is intended as a reference
book only. While author and publisher have made every attempt
to offer accurate and reliable information to the best of their
knowledge and belief, it is presented without any guarantee.
The author and publisher therefore disclaim any liability incurred
in connection with the information contained in this book.

BREED SPECIFICATIONS

Height:
Males 23–24 inches; females 21½–22½ inches.

Weight:
Males 65–75 pounds; females 55–65 pounds.

Head:
Skull should be broad without prominence of the occipital bone (that is, the bump at the back of the skull, between the ears) and in good proportion to the rest of the body.

Ears:
The ear should be fairly short and set just above and behind the eye. When brought forward, the tip of the ear should just cover the eye.

Feet:
Should be well knuckled and compact.

Tail:
Should follow the line of the back. The tip should not reach below the hock.

Coat:
Colors in shades of cream to gold.

Topline:
The back from the shoulders to the tail should be level.

Movement:
Steady, smooth and straight, without bounce.

Temperament:
Friendly and outgoing toward people and dogs. In normal, everyday conditions, should be neither timid nor shy, and should show no hostility or aggression to other dogs.

Acknowledgments

I would like to thank my husband Paul, my coauthor, researcher, and friend. If not for your help, this project may never have come to be. To my mom for watching our sons, ages two and three, while we wrote. What would we do without your help? To our dogs, who have been the inspiration for all our work thus far. To Sam, who taught us patience and made us better dog trainers. To Reggae, who made it look easy and makes us look good. To Stryker, for keeping us humble and never letting us forget to have a sense of humor. To all of our clients, volunteers, and friends, who entrusted us to teach them how to train their dogs. I hope we gave you a glimpse of what a wonderful ride this can be. Special thanks to the following people for their time and knowledge in helping us gather the information for this book:

Kathy Berube
Deirdre Doyle
Linda Hume
Donna Tagg
Suzanne Warren

• • •

Contents

INTRODUCTION . . . . **xiii**

CHAPTER 1: Is a Golden the Dog for You? . . . **1**
Origins of the Breed 1
Breed Characteristics 2
Importance of Socialization 7
Clear Rules and Boundaries 8
Training: Gently Does It 10
A Dog for Any Job 11
Exercise 12
Regular Grooming 13

CHAPTER 2: Finding the Perfect Puppy . . . **15**
Finding a Good Breeder 15
Breeder Responsibilities 18
Breeder Contracts 21
Rescue and Shelter Groups 22
The Responsible Owner-to-Be 23
Early Socialization 24
Early Housebreaking 25

**CHAPTER 3: Bringing Home Your
          New Puppy** **27**
The First Night at Home 27
Housebreaking 101 28
Using a Crate in Training 32
When Mom's Away, Puppies Will Play 33
Stopping Destructive Chewing 35
Socializing Golden Retriever Puppies 36
Food Basics 39

CHAPTER 4: Bringing Home an Adult Dog . . 41

Adopting an Adult Golden Retriever 41
The First Night at Home 42
Introducing Your Adult Dog to a Crate 43
Developing a Schedule 45
Housebreaking an Adult Golden 46
Bonding with Your New Dog 47
Feeding Basics 49
Social Butterfly or Social Outcast? 50

CHAPTER 5: Developing Social Skills 53

Socialization Is Important 53
The Socialization Window 54
Nature Versus Nurture 55
Human Socialization 56
Preventing Resource Guarding 58
Taming the Chewing Instinct 60
Dog-to-Dog Socialization 62
Getting Through the Fear Period 64

CHAPTER 6: Basic Manners 67

Training by Positive Reinforcement 67
The Clicker Training Method 69
Clicker Training Basics 71
Teaching Your Golden to Sit 74
Teaching Your Dog to Stay 75
Teaching the Down Command 76
Teaching Him to Come When Called 77
Teaching Your Golden to Leave It 79
Teaching Him to Walk Without Pulling 79

CHAPTER 7: A Golden's Life Skills 83

The Targeting Tool 83
Alone Time 85
Going to the Groomer 87
Visiting the Veterinarian 87
Teaching Your Golden to Enjoy Being Touched 89
Walking on Slippery Floors 92
Mastering Stairs 94

CHAPTER 8: Fears and Phobias 97

Why Goldens Get Scared 97
Fear Interferes with Learning 99
Helping Your Fearful Golden 99
Negotiating Scary Situations 101
Fear of New People 102
Fear of Other Dogs 103
Fear of Riding in the Car 104
Thunderstorm Phobias 105
Getting Professional Help 106

CHAPTER 9: Common Behavior Problems . . 109

Leadership Basics 109
Problems and Solutions 112
The Joy of Digging 114
Jumping for Joy 115
Using a Head Collar to Train 117
Pulling While on Leash 119
Snooping, Scavenging, and Stealing 119

CHAPTER 10: Creating a Super Learner . . 121

What Is a Super Learner? 121
Building a Training Relationship 123
Organization and Consistency 124
Creative Thinking Skills for Dogs 126
The Art and Science of Shaping 127
Shaping Project: 101 Things to Do with a Box 130
Putting Behavior on Cue 132

CHAPTER 11: Teaching Your Golden
to Retrieve 135

Natural Abilities 135
Retrieving Birds for Fieldwork 139
Teaching Tricks That Involve Retrieving 140
"Go Get Your Leash" 142
"Go Get the Phone" 142
"Find My Keys" 143
"Pull Off My Socks" 144

CHAPTER 12: Choosing the Right Diet . . . 145

A Quality Diet 145
What's in Dog Food? 147
Identifying High-Quality Foods 150
Ingredients to Avoid 151
Natural Diets 152
Dietary Supplements 155
How Much Should I Feed My Golden? 156

CHAPTER 13: Visiting the Veterinarian . . . 159

Searching for the Right Vet 159
Preparation for a Good Experience 161
Good Health Maintenance Basics 162
Spaying and Neutering 165
Vaccination Schedules 166

CHAPTER 14: Common Health Problems . . 171

Hot Spots and Skin Issues 171
Digestive Problems 173
Genetic Screening 174
Eye Problems 175
Hip Dysplasia 178
Elbow Dysplasia 180
Epilepsy 181
Subvalvular Aortic Stenosis (SAS) 182
Hypothyroidism 183
Cancer 183

CHAPTER 15: Alternative Medicine 185

A Holistic View 185
How Can It Help? 188
Finding a Qualified Holistic Veterinarian 189
Acupuncture 189
Chiropractic Therapy 191
Homeopathy 194
Bach's Flower Essences 196

CHAPTER 16: Goldens as Athletes 199

Keeping Fit and Staying Lean 199
Flyball Competition 200
Competition Obedience 202
The Sport of Agility 205
Tracking for Sport 209
Rally Obedience 210

CHAPTER 17: The Golden Retriever as Therapist 213

What Is a Therapy Dog? 213
Getting Certified 214
Training a Therapy Dog 217
Basic Obedience Skills 218
Social Skills for Therapy Work 220
Grooming and Appearance 221
The Visiting Experience 222

CHAPTER 18: Teaching Tricks 225

Natural-Born Performers 225
Elements of a Great Trick 226
Skills Needed for Trick Training 227
Kindergarten Tricks 228
First-Grade Tricks 231
Junior-High Level Tricks 235

CHAPTER 19: Golden Retriever Grooming Basics 239

Training for Grooming 239
Basic Grooming Equipment 242
Trimming Nails 245
Trimming Feet 246
Protecting Foot Pads 246
Cleaning Teeth 247
Cleaning and Trimming Ears 247
Brushing Basics 248
Giving Your Golden Retriever a Bath 250
Professional Grooming 251

CHAPTER 20: Goldens at Work 253

Beauty and Brains 253
Hunting Partners 256
Search-and-Rescue Goldens 260
Assistance Dogs 263
Work Dogs Work 265

APPENDIX A: Bibliography 267

APPENDIX B: Resources 271

INDEX 279

Introduction

▶ THE GOLDEN RETRIEVER is among the nation's most popular breed of dog—and with good reason. The typical Golden is sweet and friendly, ready to accompany you on the most mundane task or the most exciting adventure. A Golden can be the dog of your dreams, but only if you choose him carefully and are willing to exercise and train him. Goldens are not born trained and well mannered—quite the opposite, they come at life full-throttle and full of a puppy exuberance that is also part of their appeal. Golden Retrievers are not for everyone—they are large dogs that are active and mischievous and if left to their own devices will quite happily eat the couch in your absence and then knock you down in greeting when you arrive home.

In the coming pages, we hope to give you an accurate view of what life with a Golden Retriever is all about. We hope that our love for this breed doesn't sugarcoat them too much—they are amazingly lovable but they are a lot of work. In the pages that follow, you will learn how to bring a Golden Retriever successfully into your life. We hope to help your Golden find his place within your family and to keep him from getting too pushy or needy. You will learn about training and the importance of teaching your Golden the basics of living with humans. We can't emphasize enough how important it is to socialize a puppy and bring him to meet and play with all kinds of other dogs and people—it is so important to a Golden's healthy social development.

This book also gives you the basic tools you need to research this popular breed. Finding a breeder who is both conscientious and knowledgeable is crucial and can save you so much time in the long run. Choosing the right puppy for your family is another must—not all Goldens are the same. Though they share some general characteristics, their temperaments do vary. You want to choose a dog that is a match for your activity level and personality. A high-energy field dog would not be a great match for a sedentary couch potato who is looking for a television buddy.

The Golden Retriever is among the most versatile of dogs. He is a friend and companion first, but he also excels at hunting, search and rescue, competition obedience, agility, tracking, and service or therapy work. The Golden can be taught to do any activity within his physical ability, and he excels at almost any dog sport you might care to try.

Proper exercise and diet are essential to the Golden's long and healthy life. Golden Retrievers are active dogs that should be fed moderately and kept lean. If given the chance, a Golden may not be able to regulate food intake on his own. With those soulful eyes and that pushy nature, Golden Retrievers are capable of cajoling their guardians into overfeeding and underexercising them. An overweight Golden is prone to many health problems, among them diabetes and torn ligaments. Kept lean, the Golden will stay active and vital well into his senior years.

As the proud new owner of a Golden Retriever, you should take the time to research your dog's veterinary needs and your options in meeting them. It's up to you to decide on things like how often your dog gets vaccinated, the components and quality of his diet, and whether you want to use alternative therapies such as herbal and homeopathic remedies. Take the time to educate yourself. Your search for the right treatment is essential to keeping your dog vital well into old age. Options like acupuncture or chiropractic care may help you improve the quality of your dog's life and perhaps prolong it.

Owning a Golden Retriever is life at its best. They are the sweetest, most fun-loving, comic dogs around. Do your homework on the breed and breeders. Then commit yourself to training, socializing, and providing plenty of exercise, and your Golden will be the companion of a lifetime. Enjoy! ⒠

Is a Golden the Dog for You?

THE GOLDEN RETRIEVER is one of the most popular dogs in the country. According to the American Kennel Club (AKC), the Golden is second only to the Labrador Retriever in popularity. The Golden's personality and temperament fits nicely into many families, but he is not born trained. Most of the Golden Retriever's ability to become a wonderful family dog is a result of lots of socialization and training, not a miracle of nature. Make sure you are ready for this breed's boundless energy and enthusiasm for life.

Origins of the Breed

The origin of the Golden Retriever is not completely clear, but most experts agree that the ancestor of the Golden was a hunting companion bred mainly for its ability to retrieve game. Some experts think that the Golden descended from Water Spaniels, the original retrieving dog used by hunters to retrieve downed duck, goose, and pheasant. Later records show that the early Golden Retriever descended from the Flat-Coated Retriever, originating from the liver-colored variety. The Wavy-Coated Retriever (now know as the Flat-Coated Retriever) and the Labrador Retriever have a closely interwoven history, and it is believed that the Golden Retriever was derived from these breeds. There is also a made-up story of the

Golden Retriever being descendants of a troop of Russian circus dogs, which is entirely fictional.

The modern Golden Retriever was first registered as a liver-colored Flat-Coated Retriever, and it was not until the 1920s that it came to be called a Golden or Yellow Retriever. The person most influential in creating the Golden Retriever was the First Lord Tweedmouth (Dudley Marjoriebanks), who was fascinated with creating the ultimate hunting companion. Crosses to other breeds were commonly done as an attempt to improve the abilities of the breed. There are records showing that there were outcrosses made to a light-colored (yellow) Bloodhound and later to an Irish Setter. The crosses to these and other dogs were used to improve the Golden's ability to track as well as to influence the coat texture and color, which ranged from light cream-colored to a deep red.

Most of the Golden's ancestors can be traced back to England and were probably influenced by the breeds commonly used for hunting. Many of Lord Tweedmouth's dogs were given as gifts to friends and relatives who were interested in their hunting ability and some of these people went on to breed and develop their own lines.

Breed Characteristics

The Golden Retriever was originally bred to retrieve ducks, pheasants, and other upland game. When viewing a Golden Retriever as a companion, it is important to consider the dog's structure as it relates to his overall form and function. Though you may purchase a Golden strictly as a family pet and never think of your showing him in the conformation ring, your dog's overall makeup is a crucial element in your enjoyment of him as a family pet. A healthy Golden's general conformation is powerful and solid. He moves smoothly without clumsiness, which is made possible by the fact that he's slightly longer than he is tall. Having the correct conformation is necessary for the endurance and working ability he'll need to carry out any function. The proportion of the dog's body, the length of his back and legs, the levelness of his topline: These are all important factors in how your dog moves. Although you may have no aspirations to breed or show your dog, if he isn't put together well, he is not going to be a healthy, active dog that can enjoy a long life.

 **Question?**

> **What do I need to know about conformation to choose a puppy?**
> A reputable breeder should be able to point out a puppy's strengths and weaknesses. But the most important thing to remember when selecting a Golden puppy is that no one feature is more important than another—the overall balance of all the parts put together is what makes a sound dog.

70 × 0.6   70 = 105-7
7 × 6 = 42

The AKC Breed Standard

The breed standard as published by the American Kennel Club states the correct conformation of the Golden Retriever as:

- **Height:** Males 23–24", females 21½"–22½"
- **Weight:** Males 65–75 lbs., females 55–65 lbs.
- **Head:** Skull should be broad without prominence of the occipital bone and in good proportion to the rest of the body
- **Ears:** The ear should be fairly short and set just above and behind the eye the tip of which just covers the eye when brought forward
- **Feet:** Should be well knuckled and compact
- **Tail:** Should follow the line of the back and the tip should not reach below the hock
- **Coat:** Colors in shades of cream to gold
- **Topline:** The back from the shoulders to the tail should be level
- **Movement:** Steady, smooth, and straight, without bounce
- **Temperament:** Friendly and outgoing toward people and dogs

The Golden Retriever's temperament is by far his greatest quality. Their gentleness and sweetness is what has drawn so many people to the breed. A Golden Retriever should be confident and outgoing, friendly with people, including strangers and children, and should get along well with other dogs and animals (including cats). Any shyness or aggression is not in keeping with Golden Retriever character and should be avoided at all costs when considering a puppy.

Golden Retriever Personality and Temperament

The ideal Golden Retriever is an ambassador for people and other dogs. If properly trained and socialized, the Golden will get along with just about anyone. This is a dog that is even-tempered, easy to train, and willing to do whatever you want. If socialized properly, the Golden gets along with children, strangers, the elderly, other dogs, cats, and pets. A Golden can have a high energy level and may need lots of regular exercise. A walk around the block is not going to do it for this breed (though he will enjoy meeting the neighbors and seeing the sights).

 Fact

Without proper training, socialization, and exercise your Golden Retriever will not realize its potential as a wonderful family member and great companion. The more exercise and mental stimulation a Golden gets, the happier its family will be. Aim to give your Golden at least two forty-five-minute exercise sessions per day.

Goldens love to have a job to do and excel at dog sports like agility, obedience, and hunting trials. These dogs also have an amazing ability to perform and interact with people, and quickly become a favorite wherever you go. If you are a shy or reclusive person, don't get a Golden! These dogs make friends wherever they go; strangers will cross the street just to say hello to your beautiful dog.

Golden Retrievers are on the whole extroverts, eternally happy, and ready to accompany you on whatever adventure is next. This is the favorite breed of many therapy dog programs in nursing homes, hospitals, and schools. The Golden is a master at working a crowd and will make his rounds to everyone while making each person feel like he or she is the most important person in the room.

 **Essential**

> Golden Retrievers need to be socialized to all kinds of people, dogs, and other animals. They need to go everywhere and see everything, or they will not be good family companions.

The Perfect Family Pet

EVERYONE

The Golden Retriever can be the perfect family dog. With his gentle nature, great adaptability, and unlimited sense of fun, the Golden revels in the chaos of family life. This isn't a situation that develops on its own, however; each (family) needs to teach their Golden how to live with them, what the rules are, and socialize their puppies to each facet of their lives. With the proper training, your Golden will spend hours playing with the family in the yard, accompanying the family on vacations and outings, and taking part in every holiday. Here is what a Golden Retriever puppy needs to be taught to become a treasured member of the family:

- Greet family members and visitors by sitting politely for petting.
- Wait at all open doors for the signal to go through.
- Lie down under the table or outside the room during meals.
- Tolerate children of all ages and sizes and be friendly to strangers.

- Be proficient in basic obedience: sit, down, stay, leave it, come, and walk on a loose leash.
- Stay alone in the house without getting into trouble.
- Get along with other dogs of all shapes and sizes.

◀ A fifteen-week-old female puppy.

Golden Retrievers and Kids

If ever a dog was made for kids, it would have to be the Golden Retriever. Still, both the dog and the kids need to be taught how to treat one another so no one gets hurt or frightened in the process of becoming best friends. Golden Retrievers are large dogs that are capable of knocking over a young child or accidentally scratching him in play. Golden puppies can also be very "mouthy," nipping and biting young children as though they were littermates.

The best way to ensure that your child and Golden end up being the best of friends is to supervise their contact and to maintain limits with both child and dog. Children are not capable of taking full responsibility for a dog's care, but they can help take care of them with supervision and coaching. Children under four will feel more competitive with the dog than cooperative, and they may act up to make sure they get their full share of the attention at your house. If you have children this young, it is advisable to supervise all interactions. Give your child small jobs, like throwing a ball or giving the dog a cookie on a flat outstretched hand. If your child is older, he or she can help with feeding, walking, and even training.

 **Fact**

All dogs have the potential to bite under the right set of circumstances. It is essential to the development of a healthy relationship between your dog and your children that you supervise all interactions closely. Don't allow rough play or mistreatment. Make sure your puppy gets private rest time, in a crate, several times a day for the safety and sanity of all involved.

Importance of Socialization

Puppies must be socialized. For companion dogs of all breeds, socialization is vitally important. A dog that is poorly socialized will exhibit all kinds of behavior problems throughout life. It's up to the breeder and the owner to teach new pups and adult dogs that ancestry aside, they really belong to human society.

How do you socialize a puppy? You expose him, as much as possible, to the sight, smell, sound, and feel of human beings and other dogs. Breeders should make sure litters are born inside their homes, so that puppies come into the world in the heart of the home. From day one, the pups are handled, and by the time their eyes are open they are already familiar with human beings.

Clear Rules and Boundaries

If there is one thing that has been grossly underestimated about the Golden Retriever, it is the breed's intelligence and propensity for mischief. These are intelligent working dogs with a high energy level and a need to work.

 Alert!

Though Golden Retrievers are known for their sweet nature, many Goldens can be pushy with their families. The way to ensure that your dog doesn't bite to get his way is to establish yourself as leader and the giver of all good things. This is accomplished by having house rules that are not flexible until the dog is fully trained and there are no behavior problems.

If you lock your Golden Retriever in the house all day and do not provide training or appropriate outlets for exercise, your lovable, intelligent Golden will develop behavior problems. As sweet as they are, Golden Retrievers need limits, as well as boundaries and house rules. If you allow your Golden to be pushy and demanding, you will have behavior problems at some point. These may manifest themselves in not coming back when he is called, being mouthy and out of control when he doesn't want to do something, and even biting to get his way.

To prevent behavior problems and make it easier to live with your Golden, you need to provide a firm leadership structure and stick to it. Leadership is not about dominating your dog, forcing him to do things, or physically correcting him. If you behave this way with any dog, you are bound to cause more problems than you cure. Leadership is about controlling resources and setting limits. It is never achieved through violence or harsh corrections. To be a leader to your Golden, you need to:

- Establish house rules.
- Insist that the dog stay off beds or furniture until he is an adult and does not exhibit any behavior problems.
- Ask your dog to do something before you give him anything. Sit for supper, for instance.
- Limit his freedom via a crate and baby gates while you are away.
- Teach him to wait until released at all doorways and stairways.
- Restrict privileges until he has earned them by his good behavior.
- Ignore pushy bids for attention via nudging, pawing, or barking.
- Give attention to him on your own terms—for example, call your Golden to you for petting.
- Teach him basic obedience commands: sit, down, stay, come, heel, and leave it.
- Stop rough play in its tracks: If a game gets too rough, stop playing immediately.
- Don't allow off-leash freedom if he doesn't come reliably.

By setting limits on your dog's freedom, requiring that he do something before he gets anything, being first and higher, and having everything be your idea, you will teach your Golden that all good things come from you. Being your dog's leader means that he has someone to count on to help him stay safe and provide for all of his basic needs. Dogs are not democratic. They would really rather that someone else took charge so they could concentrate on being dogs and having fun. By learning how to control resources (that is, the things your dog wants access to), you will have the ability to train your dog to pay attention to you regardless of what's happening in the environment.

Training: Gently Does It

The Golden Retriever is perhaps the most willing of breeds to do your bidding. That isn't to say that some Goldens aren't more challenging to train than others, but in general a Golden is perfectly willing to do what you want if he understands the job at hand.

▲ Goldens compete well in competition obedience. This seven-year-old male performs a retrieve over the panel jump.

Rough training methods—that is, those involving harsh correction—have no place in the raising of a young Golden. Techniques involving positive reinforcement are much more effective. In general, we highly recommend clicker training for all breeds of dogs, but the Golden is an outright master of this technique. Training with a clicker and treats involves teaching your dog that the sound of the click means a food reward is coming, and this marker signal is used to help the dog identify which behaviors are rewardable. Young and old, people with disabilities, and people who have never trained a dog before can excel at this method. Best of all, there is no harm done to the dogs. (See Chapter 6 for more information on clicker training.)

As your dog's trainer, it is up to you to find the very best training method possible for your dog. Do your research, observe different group classes, and choose the class where the dogs and the people seem the happiest.

A Dog for Any Job

The popularity of the breed has led people to assume that the Golden Retriever is a house dog, meaning he lays around all day until his family shows up. Nothing could be further from the truth! The Golden Retriever is a sporting dog, bred to hunt all day with his handler. He has enough energy and stamina to run all day in all kinds of weather. The same traits that make him a great hunting dog and companion help him excel in almost any other pursuit as well. Goldens love putting their sharp minds and endless energy to work, and work is anything their people ask them to do. The best home for a Golden is one in which he gets to exercise at least some of his basic drives and instincts.

 Fact

The Golden Retriever is an ideal candidate for many different kinds of work. Different dogs have different strengths. Energy level, endurance, and maturity should be taken into consideration when choosing a dog for a particular type of work (or vice versa). Your breeder can help determine what jobs your puppy is best suited for. Other resources to consult include an experienced professional dog trainer.

The Golden Retriever is the breed of choice for many service dog organizations, including those that train therapy dogs. The Golden also enjoys regular employment with customs agents, search-and-rescue teams, and bomb and arson squads. Of all the occupations available, Goldens are happiest being with people. Not all Golden Retrievers in their youth and exuberance may be suitable for therapy work, however, but most mellow with time and make wonderful therapy dogs for those in nursing homes, hospitals, and rehabilitation centers. Think seriously about what outlet you are going to provide for your Golden's boundless energy and enthusiasm for life.

Dog sports are another possible avenue of employment for your Golden. There are many to choose from, and Goldens happen to excel at most. These include agility, competition obedience, tracking, field trials, musical freestyle (dancing with your dog!), and rally obedience. Perhaps you prefer the spotlight or the silver screen. Golden Retrievers appear very commonly on television and in the movies, thanks to their calm temperaments and willingness to learn new things.

Exercise

Most people do not realize just how much exercise active dogs require, and the Golden is no exception. Golden Retrievers require a minimum of two forty-five-minute runs a day, preferably with other dogs. This is not a breed you can exercise to exhaustion indoors or with a walk around the block. Goldens need to move, whether that means jogging by your side, swimming, running off-leash, or playing with other dogs. The goal is to keep them going until they are too pooped for mischief.

 **Essential**

If you cannot exercise your Golden Retriever enough, you need to find someone else to do it for you. Dog walkers and doggie day-care services are popping up around the country. For a fee, they can help provide the exercise your Golden needs to be a good dog.

Getting your Golden Retriever out on a regular basis will enable your dog to have appropriate outlets for his energy and save you tons of time in solving behavior problems. Among the favorite ways to exercise Golden Retrievers are swimming, playing fetch, jogging, doggie playgroups, or playing hide-and-seek with your family on a rainy day. Regardless of the method, all Goldens need outlets for their boundless energy, and the more exercise they get, the easier they are to live with.

Regular Grooming

Your Golden needs to be regularly groomed. Whether you learn to do it yourself or pay someone to do it professionally, the Golden Retriever's coat requires frequent brushing and occasional bathing. Most Goldens have full, medium-to-long coats that mat easily if not brushed every week.

The easiest time to start teaching your Golden Retriever to like being groomed is while he is still a puppy. Getting him used to being brushed, having his ears cleaned, having his nails trimmed, and being bathed is best accomplished by breaking the tasks down into tiny steps. This way, you get your dog used to each aspect of each procedure slowly and as positively as possible. (See Chapter 19 for grooming basics.)

Though spring and fall may find you with more hair on your grooming brush (and your slacks), there is no particular season in which Goldens shed. Frequent brushing during this time can help keep the volume of hair in your home to a minimum, but dog hair will be part of your everyday if you live with a Golden. Chapter 19 provides more information on grooming. Ⓔ

BREEDER

→ interest one breed – close attention norms of breed
→ ask puppies through Golden Retriever Club – if anyone has them
→ ask about breeder's philosophy
→ should know lots about breed (open about inheritable diseases)
→ has contract – exactly what expected both parties
→ requires that give puppy back if can no longer look after
→ asks about OUR life and suggests which puppy has best temperament
→ breeder should be strict on conditions for puppy
  - visiting rules: age limit & number of visitors
  - with mother until 4 weeks
  - seperate area pottying & sleeping
  - puppy area well lit & central household
→ stay clear someone claims puppy free genetic defects – cannot make such claim
→ puppy kindergarten classes
→ set up vet appointment
→ puppy proof house

Finding the Perfect Puppy

THE SEARCH FOR the perfect Golden Retriever can be daunting. Being among the top ten most popular breeds makes the choices wider but more risky. When a breed gains in popularity, the quality of the breeding tends to drop. Profit-driven folks capitalize on unsuspecting prospective owners who fail to properly educate themselves about what to look for. Being an educated consumer is the key to finding the dog of your dreams.

Finding a Good Breeder

Golden Retrievers abound in newspaper ads placed by puppy "brokers" who can dupe an unsuspecting buyer into selecting a puppy that has not had the best possible start in life. Reputable breeders stick to one breed and never have so many litters of puppies that they can't keep track of them. These are folks who usually breed dogs as a hobby and are not strictly in business to make a profit. They put an inordinate amount of time into each puppy and puppy buyer, and carefully match their puppies to appropriate homes. A good breeder is well educated about their breed and pays close attention to correct structure and temperament for their breed, even if they do not plan to show their dogs in conformation shows.

Good Breeding Matters

The Golden Retriever breed standard was set forth to offer a guideline for breeders to ensure the healthiest dogs possible. Without a standard, the Golden would be subject to anyone's opinion of what looked good, and eventually we would have many dogs within a "breed" that had few, if any, similarities, and looked nothing alike. The breed standard offers guidance about structure and locomotion, which are keys to having a healthy dog that can run, play, and live as long and trouble-free a life as possible. Without correct structure and loco-motion, Golden Retrievers fall prey to hip and joint problems, lame-ness, injuries, and lack of endurance, all of which lessen the quality of life and enjoyment as a family pet or working companion.

 **Fact**

The Golden Retriever Club of America is the largest national organization and a great starting point for finding a breeder who is truly knowledgeable and caring about the breed. Local Golden Retriever clubs can be found through the Golden Retriever Club of America and may help you locate breeders within your area.

Your best starting points for a reputable breeder are local or national breed clubs, which are made up of Golden Retriever enthu-siasts who care about the character and longevity of the breed. Most Golden clubs offer a breeder referral list with names and numbers of people in your area who currently have puppies. If you contact a breeder who does not currently have puppies, ask him or her to refer you to someone else who might. You are better off finding a Golden puppy through word of mouth at dog shows and through other breeders than through newspaper ads.

Qualities to Look for in a Breeder

Not all reputable breeders are the same. Just because someone comes highly recommended doesn't mean that they necessarily have the perfect puppy for you. Referrals are starting points only, and educating yourself about puppy development, the breed standard, and other details is still important for you to make the best possible decision.

Each breeder has a different philosophy about their breeding program, and it is important to ask him or her what that is and make sure that it matches your expectations. The best breeders are great resources for information about the breed: Not only do they know the basics of their breed's conformation and temperament, but they can talk intelligently about inheritable diseases within the breed and their own lines. No breeder, no matter how long they have been breeding and how experienced they are, should ever make any guarantees about inheritable problems in their puppies. That's not to say that genetic screening for inheritable problems isn't important—it certainly is very important—but it doesn't come with any guarantee.

To find a good breeder, look for:

- Someone who is a resource for you about the breed.
- Someone who is willing to help you find the best dog for your situation and experience level.
- Someone who has an application process to collect detailed information about what you are looking for in a Golden.
- Someone who uses a contract, which carefully spells out what is expected of each party.
- Someone who requires you to give the puppy back to him or her if you can no longer keep it.
- Someone who chooses the puppy for you based on the information you have given him or her.

Remember: The more details you share about your expectations and experience, the better match the breeder will be able to make. All puppies are cute, Goldens especially so, but they vary in temperament, energy level, and ease of trainability. This Golden Retriever is going to be a dog a lot longer than he is a puppy: You want to be sure that the choice you make is one you can live with for the next twelve years or longer!

◀ Two Golden males, ages nine and four.

Breeder Responsibilities

Breeders who have properly educated themselves about the breed can be an excellent resource to you as a consumer, but you must do your part and educate yourself as well. Time is short for breeders who are raising puppies while searching for appropriate homes for them. Before you begin your inquiries, at least get some basic education about Goldens, specifically what is required for housebreaking, crate training, and setting limits. The more you read and learn, the better prepared you will be to ask intelligent questions and find out as much as you can about the particular litter you are interested in.

Living Conditions

The breeder is responsible for setting up an environment that is clean and stimulating for the puppies. The breeder is also responsible for providing the first socialization to people, and he or she will use carefully planned visits to help puppies get to know people. Most breeders have rules about visiting, regarding age limits and how many visitors are allowed in at one time.

 **Alert!**

Though you may object to trusting the breeder to choose the perfect puppy for you, he or she knows the dogs best and is your best resource for figuring out which puppy in the litter is best suited for what you want in a family or working companion.

Golden puppies are usually exclusively with their mother for the first three or four weeks, after which many breeders begin to introduce toys and provide opportunities to explore and experience life. They should also have access to a separate area for pottying and sleeping. The area where the puppies are kept should be well lit and as close to the action of the household as possible. The closer to the action the puppies are, the better they will fit into the average household. Having heard and seen and smelled the wonders of everyday living, they will be better prepared when they are ready to explore the house.

A breeder should never sell a puppy strictly for breeding purposes and should be the puppies' advocate, first and foremost. If she feels a home would be inappropriate for a puppy, she has the right and obligation to refuse to sell the puppy to that home. Don't be disappointed if you have to wait for the right puppy: Raising the right dog to live with you for the next twelve years is well worth the wait.

Health Screening

Golden Retrievers are prone to several health problems for which reputable breeders screen. Genetic health problems can't always be avoided through genetic screening, but breeders can make more informed decisions about which dogs to breed and which to eliminate from the gene pool, based on the level of risk for a certain disease in each dog.

Some of the health screening for Goldens include clearances for hip and elbow dysplasia, thyroid problems, and heart problems. Other considerations may include the longevity of the dogs within a family, the temperament of the dogs, and whether or not there is a history of epilepsy. Buying your puppy from a knowledgeable breeder who truly cares about the health and well-being of his or her dogs does not guarantee you a healthy dog; it is, however, a better risk than buying one from a pet store or newspaper ad.

 Essential

Genetics cannot be controlled. Hip dysplasia, eye problems, heart problems, thyroid problems, and so forth can only be screened against, not ruled out completely. Nature still has a way of showing up and ruining even the best-laid plans.

Paying attention to the health of a dog and its overall physical makeup and temperament allows the breeder to choose which dogs she feels have the best chances of producing healthy puppies. Nature is never completely predictable, and genes can express themselves every once in a while, regardless of how well informed the breeder is or how healthy the dogs appear to be. Steer clear of anyone who guarantees that their dogs are free of genetic defects—this guarantee is not possible to make for a young puppy. Stay in touch with your puppy's breeder: A good breeder will want to know how his or her pups turn out so that she can make changes to her breeding program if necessary to avoid health problems in future breedings.

Breeder Contracts

Most breeders will require you to sign a contract in order to purchase one of their puppies. The contract drawn up by the breeder usually has certain terms or conditions that must be met between the buyer and the breeder. Breeder contracts can vary in their content, but their main purpose is to make sure that the well-being of the puppy is provided for and that the best possible care is maintained throughout the puppy's life.

Don't be offended by having to sign a contract in order to be able to bring your puppy home; in a sense, the contract is a promise that you will take the very best care of this animal. Here are some of the terms a typical contract might contain:

- Limited registration for pets, which means that if you breed your dog, the puppies would not be eligible for AKC registration
- A nonbreeding clause, which ensures that you won't turn around and breed this dog or sell it to someone else who might
- Co-ownership: some breeders may offer a prospective owner the opportunity to help raise a future show or breeding prospect, and maintain co-ownership rights until defined terms have been met
- Lifetime ownership by buyer
- Right of first refusal, meaning if you have to give your dog up, you attempt to give it back to the breeder before anyone else
- Food quality
- Ideal weight
- Spaying or neutering with a minimum or maximum age requirement
- Attendance at training classes
- Specifics on naming, include litter themes or use of the kennel name in AKC registration
- Specifics on veterinary visits, vaccinations, etc.

- Specifics on fencing and housing—most require the dog to live inside with you

The breeder contract has the puppy's best interests in mind and attempts to outline the best possible terms for adequate care and maintenance of the health and well-being of the puppy. Ask questions about the contract before you fall in love with a puppy, and be sure you are willing to comply with the terms. Clarify anything that is unclear or that you don't understand. Most breeders are accommodating if you have their puppy's best interests at heart.

Rescue and Shelter Groups

Golden Retriever rescue groups are operated by breeders and volunteers who love the breed and care about the dogs people give up. Local chapters can be found through your nearby breed club or through the Internet. Oftentimes, a family will not have the time to properly train and take care of a dog. Other times, the owner may have a health problem, be going through a divorce, or have another family situation that makes dog ownership low on their list of priorities. Many good Goldens are given up to shelters and rescue groups in the hopes of being re-homed, and many dedicated people work diligently to ensure that the next home will be a permanent one.

 Fact

Although the dogs given up to rescue or shelters are usually carefully screened for health and temperament problems, many of the dogs given up have never had any formal training and many are undersocialized to other dogs and people.

If you decide to adopt a Golden through a shelter or rescue group, be sure to do your homework and read up on the temperament and energy level of the breed. Many rescues require that potential adopters fill out an application first and then schedule an at-home interview. The purpose of the interview is to determine your lifestyle and whether or not you would make a suitable candidate for adopting one of their rescued dogs. Don't be offended by the thoroughness of this application process: It protects both you and the adopted dog, and tries to make sure that the dogs that the group places stay in their next home for the rest of their lives.

On the flip side, you should be equally as thorough in making sure that the rescue or shelter aims to place dogs that are free from temperament and aggression problems. Undersocialized dogs that are afraid of everything or dogs that are aggressive toward other dogs or people are a nightmare to own. They require constant training and supervision, and they are never socially normal. Be bold about stating what you are looking for and be willing to do your part in making the match a success, and you will get the right dog.

The Responsible Owner-to-Be

As a prospective dog owner, you have a responsibility to educate yourself on the breed, its care, training, and socialization. Start with the appendix at the back of this book for a list of great books to get you started. The better educated you are about the care and training of a dog, the better able you will be to evaluate a breeder and see if she has the Golden Retriever you are looking for.

Research puppy kindergarten classes so that you can enroll your puppy within the first few weeks that you bring him home. Make sure that you have determined what veterinarian you will visit and set up that appointment as well. Learn about the basic veterinary care your puppy needs to receive, as well as socialization and early training needs. You may also want to hire a pet sitter or dog walker to help you take care of your puppy if you work full-time or will be away for periods of time, to help you maintain your puppy's housebreaking schedule.

On the home front, inspecting and puppyproofing your house and yard is essential. Though your puppy won't be given free reign unattended in either place, it is important to consider fencing, gating, and otherwise preventing him from getting into trouble. If you have children or a large family, you may want to plan who will be responsible for what, and designate a job for each person so that your puppy's first few weeks at home run as smoothly as possible. Children should never be expected to have full responsibility of a puppy, of course. An adult should always be available to assist and supervise the care, feeding, and training of this puppy to ensure his best possible start in life.

 **Question?**

What is the best age for children to enjoy raising a puppy?
The ideal age is six or older. Children younger than six tend to still require large amounts of time and care from their parents, and will often view the puppy as competition rather than a companion.

Early Socialization

Before you ever bring your puppy home, the breeder should have provided an environment where it was possible for your puppy to begin his socialization to people and experience life, albeit on a limited basis. Locking puppies in the basement or furnace room until someone purchases them is disastrous to their ability to become great family companions. Dogs need to be socialized to people from the beginning, and they need to be underfoot around the house as much as is reasonable. In this way, they are exposed to the sights and sounds of normal family life: They learn the ins and outs of noises, such as dishwashers, vacuums, traffic, children, television, music, and so forth. Without this early exposure, the puppy will never reach his full potential as an adult.

A lack of early socialization literally retards the dog's development, making it harder for him to adjust to a new environment at a later date. Ian Dunbar, a well-known behaviorist, dog trainer, and veterinarian, recommends that dogs meet 100 people before they are twelve weeks old. Although this is a tall order, breeders should be doing their best to introduce their puppies to a wide range of people as early as possible. Educate yourself on puppy developmental deadlines so that you can ask the breeder appropriate questions.

 **Fact**

Providing stimulation—in the way of toys; things to chew on; and things to climb over, around, and through—is crucial, as these activities stimulate the puppy's brain and fosters the beginnings of problem-solving abilities.

Having adult dogs interact with puppies is also an important part of their development. Adult dogs teach young puppies the rules of being a dog, and give feedback on using their mouths gently. Adult dogs will not tolerate puppies biting their sensitive ears or feet for long without disciplining them (gently) or simply removing themselves from the puppies. This is an important lesson for puppies to learn, since it correlates directly to how much mouthing and biting they will do with you. Learning the rules of living with humans while they are still with their littermates makes your job that much easier when you bring your new puppy home.

Early Housebreaking

The way a breeder raises a litter can make housebreaking your puppy an easy or difficult task, depending upon the circumstances. If puppies are raised in an environment that is kept meticulously clean, and as they mature, a separate potty area within the whelping box is provided and maintained, then housebreaking is easy on the new owner. If, however, the breeder was careless and less than meticulous about cleaning up soiled shavings or newspapers quickly, the job of the new owner will be much more difficult.

Dogs come with an inborn housebreaking mechanism that works in our favor if we don't foster it. Innately, dogs want to sleep in one area and use another area as their toilet. If there is no clear area for toileting, you end up with a dog that bypasses this instinct and goes wherever and sleeps wherever. Though the instinct to eliminate away from the sleeping area is innate, it must be fostered with the proper designation and maintenance of sleeping and potty areas. Dogs raised in cages in pet stores are probably among the hardest to housebreak, since they are used to sleeping and going to the potty in the same area.

Bringing Home Your New Puppy

THERE IS NOTHING QUITE LIKE a Golden Retriever puppy. It may be hard to conceive of now, but this cute little bundle of fluff that you hold in your arms will soon grow into 60 to 75 pounds of big dog. You may find his antics adorable now, but they'll be barely tolerable when he's big and strong enough to knock you flat. Remember that everything you do now with socialization, training, and setting limits will help your sweet little Golden puppy grow up to be a superior adult dog.

The First Night at Home

Being away from his mom and littermates for the first time can be a stressful time for a puppy, and his first night at home may be less ideal than you imagined. Most puppies cry in their crate the first night and will probably need to get up at least once or twice to go out in the middle of the night.

Using a crate from day one is a must if you are going to raise the best possible companion. Goldens need to know their limits, and this is the first way you are going to show them that there are rules. The crate can go anywhere, but ideally it should be placed in a fairly high-traffic area (like the kitchen), especially during the day. In the evening, if you'd like to crate your Golden puppy in your bedroom, you might want to cover the crate with a towel or blanket. This way your puppy will realize it's time for sleep (not time to play). You may want to put a towel or soft blanket in the crate that first night or two, but eliminate it after that so that your puppy doesn't chew it or soil it. Having a towel that smells like you will be reassuring to your new Golden puppy, but he'll only need this for a night or two until the strangeness of this new place wears off. A great way to have the towel pick up your scent is to put it in the laundry hamper for a few hours or put it on your pillow and sleep on it the night before you get your new pup.

Housebreaking 101

There is nothing all that complicated about housebreaking a puppy, but the job is time consuming. The speed with which puppies pick this up depends on two factors: their physical development, and the predictability of their potty schedule. Just like human children, puppies need to develop the muscles necessary to "hold it," and they have to learn to "go" in the appropriate places.

 **fact**

Paper training your puppy is a terrible idea. Most dogs that are trained to go potty on newspaper will never be reliably housebroken. Take your puppy outside to eliminate from the first day, ignore mistakes, and reward everything that is going right.

Ignore your friends and neighbors who claim their dog was housebroken in a week. No puppy is physically capable of developing that quickly. These dog owners have learned to read their puppies' "gotta go" signals and have them on a very consistent schedule. The humans here deserve the credit for learning what they need to do to teach their dogs, but the dogs will not be reliably housebroken for at least the first year. This doesn't mean they will have accidents every day, but it does mean they will have occasional relapses. Until he's about a year old, your Golden will need his humans to be predictable and vigilant about taking him out.

Keep a Schedule

The easiest way to housebreak your Golden is to put him on a predictable schedule and keep track of it. A simple yet effective means of doing this is to keep a chart on the refrigerator with the time the puppy went out and what he did. Young puppies between seven and twelve weeks of age should go out every hour, after every meal, after coming out of the crate, and after playing. Everyone in the family should help keep track of this, and if there are accidents, those should also be written on the chart. After a few weeks of keeping track like this, it will be obvious when you look at your chart what your puppy is ready for. From looking at the mistakes and successes, you will be able to tell when in the day your Golden puppy needs more walks, when he is ready to go a little longer between breaks, and when he has earned a little more freedom.

Choose One Spot

To start, you should choose one spot in the yard for potty breaks. Have your puppy on a leash each time you take him there. Give him at most one to two minutes to do his business; if he goes, he can have some freedom inside or out. If he doesn't go, he should stay with you on a leash or go back in his crate (if you can't watch him) for ten to twenty minutes before you try again. The rule here is no freedom until he's had a successful potty break. After a week or so of this routine, most pups really catch on, and you can start to extend the time between breaks to two hours or more at a time.

Potty on Command

Teaching your Golden to go to the bathroom on command is simple to accomplish. Be sure in these early weeks to take him out on leash and say your potty command just before he goes. Dogs need to hear words many times before they associate them with actions, so be patient—this could take a while. You can call each function by a different name if you'd like. This will make it easier to be sure your dog is completely empty before giving him freedom in the house. Some common phrases to consider are "go to it," "hurry up," "get busy," and "go now." Whatever command you choose should be said right before the dog begins to go.

Be sure you label the functions so that even in inclement weather or while on vacation you can get your dog to go quickly. By sticking to one spot in the yard you are helping your puppy learn why he is outside, and leaving his scent in one area continually will help him use that one spot for his potty needs instead of the whole yard.

◀ A three-month-old male Golden puppy.

Middle-of-the-Night Potty Trips

The first few weeks, you will have to get up in the middle of the night to let your puppy out to potty. Do this with him on a leash, and make it as quick and businesslike as possible. The lesson you are hoping to convey is that it's no fun to get up in the middle of the night and go outside in the cold. Put your puppy right back in his crate after he does his business—no drink, no cuddling, no playtime. Puppy goes straight back to his crate, you cover it, and it's back to bed for everyone.

Your puppy needs you to adjust your schedule to his, but as he approaches adulthood, you can begin adjusting him to yours. One example of this is delaying the speed with which you get him out in the morning so that he is gradually getting up later instead of at the crack of dawn.

Cleaning Up Accidents

Keep track of accidents on your chart to see if there is a predictable pattern. If you find that your Golden pup poops at noon every day, chances are he needs another walk added in around that time.

 **Alert!**

If you were making good progress with your housebreaking but are having a sudden backslide, consider taking a urine or stool sample to your veterinarian for testing. Dogs that are housebroken and begin having accidents again may have a urinary tract infection or an intestinal parasite called coccidia. Both are easily treated with medication.

Cleaning up accidents thoroughly is essential to helping your dog stay on track. When your puppy has to go, he will be attracted to any spots on the carpet or floor that smell like he has gone there before. The odor of a previous accident may attract your puppy back to the same spot if he has to go again.

Cleaning up thoroughly after each incident is crucial to house-breaking progress.

If the accident is on carpeting, blot up urine and/or pick up the poop with paper towels. Pour a glass of plain water over the spot, and blot until the color is clear. You can then use a spray-on carpet cleaner and a scrub brush to clean the spot. On tile or linoleum simply wipe up, and use a spray-on solution.

You can also buy specially formulated products designed to break down the enzymes in these stains. As a result, your dog will not be able to scent the mess he left behind, and he will be much less likely to choose that spot again. These products are easy to find at pet supply stores or through catalogs.

Using a Crate in Training

The most wonderful tool available for helping you train a dog is a crate. Think of it as your puppy's safe haven and den, a place where you can know with complete certainty that he is safe. Except for the first two nights at home, there should be no blanket or towels in the crate. The idea here is that if your puppy has an accident, he will be wet and uncomfortable until you come to rescue him. Lest you think this harsh, remember that you are walking him every hour so an accident should be a rare event. When your pup is dry and clean for two weeks straight, then you can try giving him a towel and see how he does.

The crate is not only used to help you housebreak a puppy but also to help you establish yourself as leader and set clear limits for your young Golden. A puppy that isn't crated gets into lots of expensive trouble before he is full grown. Dogs don't suddenly outgrow destructive chewing and getting into things, so it's best that they never learn they can chew or destroy furniture or other valuables.

The rule for puppies between seven to fourteen weeks old is that they are in their crate more than they are out. When they are out, they are confined to a puppyproof area and under close supervision. If no one is available to watch, the puppy does not get freedom.

After about fourteen weeks, you can start to be a little less vig-ilant and see how it goes. If your Golden puppy is getting into trouble, back up and limit his time out to supervision only. Gradually, you are working toward having your puppy out for longer and longer periods of time without getting into trouble. Do not give him the run of more than one room for now.

 Essential

Though it will break your heart at first to hear your Golden puppy cry in a crate, it is essential that you do not give in and take the puppy into bed with you. To prevent future behavior problems by giving privileges too soon, your puppy should sleep in a crate from day one. The crate can be in your room, but your puppy should not be allowed to sleep with you.

As he gets close to a year old, you can gradually leave your Golden out longer while you are home with less supervision. However, make sure you check on him frequently to be sure that he isn't getting into trouble. Crate him when you leave the house, at least for the first eighteen to twenty-four months of his life.

When your Golden Retriever has proven that he's trustworthy while you are home, you can then begin to wean him off his crate while you are out. Start with short periods of time. Eventually, when he can handle small amounts of time, you can extend his free times to longer and longer periods, until he can be home alone several hours of the day.

When Mom's Away, Puppies Will Play

There are so many dog services now available for working people trying to raise a puppy. If you work and can't be home with your new puppy all day, chances are that you are going to need to hire someone to let your Golden Retriever out in the middle of the day.

Pet Sitters and Dog Walkers

A reliable dog walking or pet sitting service will come to your house to let your puppy out to play and go potty, which will allow you to keep your job and housebreak your puppy in the shortest time possible. It's worth every penny for this service, which is a must if you work full time.

People who work and are away from home for six hours or more usually hire a dog walker for the first two months or so until they can get their pups to hold it for longer periods of time. If you work a longer day, you will probably want someone to come home and let your dog out in the middle of the day for a little fun and exercise a few days a week.

Doggie Day Care

Doggie day care is another excellent option for puppies, especially if you work full time. A well-run canine day-care facility will allow your puppy to socialize with other dogs and humans as well as help maintain your Golden's housebreaking routine. As your puppy grows up, you'll probably like the idea that for at least a few days a week he has something fun and exciting to do while you are out.

Make sure you visit the day care and see where your puppy will play. Talk to the staff and find out who will be supervising the dogs and how they are broken up for playtime. Steer clear of places that claim they don't use crates or confinement. Most dogs like having down time, and they should have somewhere private to sleep and rest when they've had enough of the other dogs. All dogs should have their own water bowls and be allowed out to potty every couple of hours. Big groups of dogs playing for long periods of time is less than ideal; puppies absolutely need to have downtime and to learn self control via crate rest or naptime. Be selective about where you choose to leave your puppy, and make sure the facility can best meet your puppy's needs.

Stopping Destructive Chewing

Puppies use their teeth to explore their world. Given the opportunity, they will rip and shred just about anything they can get their paws on. Punishment for such behavior is totally unacceptable and will only hurt your relationship in the long run. From about seven to twenty weeks, puppies chew with mostly immature baby teeth. Their destructiveness is minimal because their chewing equipment hasn't fully developed yet. A puppy's baby teeth are sharp and pointy, but they are not yet set deeply in the jaw. Puppy teeth typically fall out starting around fourteen weeks, and they are almost completely replaced by adult teeth by six months of age. The chewing a Golden does at this stage is minimal compared to what he will be capable of later.

 Fact

Using a gate or some other kind of barrier is an excellent way to ensure that your puppy will not destroy something valuable or limit access to a child's bedroom, toys, or other valuables. Puppies are inquisitive and need barriers to help them figure out where they belong in your household.

Yes, a Golden can eat a whole couch. It is not a pretty sight and should be considered an expensive lesson for the person who goofed in the management of a young dog. Once your Golden puppy's baby teeth fall out and he gets his adult teeth, his need to chew increases greatly. This is also right around the time your puppy becomes an adolescent dog (five to six months of age).

Without a routine and careful management, the adolescent Golden Retriever will get into a lot of very expensive trouble. This is a great time to keep your dog crated when you are out or when you will be unable to watch him. You probably won't have to be as vigilant as when he was a young puppy, but you will have to be careful not to allow too much freedom too soon.

Socializing Golden Retriever Puppies

Puppies of any breed are cute, but Golden puppies are by far the cutest puppies on the planet (no bias here!). The ideal Golden Retriever has a friendly temperament. He loves people, kids, other dogs and cats, and going all kinds of places with his beloved family. In short, he is well socialized.

Teaching Your Puppy Social Skills

Socialization does not happen on its own. Despite the Golden Retriever's reputation for friendliness, genetics alone does not guarantee that your Golden puppy will grow up to be a friendly and sociable adult dog. It is your job as your puppy's guardian to provide numerous and varied social experiences now, while he is still open to learning about new things.

The ideal time to socialize a puppy to people and other dogs is between the ages of seven and eighteen weeks. At this stage in his development, a Golden puppy is completely open to accepting just about anything as part of his normal environment. Even people or animals he seems unsure of at first he will learn to enjoy if you consistently give him lots of good experiences.

 Essential

Dogs that are given too much freedom too soon are bound to get into trouble and learn to be destructive. Many behaviorists and dog trainers agree that separation anxiety can be triggered by failing to set boundaries and limit freedom when a dog is young. Separation anxiety can also have a genetic component, but a young dog that does not get too much freedom too soon can learn to be alone without becoming destructive.

Puppies need to meet people of all shapes and sizes: young and old; male and female; people in uniform; people of different races;

and people doing different things. You need to expose your puppy to lots of different noises and things that move, such as trash cans that bang, cars that backfire, or a schoolyard full of running, screaming children. Your puppy needs to meet all kinds of dogs of all different sizes, breeds, and mixes. He needs to be comfortable around dogs on leash and dogs running free. The more your puppy gets to try out his social skills, the better he will be at being able to get along with all kinds of dogs for his entire lifetime. This doesn't mean that you are done with socializing your dog at eighteen weeks, but it does mean you must start the process early.

Fun Ways to Teach Socialization Skills

Ian Dunbar, D.V.M., a renowned veterinary behaviorist and author, recommends that in order to be socially normal, all puppies should meet at least 100 people—other than those in your family—and at least 100 other dogs before they turn eighteen weeks old. We realize this is a tall order, so get out there and get busy, no matter how old your puppy is now. Teach your Golden that new people, places, and things are fun and exciting, and he will look forward to new things. It's really that simple.

Keep in mind as you introduce your puppy to new places that his vaccination schedule will not be complete until he reaches fourteen to sixteen weeks of age. Until then, he is susceptible to several highly communicable diseases, including the dreaded parvovirus. Doggie diseases are commonly passed in urine and feces, so don't take your young pup to the dog park quite yet, and keep away from areas where you know a lot of other dogs have done their business. His little system isn't quite ready yet to fend off major illnesses by itself.

In the meantime, there are plenty of ways you can show your puppy what a wonderful world it is. Here are a few ideas:

- Sign your dog up for doggie day care so he can practice his social skills all day long.
- Stand outside a grocery store with treats and let people feed and pet your puppy.

- Carry your puppy into the video store next time you get a movie; let the staff love him up.
- Take your puppy into the bank and let the clerks give him treats and kisses.
- Take your puppy in the car to a full-serve gas station and let the attendant give him a treat.
- Sign your puppy up for a well-run puppy kindergarten.
- Go to the pet store twice a week and let him meet as many children and adults as he likes.
- Take a ride on public transportation with your puppy. In Boston, the subway and buses allow well-behaved dogs to accompany passengers.
- Go to the downtown area of your town and sit on a bench or outside a store, and let your puppy watch the world go by.
- Sit outside your local library and let your puppy meet whomever comes your way.

Puppy Kindergarten

By far, the best thing you can do for your Golden puppy is sign him up for puppy kindergarten. Even if this is your third puppy and you've been through it all before, there is nothing quite like taking your puppy through a well run puppy kindergarten. Most puppy kindergartens have a group playtime during which your puppy gets to meet lots of different puppies and begins to learn his own language. Training exercises usually take you through the basic obedience exercises of sit, down, stay, come, heel, and leave it, as well as handling and gentling exercises in which your puppy learns to like being handled.

Clicker training classes are a great choice because the method is gentle and teaches your puppy to think. Using a clicker to train your Golden puppy is an exciting introduction to learning how to train a dog, and best of all it builds a strong, healthy relationship that will last a lifetime.

 **Essential**

Most puppy kindergarten classes limit the size of their groups to ten to twelve puppies or less. Avoid larger classes. You won't get as much attention, and your puppy will get lost in the shuffle. Make sure if there are more than six puppies in the class that the instructor has an assistant.

The duration of puppy kindergarten varies greatly from trainer to trainer. Six weeks is about the right amount of time for you to learn the basics of dog training, and it's enough for your Golden Retriever puppy to start to understand the exercises you are teaching him. He will need more training, of course, but after the initial six weeks you should be well on your way toward making your Golden puppy a wonderful companion.

Food Basics

Puppies between seven to fourteen weeks normally eat about one cup of dry food three times a day. As they reach the fourteen-week mark, most puppies can give up their midday meal. They will still get the same amount of food, just split into two feedings. Golden Retriever puppies are always ravenous, and they will bolt down their food as fast as their little mouths will allow them. A Golden can literally eat himself sick. Don't be tempted to fill your puppy's bowl up to the top and walk away. It is important for your puppy's physical development that he not overeat.

Use a measuring cup to scoop out your puppy's food, and watch him closely to see whether you need to adjust his intake according to his appearance. In our experience, the side of the bag of dog food will tell you to feed your dog a lot more food than your puppy really needs. Overfeeding your dog will make him eliminate more than normal (more than two or three times a day) and could cause structural abnormalities as he grows up. Keep your puppy on the lean side to ensure the best chance for him to grow up healthy and structurally sound.

There are a staggering number of dog foods on the market today. Trying to choose the best brand for your puppy can be an intimidating task. First off, should you buy puppy food instead of adult dog food? Most modern research actually advises against feeding puppy food because the fat and calorie content is high, which tends to make for faster growing puppies. The nutrients in puppy food and adult dog food are essentially the same; feeding adult dog food will not harm your puppy, and slower growth may mean a healthier adult dog.

After raising Golden Retrievers for years now, we are convinced that you do indeed get what you pay for. The quality of the ingredients that go into your dog's food will have a direct effect on how often your dog visits the veterinarian. The lower the quality of ingredients in the food, the more allergies, skin problems, and digestive upsets your dog will experience. Take the time to educate yourself about dog food (see Chapter 12) and make an informed decision about how you feed your best friend. 🐾

Bringing Home an Adult Dog

ADOPTING AN ADULT DOG from a Golden Retriever rescue group may be the answer to all of your prayers. Golden Retriever rescues are run by volunteers who love and know the breed inside out. There are many wonderful Goldens waiting for just the right family to adopt them.

Adopting an Adult Golden Retriever

It is very common for people to want a new Golden but not want the problems that come with new puppies. Beware, however, that this active breed may have been given up because of its high exercise requirement and need for training. Be sure you spend time with your new potential pal and have a clean view of just how much training and exercise he will require. Older Goldens are usually harder to place in new homes because many people are looking for a puppy, but adopting a middle-age or adult dog can be a walk in the park—literally!

The folks who run the Golden Retriever rescue groups are the best source for information about a particular dog you might be interested in. Volunteers usually foster a Golden for a period of time to learn what he needs as far as training. Dogs are carefully observed to see if they have any serious behavior problems that would make them dangerous or otherwise unadoptable. This screening by people familiar with the breed is very important. You should ask plenty of questions about an individual Golden before you adopt to be sure he is the right fit for your family.

 **Essential**

Planning ahead is the key to a successful first night with your new Golden Retriever. Have all your supplies ready, with a feeding and exercise schedule all planned out. Your new companion will feel more secure if he knows what to expect from you.

Don't be surprised if the rescue group has a list of criteria that you have to meet. A well-run rescue will put you through the wringer before they place a dog with you. The rescue people have seen a lot (and it isn't always pretty). Their goal is to find the best homes for their Goldens because these dogs have already been through enough.

A good approach to adopting is to sit down with your family and develop a profile of your ideal dog. Pass it on to the rescue folks so that they can match your family to the right rescue. Be as logical as possible, and try not to make decisions based solely on emotion—feeling sorry for a dog is not a good reason to adopt. A few of these rescue Goldens lost their homes because their previous owners acquired them strictly on an emotional whim. Go into this with eyes wide open, and be patient. The right dog may be difficult to find, but he will be well worth the wait.

The First Night at Home

The first night in a new place can be scary for anyone, and dogs are no exception. Planning for your adopted dog's arrival is essential for a smooth transition to your household. You'll want to have all the supplies you need on hand so that you won't have to leave your new Golden alone that first night. Make sure you have at least a three-day supply of food, bowls for water and food, toys, a blanket, a crate, a leash, and a flat collar. Decide who will walk the dog, who will feed him and when, and make sure everyone knows what to do. If children will be taking on some of these jobs, they should be supervised by an adult to be sure they are comfortable with the dog and that things get off to a good start.

Prepare your yard, and clearly mark out a potty spot so that everyone knows where to take your new Golden when he goes out for potty breaks. Keep the chaos to a minimum those first couple of days so that your new Golden Retriever can settle in and learn your family's routine. It is strongly advised to use a crate with your new adoptee even if he is already housebroken and past the chewing stage. Most dogs feel more secure in a confined space with a predictable schedule, and this way you won't have any accidents or stress-related chewing in your absence. Dogs who are past the chewing stage and are housebroken can regress when they are stressed, and there are probably few things more stressful than moving to a new home.

If you have friends and relatives who are dying to meet your new family member, have them hold off for about a week. Give your Golden time to first learn who his family is. Being overwhelmed with visitors, with all the noise and chaos this can bring, is a frightening introduction to a new family. Once your dog has had a week to settle in, however, by all means have a "Welcome to our home" party, and invite your relatives and friends to meet your newest member. By that time, your dog will have settled in a bit and be much more comfortable meeting new people and putting on his best Golden charm.

Introducing Your Adult Dog to a Crate

The rescue group where you adopted your Golden will know whether he has been exposed to a crate. If they don't know, you can try introducing a crate and see how easily your dog accepts it. Some adult dogs who have had a bad experience or suffer from separation anxiety cannot be crated, but most dogs can learn to accept the crate and even come to like it.

 **Question?**

How long can I leave my dog in his crate?
Once your dog accepts the crate, he can be left up to four hours at a time. If you'll be away longer than four hours, hire a pet sitter to let your dog out for a potty break and to stretch his legs.

Here are some tips for successfully introducing an adult dog to a crate:

- The crate should be big enough for your dog to stand up and turn around in. Place it in a part of the house where your dog can see what's going on.
- The crate can be wire or plastic, depending on your taste. Put a soft towel or rug in the bottom of the crate to make it more inviting.
- Feed your dog in its crate for the first two weeks so he associates the crate with good things.
- Teach your dog to go in and out of the crate with the door wide open; offer a treat when he goes in the crate but not when he comes out.
- Put your dog in his crate for ten minutes of every hour that you are home so that he doesn't get anxious about going in the crate when you leave for work. Minute by minute, build up the time he spends in there. If he tends to bark or whine in the crate, cover with a beach towel or sheet.

Dogs that are crate trained can be taken just about any-where. Many hotels accept dogs that are crated, and there will be times when you are traveling by car when the safest place for your dog is a crate. If your dog must stay overnight in a kennel or at the veterinarian's office, being comfortable in a crate will be to his benefit. Even if you are sure your Golden will never need to be crated, introduce it to him anyway, you never know what life may bring.

▲ This male four-month-old Golden puppy and his "pal" enjoy the comforts of his crate. Crate training is a great way to housebreak a puppy.

Developing a Schedule

Golden Retrievers respond well to predictability and love having things happen at scheduled times. You don't have to be rigid about it, but feeding, walking, and exercising your Golden on a relatively predictable schedule will help him learn to trust that all his needs will be met. Having a routine is a great way to build confidence and help your Golden learn to be alone.

When introducing a new dog to your home, try bringing him home on a Friday afternoon, and free up the weekend to be with him. Decide where and when he will be taken out to potty and where his crate, bed, toys, and food dishes will be put. Feed your Golden twice a day, in the morning and again around dinnertime. Keep a chart to track his potty trips.

Housebreaking an Adult Golden

People normally associate housebreaking with puppies, but adult dogs can experience periods of regression, or some were never taught where to go in the first place. To successfully housebreak an adult Golden, you need to develop a predictable schedule; keeping a chart and recording what happens during each potty trip will help immeasurably. If there are any accidents in the house, put those on the chart as well. After a few weeks, you will be able to see those times when you need to put in more walks and those when your dog can go a little longer between trips.

An adult dog will usually be housebroken much faster than a puppy. At the same time, remember that his body is still learning a new skill and the muscles necessary to "hold it" may need time to develop. If your adopted dog lived outdoors or in a kennel, he went to the bathroom anytime he needed to. Teaching your adult Golden to hold it and go outdoors will be a new concept for him, and he will need time to get good at it.

Here are some tips for housebreaking an adult dog:

- Take your new Golden out to potty once an hour for the first three days. Chart his potty activities, including accidents. After the first three days, modify your schedule as necessary.
- Crate your new Golden when you are going to leave the house.
- Walk your Golden after meals, exercise, and play sessions.
- Limit access to water and food; feed on a regular schedule.
- Go to one place in the yard for potty breaks, and give him only a minute to do his business. Praise him ("Good potty!") when he goes.

Housebreaking is not rocket science, but it is time consuming. The good news is that adult dogs pick up the skill much faster than puppies. If you feel like you've followed these guidelines but are still not making progress, consider consulting your veterinarian.

Some dogs, especially when they are under stress, develop urinary tract infections that make their need to eliminate more frequent and less predictable. Some intestinal parasites can also go undetected and can interfere with even the best housebreaking plan. With patience and time you will see that Goldens are a quick study; unless there is a medical problem, your new Golden will be reliably housebroken before you know it.

Bonding with Your New Dog

Making friends with your new Golden Retriever involves spending quality time together, learning about each other through training, play, and quiet time. A balance of these is essential to getting your relationship off on the right paw. Regardless of your dog's previous history, it will take time to learn about his likes and dislikes, his bad habits, and his strong suits.

Training

Even a dog that has had some previous training can benefit from a refresher course. A good, upbeat training class can help you develop a wonderful relationship as you learn about each other.

 **Alert!**

A good way to tell if a particular class is right for you is to watch and see whether the students are smiling and having fun. A good instructor will make sure that everyone gets enough attention to be successful.

Search for a class in your area that offers clicker training classes (see Chapter 6 for more details) and ask to observe a class to see if it's for you. Most well-run training classes have a student-to-teacher ratio of about six to one, and the atmosphere is upbeat and fun. The class participants should be enjoying themselves and smiling a lot, even if their dogs are not perfectly behaved. Most beginner's classes cover the basic commands of sit, down, stay, come, and heel, and this is where you'll want to start if you've never trained a dog before. If you've trained other dogs before and your dog has a grasp of the basics, you might consider taking a more advanced obedience class or a fun class like tricks or agility.

Play Time

Every dog needs exercise, but Golden Retrievers in particular need lots. These are active, social, and happy dogs that need to work off their boundless energy. Otherwise, they will channel that energy into behavior problems like barking, digging, and destructiveness. This is not a dog that will be tired out by a walk around the block; a fenced yard or a nearby park are essentials.

 **Essential**

> The more exercise you provide, the easier your dog will be to live with. Play also provides a wonderful outlet for stress, and there is nothing quite as stressful as moving to a new home.

Goldens love to play fetch with just about anything. Balls, flying disks, sticks, bumpers—if you can throw it, they will usually bring it back. Playtime also allows you to learn about your new dog: how he thinks, how he works things out, what his passions are.

Most Goldens need at least two forty-five-minute runs per day, during which they are actively running, chasing, fetching, swimming, or playing with other dogs. Providing enough exercise for your Golden Retriever means that it is possible for him to realize his full potential as a companion, because his most basic need for activity has been satisfied.

It isn't easy to live with a dog that isn't getting enough exercise. Like most highly social dogs, Goldens will not exercise unless you're in on the fun. They should not be left unsupervised in a yard or kennel for extended periods of time.

Quiet Time

This could also be referred to as "cuddling time" and should be part of every day. Goldens don't just love being with people—they demand it. They will nudge you to be petted, rest their noble heads on your knee, and always seem to be in close proximity to any activity around the house. There is nothing quite like that soulful look of a Golden to stop you in your tracks for a quick moment of pure bliss. Finding time to relax and hang out with one another is crucial for developing a great relationship. Golden Retrievers are masters at reducing stress and slowing us down, especially when we feel like the world is spinning out of control.

Quiet time for you might include watching television, giving your dog a massage, grooming, or just resting quietly together. Whatever the activity, your Golden will enjoy being in your company and learning that he will get his one-on-one time from you on a regular basis. All dogs love this, but the Golden Retriever lives for it. Some activities that you might like to try with your new Golden include taking a swim in the ocean, a lake, or a pond. Go for long walks or hikes in the woods. Take your Golden on a picnic, learn to do canine massage, or sit in the sun on a warm day and read a book. Goldens are great snuggle buddies and will gladly spend the day with you on the couch watching old movies or cartoons.

Whatever the activity you choose, the Golden Retriever is the most soulful of breeds. If you open yourself to them, they will teach you things about yourself you never knew. Enjoy the wonderful experience of bonding yourself to this wonderful canine soul. May your experiences together be the best you ever dreamed possible.

Feeding Basics

Feeding your new Golden Retriever will be the highlight of his day. Most Goldens are big eaters that will happily eat themselves into oblivion if you let them. These are not dogs that you can free feed (leave their food down all day). Instead, you must carefully measure out a small amount of food for each meal. Goldens should be fed twice a day as adults to help maintain a level blood sugar level and for optimum health.

 **Fact**

You will have to adjust how much you feed your Golden Retriever according to his activity level. You may find this to be seasonal. In the winter months, he may not get as much exercise and therefore he needs fewer calories, but during the summer, he may get lots of exercise and be able to eat a bit more without any changes in weight.

The type of food you feed your dog will determine how much is too much and how much is enough. The higher the quality of food, the more calorically dense it will be, and the less you should feed. The lower the quality of the food, the more filler it contains and the more you must feed. Make a commitment to feed your dog at the higher end of the quality spectrum. Not all dog foods are created equal, and many health problems can be avoided by feeding a better quality food from the start. (See Chapter 12 for more details on canine nutrition.)

You should always use a measuring cup to measure out your dog's food. Vague measurement techniques, like a handful or a scoopful, are not an accurate way to make sure you maintain your dog's ideal body weight. In general, assuming that you feed a better quality food, you would give your female Golden Retriever two feedings of ½ to ¾ cup of dry food. Your male Golden needs ¾ to 1 cup twice a day to maintain his optimum weight. There are exceptions of course, but this is a very general guideline to help your Golden maintain a healthy weight.

Social Butterfly or Social Outcast?

Golden Retrievers are one of the few breeds that are almost unanimously extroverted. Most Goldens love everyone and seek new people out on a regular basis to add to their friendship circle. Not all Goldens, however, have had the best start in life, and some can be shy toward strangers and unfamiliar people. Don't fret if your adopted Golden is more of a social outcast than a social butterfly. With the right training and enough patience, he will learn that new people can be a host of happy surprises and fun.

 **Essential**

A Golden with limited social experience is likely to be afraid of new people and places. Fear inhibits his ability to think and make sense of things. If you push your Golden into fearful situations, you will not make progress in your training program.

Learning to Socialize

Even if you feel your Golden Retriever is very social, it's always a good idea to get him out on a regular basis and let him socialize a bit to keep up his people skills. Without frequent exposure to new people, many dogs lose this ability. Here are some tips for helping your social outcast become more socially accepting:

- Associate all new people with tasty treats, toys, and happy talk.
- Have new people stand or sit facing sideways to your Golden. They should not look directly at him, which is intimidating, or reach for him.
- Let your Golden decide when to approach the new person. If you're out in the open, keep your leash loose and allow him to move away if it's uncomfortable.
- Have the new person drop really yummy treats all around their feet.
- Start with short sessions of five to ten minutes.

For more details in rehabilitating a shy Golden Retriever, refer to Chapter 8.

Visitors

Having company and sharing your new Golden Retriever with them is one of the great moments of dog ownership. It is important to keep in mind, however, that not everyone is a dog lover who will want 75 pounds of dog in his or her face. It's a good idea to ask your company if they would like to meet your dog and then do so on leash after they are seated and comfortable. This would be a great time to work on your new Golden's greeting manners by stepping on the leash and having visitors offer him cookies for sitting. This way you are teaching your dog that new people are fun, but there are rules about how to behave around them.

Try not to overwhelm the newest member of your family by having a lot of people over at once. Instead, plan smaller get-togethers to help him learn that visitors are a welcome part of everyday life. With time, patience, and training, it won't be long before your friends ask how your Golden is doing before they ever ask about what's happening with you.

Developing Social Skills

PUPPIES DEVELOP ON A TIMELINE that is fairly universal among all breeds of dogs. In general, puppies need to learn some basics about living with humans and other dogs in order to be socially normal and not develop aggression problems. The window for this social development is narrow. A puppy's social development should be well underway by eighteen weeks in order for him to mature into a healthy adult dog.

Socialization Is Important

Some people debate how much of a puppy's temperament is a result of his genes, and how much can be influenced by the environment where the puppy is raised. There will never be a complete consensus on which aspect is more influential, but researchers agree that if a puppy lacks a nurturing environment, he will never grow to his full potential. This means that you can have the most social and confident puppy in the litter and still encounter behavior problems later in life if you don't socialize him properly early in life. For starters, give your dog:

- Plenty of social opportunities with people, especially men and children
- Plenty of social opportunities with other dogs, all ages, all sizes, all breeds

- The opportunity to go new places and see new things weekly
- The opportunity to investigate novel objects
- The opportunity to be in the middle of the household action
- The opportunity to be around the sights, smells, and sounds of daily living
- A rotating variety of toys to play with
- Training that requires him to think and problem solve
- Outlets for energy and playtime with his owner
- Limit-setting that is fair and consistent: gates, crates, and pens
- Plenty of opportunities to be handled by lots of different kinds of people
- Car rides, train rides, boat rides, elevator rides
- Walks in the neighborhood, downtown, on the beach, and in the woods

The Socialization Window

The timeline for puppy social development is fairly short. By eighteen weeks of age, your puppy should have met all kinds of different people—men, women, children, people of different races, people dressed in uniform, people wearing hats. The more varied your Golden Retriever puppy's social experience, the more friendly and social he will be, and the less risk of aggression or other serious behavioral problems you will face.

Dog-to-dog socialization is ongoing as well. You want your Golden Retriever to be socially normal around dogs, meaning he is able to interact and play with them without becoming frightened or aggressive. To reach this goal, he must play with all different types of dogs on a regular basis. The dogs in the neighborhood are a good start, but your puppy must meet and play with as many different types of dogs and puppies as possible. Your Golden depends on you to help him develop the social skills he needs to get along with other dogs.

Golden Retriever puppies are not couch potatoes. Energy levels vary from one pup to the next, but most Golden puppies are highly energetic long before they actually mature into calm, well-mannered adults. But left to their own devices, your Golden will never grow out of his bad habits. He will become more and more of a nuisance if not given the right guidance. Start your Golden's socialization and training now—he's getting bigger every day.

 **Essential**

> It's a good idea to enroll your Golden puppy in a puppy kindergarten class at about twelve weeks. At this point, he and the other puppies in the class will have had at least their first round of vaccinations. They should all be able to enjoy each other's company safely.

The crucial point to understand about puppy social development is that you have a very limited time to get things started. You cannot wait until your puppy has been fully vaccinated to socialize him to other dogs.

After the eighteen-week mark, the window for socialization starts to close. If you haven't started socializing your Golden to other dogs and various types of people, he will develop behavior problems (usually aggressive in nature) that will be a permanent part of his personality. It is so much easier to start out right from the beginning than try to fix it later.

Nature Versus Nurture

Nature gives each puppy a certain personality, whether pushy or soft, bold or cautious. However, it's the environment and social experience you provide that determine what kind of adult Golden your puppy will become. You can take a mediocre puppy with a lack of confidence and make it a confident, well-mannered adult dog. Conversely, you can also take a very bold, confident puppy and turn it into a fearful and aggressive dog, simply by not providing enough social experience and a stimulating environment to grow up in.

fact

> Puppies can be temperament tested at age seven weeks or later. This test gives you an inkling of the adult Golden your puppy will become. Make sure the litter you choose is being temperament tested and that the breeder is familiar with temperament differences in puppies.

Poor socialization is almost always at the root of any aggression a Golden might show toward people or dogs. To be properly socialized, your Golden must meet, greet, play with, and be loved by all sorts of people and other dogs. These are the experiences that teach him how to cope with life. The more good experiences your Golden has had, the less likely it is that an unpleasant encounter will alter his behavior. It's your job to teach your Golden that though bad things might happen sometimes (other dogs bite, people are sometimes scary), the world overall is an exciting, happy place.

By providing your Golden with an environment that stimulates all of his senses, you are making his world a comfortable and safe place. By overprotecting him, and not letting him experience the sights, sounds, and people of the world, you are severely limiting his potential to adapt to new environments. This limitation is the cause of many aggression problems, fear issues, and other under-confident behavior.

Human Socialization

Human socialization must have been started by the time your dog is four weeks old. Puppies should be handled several times a day by their breeders and caretakers, and they should begin to meet different people by the time they begin their fourth week of life. If the puppies are raised in a kennel (or the garage or basement) with very little social contact, chances are that they will be fearful and tentative around new people and in new situations.

◀ A four-year-old male Golden.

It is crucial that you notice these things when you are shopping for a puppy, for they will influence the way your Golden turns out. Walk away from Golden puppies that were not raised underfoot in the home, right in the middle of the household action. You want a puppy that has been hearing the sounds and seeing the sights of life. A puppy that grows up hearing the vacuum, the banging around of pots and pans, or the ringing of a telephone, will adjust to life much more easily than a puppy raised in the basement or outside in a kennel run.

Once your Golden Retriever puppy comes home, the real fun begins. Your puppy is ready to meet people and learn how to act around them from the start. The first thing you'll want to teach your Golden puppy is that people mean good things. Right from the start, you can have visitors teach your puppy to sit for treats. In this way, you can start teaching good manners right away. Put your

Golden Retriever puppy on leash, and have the visitor put his foot on the leash. This will prevent jumping while your guest lures your puppy into a sit with a food treat.

 **Esseńtial**

Keep good treats on hand for when you have visitors. Allow visitors to feed these special treats to your puppy so that he learns to look forward to being handled and petted by strangers.

Invite friends, coworkers, and family members over on a regular basis. Company is fun for you, and it will also help your Golden puppy learn to accept handling and restraint. Take turns touching the puppy all over: ears, feet, mouth, tail, belly, legs, and back. Supervise closely to be sure your puppy doesn't become overwhelmed with this. You can also show visitors what to do if your Golden does seem a little scared—lots of really yummy treats usually keep this from being a problem.

Preventing Resource Guarding

All dogs come with the ability to defend what's theirs. If they didn't have this ability in the wild they wouldn't get to eat. A Golden guards food, toys, or bones for reasons having to do with confidence (or lack of it) much more than issues about the dog's rank or position within the group.

What Is Resource Guarding?

A Golden with lower confidence usually feels the need to guard his things from his owners and sometimes from other dogs as well. This behavior is known as resource guarding, with the resource being something the Golden values—his food bowl, a toy, the ball, or a bone. When the resource is in his possession, the Golden will usually growl, bare his teeth, and possibly snap. His goal is to let you know that this resource is *his,* and he does not want to share it. If you attempt to take the resource away, your Golden might bite you.

Punishment is the wrong way to stop your Golden from resource guarding. In fact, it could make him more dangerous. What you are actually punishing is the growl or snap. You may teach your Golden not to do those things, but he is still stuck with the need to be overly protective of his resources. He may feel he has no choice but to skip directly to the bite.

The right way to stop resource guarding is to build up your Golden's confidence. You want him to learn that giving up resources produces better results than guarding them. In the meantime, you must try your best to prevent the dog from practicing the undesirable behavior, which may mean not making the resource available (or at least not challenging him for it) while you are retraining him. By far the best solution to the problem of resource guarding is to prevent it in the first place.

Food-Bowl Etiquette

To keep your Golden puppy from becoming overprotective of his food, feed him in the middle of the kitchen, not in a corner or in his crate. Start by putting just a little of his meal in the bowl, and add to it while he is still eating. If your puppy growls during this process, quit adding food and leave the pup alone. You can count on the Golden's hungry nature to teach him quickly that growling means no more food. At the same time, he will learn that hands around his fool bowl are a good thing.

As your puppy is eating, you can also add a delicious treat like a teaspoon of yogurt or a liver treat. Pet your puppy with your free hand. Practice this exercise at every meal until any growling disappears and the puppy looks forward to people approaching his bowl.

Giving Up the Bone

Some dogs guard any favorite object, which might include bones or other things they chew on. There are several things you can do to prevent guarding behavior from becoming a problem in your Golden puppy. Let your puppy chew the bone while you are holding it, and then trade the puppy for the bone with a delicious treat, like freeze-dried liver. Occasionally give the puppy the bone for a few seconds, and then trade again for liver. Repeat this constantly, until your puppy willingly gives up the bone upon your approach. Also, be sure you perform this exercise with other family members and pets present.

 **Alert!**

The best way to prevent your puppy from growing into an adult Golden with a guarding problem is to give a clear message from the beginning that all resources belong to you first. It's up to you whether your Golden gets the privilege of chewing his bone or eating his dinner.

If you know that your Golden already tends to guard an object, avoid giving it to him until you have some control over his behavior. Never ever take something away from a dog that is growling and snapping at you, as this will likely result in the dog biting you. Consult a professional trainer for help with your Golden if his behavior is aggressive or threatening.

By teaching your puppy that he can trade in prize possessions for delicious treats, and by varying your timing in giving the original resource back, you will end up with an adult Golden that does not have a resource guarding problem. This means he can be safely around all different types of people in all kinds of situations.

Taming the Chewing Instinct

All puppies need outlets for their energy, and all puppies have a tremendous urge to chew anything they can get their mouths around. Golden puppies seem to take particular pleasure in a good chew. How much of a problem this is directly relates to the limits you set with your Golden puppy from the start. Allow your Golden pup free run of the house too soon, and he will chew his way through it. A chew-happy Golden can end up causing a considerable amount of damage before he is through.

Contrary to popular opinion, Goldens don't simply outgrow their need to chew everything in sight. Without the proper training and guidance, they will chew right through adulthood. Prevention is a big part of the solution. Your Golden Retriever puppy can only chew the mahogany paneling, your Italian sandals, or the Bruce Springsteen boxed set if you give him access to these things. Use crates and gates to greatly cut down on the amount of destruction your pup can do. These tools also make it easier to train your puppy to chew on his own toys and bones, leaving your stuff alone. Provide a variety of toys, and rotate them on a regular basis. When your Golden puppy starts to get into trouble, redirect him onto a more appropriate chew toy, and praise him for chewing on it. In addition, be sure your Golden gets plenty of exercise and opportunity to play with other dogs. You want him tired at the end of the day. Lastly, make sure that your puppy is getting sufficient downtime for napping.

 Fact

Overtired puppies—those that have had too much freedom for too long—tend to get into things. They are not easily redirected. Like overtired toddlers, they stop hearing "No!" and continue to get into mischief. Your ability to control destructive chewing depends on supervision and limit setting.

The first stage of chewing is puppy chewing, which occurs between two and six months. This is an exploratory stage of development, in which your Golden is using his sensitive mouth to explore his environment. Though it's painful when he uses his teeth to explore you, in this stage he isn't likely to cause extensive damage to your property.

At about six months, a Golden's adult teeth have come in and are beginning to set in the jaw. This is when the urge to chew is greatest. At six months, therefore, be on the lookout for your Golden to be tempted into some very destructive, damaging chewing. Just because your puppy is housebroken doesn't mean that he is ready to be out of a crate. Goldens in particular are fairly slow to mature. Give your Golden too much freedom too soon, and he will show you just how much trouble he can get himself into.

Dog-to-Dog Socialization

To be socially normal, your Golden puppy must play regularly with other puppies and adult dogs. Otherwise, not only won't he be very playful with other dogs as an adult, he might even be aggressive toward them as well. Once the window for socialization closes at around the eighteenth week, you can't open it again. You can do remedial training to help manage any problems, but your Golden will have lost a big opportunity to learn how to communicate and play with other dogs.

The key to preventing this from being a problem is to get your puppy around other puppies and adult dogs of all breeds, sizes, and shapes. Playing with other dogs is not just for fun. The more you allow your Golden Retriever to play with other dogs, the more social he will be. *JILL - BORDER COLLIE VERONICA - SPANIEL CLARE - TERRIER RUTH - GREYHOUND*

Bite Inhibition

Wrestling and play-fighting teach puppies a very critical skill called bite inhibition. Bite inhibition is the limiting of the force of a dog's jaws, which prevents injury to the person or animal being bitten. By practicing mouthing and nipping on other dogs, a puppy learns how to inhibit the force of his bite, thus preventing any real injury from occurring.

Bite inhibition must be learned during the puppy stage. You can help teach this skill by yelling "Ouch!" and leaving the room when your Golden puppy bites, but this lesson is best taught by other dogs. Dogs that have bite inhibition can safely be around people and other dogs. Even if they bite out of fear or if they are in pain, they will not cause significant damage.

Essential

It is imperative that you make sure that your Golden Retriever plays with other dogs on a regular basis throughout his life. This is how he learns to inhibit his bite and also to maintain his social skills.

On the other hand, dogs without bite inhibition are like a time bomb. The reason for this is that they never learned to inhibit their bite through play with other dogs. Typically, these pups do very little nipping and biting as puppies, and the little that they do is discouraged. Instead of learning to change the pressure in their jaws, they skip this step altogether. This at first seems like a good thing, since everyone hates those needle-sharp puppy bites. But without this kind of interaction with other dogs, these pups have no idea of the power in their jaws. These dogs may have been socialized to lots of people and never show fearfulness or aggression. Still, any dog that becomes frightened or hurt is likely to bite. If this happens, they could cause serious injury requiring medical attention.

Play Dates and Doggie Day Care

If you work full time or live in a neighborhood with very few other dog owners, you can employ a dog walker or doggie daycare provider to help ensure that your dog is getting enough time with other dogs. If your dog doesn't get regular off-leash play with other dogs, he will not maintain his good social skills. Dogs are similar to people in this respect. Just as we can get a little cranky if we don't get out much, dogs can lose their ability to communicate effectively if they don't get to practice their skills.

If you do live in a neighborhood where there are other dogs (or you have friends with dogs), by all means make play dates. Let the dogs mix it up as often as possible. It's important to pay attention to other dog's play styles when you are getting together on a regular basis. If there is a dog in the group that tends to get everyone else riled up and overexcited, break up the play. Direct the dogs into another activity before letting them go back to their play.

Alert!

When searching for a doggie day-care facility, make sure you visit and ask questions about how the place is run. Dogs should play in small groups (of no more than eight to twelve). Multiple staff members should be on hand to redirect inappropriate behavior or rearrange a group in which one dog is bullying the rest.

The ability to break away from play and respond to you is a crucial element of your Golden's self control. This doesn't mean you must constantly interfere and interrupt his playtime. But if he gets rowdy, you should be able to call him away from the other dogs. This will ensure that your Golden does not learn he can get out of control and stay that way.

Getting Through the Fear Period

All puppies go through their "fear period" at about the eighth week. In earlier development, they only knew the world as an interesting place worthy of exploration. In week eight, they suddenly become aware that there are scary things out there, too.

During the fear period, if they experience something scary or stressful it can affect them well into adulthood. This is why many breeders prefer to send the puppies home at the seventh week or hold onto them until about nine weeks of age. If you take your Golden puppy home on or before the eighth week, you must be absolutely certain that he doesn't get frightened or overly stressed by anyone or anything. The fear period only lasts about a week; when it's over, it's done and the puppy goes back to being his own inquisitive self.

The message here is to go slow with your puppy during the eighth week. Not all puppies will show overt signs of being leery of new situations, but most do. This doesn't mean that you should shelter your puppy forever—just go slow during the eighth week, and go back to a busy socialization schedule the following week so that your puppy can grow up to be a happy, confident dog.

CHAPTER 6

Basic Manners

EVERY DOG NEEDS TO HAVE some basic manners in order to be an enjoyable family pet. Golden Retrievers are no exception to this rule. It's never too early to start training a Golden. A Golden with good manners is a welcome guest and a polite companion at home and on the street. A dog that responds to basic obedience commands, like sit, down, come, stay, and leave it, is a joy to live with. The benefits of a well-trained dog are endless.

Training by Positive Reinforcement

The Golden Retriever was bred for his intelligence and desire to please. The Golden Retriever is a willing partner in the learning process, and though you can train him with any method, those that involve teaching him how to think are the most exciting and fun ways to train him to be a polite companion. Harsh corrections have no place in the training of any dog, but especially one as willing as the Golden. That is not to say that you should be permissive with Goldens, for they can be pushy to get their way with people. Setting limits is essential to raising a dog that will be a happy companion, is easy to live with, and knows the rules. See Chapter 9 for more on setting limits and establishing leadership.

◀ A sixteen-month-old male Golden.

Get Recommendations

Searching for the right training class can be a daunting task. In general, it's a good idea to find a place that several sources have recommended. Your veterinarian, fellow dog owners, or your groomer may be good resources since they are often exposed to both good and ill-behaved dogs. If you start asking your neighbors and people at the park, you will find out what trainers are in your area and which style best suits your personality. Since many trainers offer classes as a part-time small business, a referral may put you in touch with someone you may not have found on your own.

Observe a Class

The best way to be able to tell whether or not a trainer's style and methods will work for you is to ask to observe a class in session. Most trainers are happy to oblige and the experience will help you get an idea of whether or not you are comfortable with how they run their classes. There are lots of different dog training methods and techniques; the best methods utilize very little, if any, force; lots of management to prevent mistakes; and lots of positive reinforcement (via food, toys, games, and play) when the dog gets things right.

 **Essential**

Training a dog is about establishing a relationship and developing a way of communicating with one another. It should not be about force and bullying, but about cooperation and teaching. Spend the time to find the right fit—your dog is counting on you!

You should avoid trainers who tell you that using food will ruin your dog—it's simply not true. Also, steer clear of trainers who tell you that you must be physical with your dog in order to get him to respect you—that's also untrue. Look around at the students enrolled in the class. They should be happy and smiling. If an instructor is doing her job right, the students should be comfortable and willing participants.

The Clicker Training Method

The use of positive reinforcement, through the use of an event marker like a clicker, is the best method for training dogs. Other methods can and do work, but this method is fun and results come much quicker. All ages and abilities can learn to apply its principles. Becoming a great clicker trainer does not depend on physical strength or asserting your will over your dog.

The clicker is a small plastic box with a metal tab that makes a clicking sound when you push down with your thumb. The sound of the click is paired with a food reward by clicking the clicker and giving the dog a treat. After a few repetitions the dog learns to associate the sound of the clicker with a food reward. The click (and pending food reward) is then used to mark the behavior you are working on, to identify in "language" your dog understands which behavior earned the reward.

You will find that your dog will work for the sound of the click rather than just the presence of a food reward. When the dog begins to understand clicker training, you can use other rewards, such as balls, tug toys, etc. Starting out with food is faster and makes your training more portable than using toys and games.

 **Question?**

My dog isn't getting it. What am I doing wrong?
You may want to keep a notebook of your progress so that you can refer to it when you run into trouble. Keeping track of your progress will allow you to see when you've made it too hard to earn the click and how to break things down into simpler steps.

By pairing the clicker with a food reward, we have created a powerful way to specify to the dog (especially a very active breed like Golden Retrievers) exactly which of the behaviors he offers are rewardable. Since dogs are always on the move, clicker training will save you lots of time.

Canine University® has successfully trained more than 2,000 dogs using clicker training. Golden Retrievers are smart and willing partners in the learning process and are only limited by the amount of time you dedicate to the task. You do not need force to train any dog, but especially not a Golden. You will love training your Golden using this method and enjoy watching him really learn how to think and problem-solve. Even after all these years, it still gives us chills to see how dogs come alive when they really understand what you want.

Clicker Training Basics

The sound of the click is unique and like no other sound that the dog has ever heard. This is part of the key to its success in shaping behavior and helping dogs understand what it is that's going right. People often ask about using their voice instead of the clicker to mark the behavior they are looking for. In the initial stages of training, your voice is not a good event marker. Because you talk to your dog all the time, your voice lacks the startling effect that the clicker invokes.

The clicker is a unique sound that most animals have never heard before, and its uniqueness reaches a part of the brain that is also responsible for the fight-or-flight response. In short, it really piques the dog's attention.

The process of shaping behavior is what clicker training is all about. Shaping is useful in all types of training, but it is crucial in teaching tricks and more complex behaviors (e.g., down on recall). Shaping behavior helps Goldens learn how to think about what they did to earn the reward. By not helping them or physically manipulating their bodies, they learn faster and more permanently by trial and error. We tell them by clicking and the absence of clicking which behaviors will be rewarded and which will not.

Labeling Behavior

The one major difference between clicker training and other types of training is that you don't label the behavior right away. The reason? The early versions of the behavior are not what you want for the final behavior.

 Alert!

If you label behavior too soon, you will get a wide variety of responses from the dog when you ask for that behavior in the future. Wait until the behavior looks close to perfect before labeling it.

The first click for heeling, for instance, is a far cry from what the finished behavior will be. Saving the label until your Golden is readily offering the behavior will ensure that the dog connects his behavior to what is being clicked. The label can come as a verbal cue, a hand signal, or both, but should not be introduced until the dog is offering a decent-looking version of it.

Using Lures in Training

A lure is a piece of food used to elicit behavior. Its goal is to help the dog get into the right position in order to earn the click and treat. In the beginning stages of training a dog, it is often frustrating and time-consuming to wait for your dog to offer the right behavior as more experienced trainers do with free shaping. Thus, you may be tempted to resort to using a food lure to get things going and help the dog into the right position. The problem with food lures is this: Unless they are discontinued relatively quickly, the dog (and humans) become dependent upon them in order to perform the behavior. This is not the appropriate use of a food lure, and if lures are not phased out, you will not have a trained dog that can perform behaviors on cue—you will have a dog that follows food.

 **Fact**

For some dogs, the use of a lure is more of a distraction and a hindrance than helpful, and these dogs may do better without a lure as help. Your goal if you do use a food lure is to help the dog into position six times in a row and then on the seventh repetition hide the lure to see if he offers the behavior on his own.

A good general rule of thumb is to lure the dog six times in a row and then on the seventh repetition, do all the same motions with your body, but without the food lure in your hand. If the dog performs the behavior correctly, click and treat. If he doesn't perform the behavior correctly, go back and lure him six more times and try it again. You are giving the dog a mini-drilling session on how to perform the correct behavior and then you are seeing if he understands what he's being clicked for.

When you take the lure out of your hand, you can start phasing it out gradually by putting it on a nearby table and running to get it after the click. The beauty of this technique is that the dog knows it's there and is excited about it but is not dependent on you waving it around to get him into the right position. Using this method to wean your dog off lures means that you get the dog to perform the behavior, click, and then run to get the treat. Doing this exercise will help your dog learn that he is working for the click, and that the treat is an afterthought. Our own dogs sometimes become so engrossed in playing the clicker game that they forget to come and get their treat every once in a while and repeat the behavior over and over, ecstatic that they are right. At this stage of training, however, you should always treat after the click.

Weaning Off the Clicker

The clicker is meant as a learning tool, a marker signal that identifies for your Golden Retriever which behaviors will be rewarded. When your dog is performing the behavior on cue and reliably (meaning that you ask for a behavior ten times in a row without clicking and treating and he performs it perfectly all ten times), he is ready to be weaned off the clicker and treats.

The click and treat always go together. You shouldn't click without treating because the value of the reward marker (the click) will become diluted and less meaningful to the dog. One way to begin the weaning process is to have the dog repeat the behavior more than once before you click and treat. This gives the dog the idea that he must continue to perform the behavior until he hears his click.

Once a behavior is well established and the dog is performing it reliably, you can begin to use real-life rewards instead of food in some instances. Some examples of real-life rewards: the opportunity to go greet a guest after sitting, being released to go play with other dogs after coming when called, or having a door opened after sitting. If there is any regression, go back and show the dog what you want him to do until the behavior is reliable again.

 **Essential**

The worst thing you can do when you are weaning your Golden off the clicker and treats is to do it cold turkey. Getting rid of rewards and information that he is performing the behavior correctly all at once is too abrupt and will result in a frustrated dog.

Teaching Your Golden to Sit

Sit is a handy command and one that is easy for any dog to master. It involves the use of a lure to get the behavior started and a click and treat to let the dog know when he has accomplished the task.

Here are the shaping steps for teaching Sit:

1. Show the dog the treat at nose level and raise it slightly above his head.
2. Put your foot on the dog's leash to stop him from jumping.
3. When his fanny hits the floor, click and treat.
4. Repeat this until your Golden is sitting as soon as you move your hand.
5. Label the behavior Sit as your dog's bottom hits the ground; click and treat.
6. Take the food out of your hand and cue the sit; click and treat if he sits.
7. If he doesn't sit, go back to food in your hand for three to four reps and try again without it.
8. Take the food off your person and cue the sit, then click and run to get the treat.
9. Cue the sit multiple times in a row before you click and treat.
10. Add distractions.
11. Try the behavior in new environments.

🐶 Alert!

If at any point your dog doesn't sit, go back to the previous step for several repetitions before trying to move forward. It is really important that you stay at your dog's pace and not push him to move at a speed he isn't comfortable with yet.

Teaching Your Dog to Stay

Stay is a nonaction command that is difficult to explain to a dog that is in perpetual motion. Stay means hold your position, until the trainer gives the release command. Stay actually has two parts, duration (the time the dog has to wait between each click and treat) and distance (how close or far you are relative to the dog). These concepts should be taught separately and only combined when the dog can do each part individually and well.

Here are the shaping steps for teaching Stay:

1. Start with your dog in a Sit or a Down, and count to two before you click and treat.
2. After you give the treat, count to two again and click and treat.
3. Repeat step 2 and gradually increase the number of seconds until you can get to ten seconds between each click and treat.
4. If the dog gets up, start over and lower the number for a click or two before increasing it again.
5. When you can consistently get ten seconds between each click and treat, label it "Stay."

Shaping steps for adding distance to the Stay command:

1. Now that you are working on a different aspect of stay, lower your standards for time.

2. Start with your dog in a sit or down and shift your weight slightly left or right; click and treat if he maintains the stay.
3. Shuffle your feet around, and click and treat your dog for holding the stay.
4. Move one foot to the left or right, and click and treat if he holds the stay.
5. Move backward and come right back, click and treat if he holds the stay.
6. Gradually take more steps, always clicking and treating on your way back.
7. Gradually lengthen the time you are away as you see your Golden start to get it.
8. Add in the label "Stay" as the behavior starts to look the way you want it to.

Teaching the Down Command

The Down command comes in handy in so many situations and should be taught in many different environments so that your dog will lie down anywhere you ask him to. A dog that knows how to lie down will be a joy to take anywhere, even if he is very active and bouncy. The better he knows Down, the more self-control he will have in new situations and the more pleasant a companion he will be.

The shaping steps for teaching Down are:

1. Start with your dog in a Sit and, using a treat, lure his head halfway to the floor; click and treat.
2. If his rear pops up, it means you lured him too far, so try again.
3. Click and treat only if he lowers his head while keeping his rear on the floor.
4. Gradually try to lure him lower to the ground with a treat held in your fingers or fist, and click and treat any attempts to be lower than before.
5. Eventually your puppy will flop to the ground; click and treat.

6. Repeat this exercise until your dog will flop to the ground on a regular basis on the first try; click and treat.

7. Remove the treat from your hand and tap the ground. Click and treat your pup for lying down without the treat in your hand as a lure.

8. When he has mastered that step, phase out the tapping by pointing first without touching the floor and wait a second: if he makes any attempt to lie down, click and treat.

9. Phase out all tapping until your dog will lie down with a pointed finger signal; click and treat.

10. When he's lying down regularly, label the behavior "Down" as he begins to lie down.

11. Go to new places and practice around new distractions.

12. If at any point he falls apart, go back to an easier step for a few repetitions before moving forward.

 **Fact**

Though most dogs may be able to sit when there are no distractions, this doesn't mean your Golden will be able to sit when a kid with a hot dog approaches him or when he sees his favorite person. Dogs need to be taught by degrees around gradually more stimulating distractions, they don't automatically generalize their behavior to all environments.

Teaching Him to Come When Called

The Golden Retriever is a hunting dog, and with that retrieving ability comes a great nose that likes to hunt up dead stuff to eat and roll in. These are not dainty dogs: They love to get muddy and smelly and will take any opportunity to go out and perfume themselves with nature. This makes it a challenge to teach your Golden to come back reliably when he is called. Remember that dogs do what works, and if it works for your dog to run off and reward itself by eating garbage and rolling in dead stuff, it will, over and over again.

Coming back reliably when called is partly training and partly about your relationship. See Chapter 9 for more details on improving your relationship through leadership. Here are the basic steps for teaching your Golden Retriever to Come:

1. Always start this command while the dog is on a leash to prevent him from running off.
2. Stand with your dog on leash in a mildly distracting environment, and click and treat him whenever he looks in your direction.
3. Put the treat between your feet so that he comes all the way to you.
4. When he is no longer distracted, increase the difficulty by going closer to the distraction or change to a more distracting environment.
5. Don't say anything to him at this point, just watch closely and click and treat him for looking back at you instead of at the distraction.
6. Once he's good at this in a moderately distracting environment, click him for looking at you but then run backward for a few steps and put the treat at your feet.
7. Label the behavior "Come" as it is happening, just before you click and treat.
8. Change distractions, or go closer to the distractions, and repeat from step 1.
9. Change the length of the lead to 12 or 20 feet and repeat from step 1.
10. Gradually work up to dropping the leash and rewarding him for checking in on his own.

At the same time you are training your dog to come to you, be sure you are also following the leadership guidelines in Chapter 9. You will not see a lot of improvement in your Golden's recall if your leadership structure is not in place.

Teaching Your Golden to Leave It

Of all the commands that you will teach your Golden, this one is the most useful for dogs that love to pick up and eat just about anything they can get in their mouths. Owning a Golden Retriever is a lot like walking a vacuum cleaner down the street. If not trained properly, their scavenger qualities come out and they become eating machines. You can train your Golden not to eat everything in sight by teaching him the Leave It command.

The shaping steps for teaching Leave It are as follows:

1. Start with a food treat in your fist and offer it to your dog at nose level.
2. When he gives up trying to get the treat out of your hand, click and treat.
3. Repeat this until he is backing off without even trying to take it.
4. Now, put the treat on the ground with your hand nearby to cover it up.
5. Click and treat him for not trying to take the food.
6. Repeat this until you can move your hand away from the treat.
7. Label the behavior Leave It when he is backing off regularly.
8. Restraining your dog with a leash, throw the food just out of reach, and click and treat him for looking back at you instead of lunging toward the treat.
9. Practice with different Leave It items—such as cats, kids with food, smells, squirrels, other dogs—until your dog will turn easily away from them and look at you.
10. Label the behavior Leave It when he's looking back at you.

Teaching Him to Walk Without Pulling

Goldens are the ultimate sled dogs. They are energetic dogs with places to go and things to do, and they will pull on a leash to go where they want to go. To prevent pulling, it's essential to use a head collar. The head collar is a training device similar to a halter on a horse, and it allows you to prevent pulling by controlling the dog's head. We have had great success with these collars if they are introduced slowly and the dog is taught how to wear it. See Chapter 9 for more details on introducing a head halter. Keep in mind that any training device, be it a training collar, pinch collar, or head halter, is just that—a training device—and in and of itself does not teach your dog how to walk without pulling.

 **Essential**

If you want to teach your dog not to pull, don't give him the opportunity. Eliminate his on-leash walks until you are getting somewhere with his leash manners.

The shaping steps for teaching your Golden how to walk without pulling are as follows:

1. With your dog on a leash, walk briskly.
2. Change direction every time your dog gets in front of you.
3. Click your dog when he catches up with you, and stop to give the treat.
4. Repeat this over and over again until he is trotting next to you; click and treat.
5. Gradually increase the distractions, clicking and treating him for being with you and changing directions when he is not.
6. If your dog puts on the brakes and stops, keep the leash tight but don't drag him; wait it out.
7. As soon as your dog steps forward, even if it's a fraction of an inch, click and treat.
8. Gradually lengthen the time your dog is with you before you click and treat.

Teaching your dog to walk without pulling is time-consuming and, frankly, kind of boring, but well worth the effort. Being able to go for a walk without being dragged down the street is essential to your enjoyment of being outdoors with your companion. You may want to start this exercise indoors in a hallway or basement and then gradually work up to an empty parking lot or driveway.

 **Fact**

When you begin to introduce the outdoors, keep your goals low. Maybe for the first session out in front of the house, you go as far as the first house to your left, and the next session you go the length of a house on each side of yours.

If this seems like a long and time-consuming process, it is. You may find that using a head halter (the brand Canine University® sells and recommends is the Gentle Leader Headcollar) helps you prevent pulling while you are training your puppy to walk nicely on a leash.

▲ A 1½-year-old male, an 8½-year-old male, a 10½-year-old female, and a 5½-year-old male.

Golden Retrievers are big, active, friendly dogs that love to be with people. If they are untrained and unruly, they can be a challenge to control. Sixty to eighty pounds of dog trying to cuddle up to someone he meets on the street can be a scary experience for a non-dog person. The more training your Golden has, the more his gregarious qualities will be appreciated and the less apt he is to injure someone when he tries to "love" them. It's no fun to be greeted if it involves being knocked over by a large, exuberant dog with no manners. Giving your Golden some basic good manners will ensure that he is welcome wherever you go.

CHAPTER 7

A Golden's Life Skills

BASIC OBEDIENCE IS USEFUL and important, but life skills are more important for the mental and emotional well-being of your Golden. A dog that accepts having its feet, ears, nails, eyes, and tail examined is more likely to have a good experience at the vet and the groomer. Teaching a scared dog how to cope with loud noises, stairs, or a slippery floor is essential to his emotional health and well-being and will definitely make him a better pet.

The Targeting Tool

By far the best tool for teaching a dog to accept something new is targeting. Targeting involves teaching your dog to touch his nose to your hand. Once this behavior is built, you can then use it to teach your dog to touch other objects, move from one place to another, or meet new people.

The steps for teaching targeting are as follows:

- Put a treat in your hand and when your dog sniffs your hand, click and treat.
- Repeat this six times in a row with the treat in your hand.
- Remove the treat from your hand and offer it to your dog— when he sniffs it click and treat.
- Repeat this until your dog is pushing his nose into your hand with purpose.

- Move your hand around and see if your dog will follow it to touch it for a click and treat.
- Change your position so that you are sitting, standing, or kneeling.
- Take it to a new location and practice it from the start.
- Label the behavior "touch" when your dog is doing it reliably.
- Transfer "touch" to another person by starting off with a treat in both of your hands.
- Gradually increase the distance between you and your helper until your dog will run across a room to touch someone's hand.
- Change positions so that your dog will touch hands regardless of the person's posture.
- Transfer "touch" to an object by placing your hand closer and closer to the object you want your dog to touch.
- Once your hand is on the object, withhold your click until your dog touches the object with his nose, then click and treat.
- Gradually build up your dog's repertoire for touching anything you point to.

 Essential

One of the best tools you will have for teaching your dog basic life skills is your clicker and treats. The clicker will be used throughout the process to mark progress toward your end goal. Since the clicker is an event marker, it emphasizes for the dog what is going right at the moment he is doing the behavior and is a powerful way to communicate that he has made the right choice.

Once your dog understands the "touch" command, you will have a useful tool for helping him to get over fears, make new experiences positive, and in general communicate to him that investigating the unknown is safe. Teaching your dog to target will help him get over his fears much more easily. Now you have a way to actually get him to discover that for himself.

Alone Time

Lots of dogs don't know how to be on their own. Often they have an unhealthy overattachment to their owners. This is a stressful problem for both dog and owner. There are usually problems associated with this stress, like excessive barking, chewing, and destructiveness as the dog tries to relieve his anxiety. There are lots of ways that you can teach your dog to be alone and be content.

Puppies that have had a good start in life can suddenly seem to stress when they are left alone, and often this is because their owners give them too much freedom too soon. Puppies who don't really know how to act or how to be alone will often relieve their anxiety by chewing on something. This becomes the dog's way of relieving stress when he is alone. If there is no one there to supervise or he is not confined to a crate, he often uses his mouth throughout the house, causing lots of expensive destruction.

 Fact

If you have a dog that barks in his crate, try covering it with a blanket, putting on soft classical music, and leaving a stuffed Kong toy with him to keep him occupied. In the warmer months you can even freeze the Kong (stuff it with dog food and peanut butter) before you leave it with your dog.

When your Golden puppy hits the seven- to nine-month mark, he can have longer bouts of freedom. Someone should still be watching him. At about twelve to fifteen months, you can ease up on the supervision, but he's still not ready to have free run of the house when you are out. A good way to judge whether or not your

Golden is ready for more freedom is to leave him loose in the house for short periods of time, maybe while you work in the yard or mail a letter. If he is into trouble upon your return, you'll know he's not ready for complete freedom. Be stingy with freedom. Your Golden has to earn it by proving that he can be alone without destroying anything.

 **Question?**

Is it cruel to crate my dog?
No. Crating and gating dogs and limiting their freedom is a way to say you love them enough to set limits on where they can be in your home.

The behaviorist Ian Dunbar, D.V.M., recommends that all dogs be taught to be alone by leaving them with their dinner/breakfast stuffed into a Kong toy. They will spend their day unpacking the Kong that you have stuffed with their dog food and peanut butter and leave the furniture alone. The use of crates, gates, and pens is essential when training your Golden to be alone, as you can determine just how much room to give him and make certain areas of your home off limits. Here are more tips for helping your dog to like being on his own:

- Rotate his supply of toys on a weekly basis so that he always has something different.
- Leave him with his Kong only when you are leaving and not when you are home.
- If you work from home, crate or confine him away from you for several hours a day.
- Don't spend all your waking moments petting and having him follow you everywhere.
- Crate him for several hours a day on the weekends, too.
- If you work a long day, hire a dog walker to come in and

break up the day or consider a doggy day-care service at least once a week.

- Practice leaving without an overemotional goodbye.

Going to the Groomer

Goldens need to be groomed on a regular basis depending on the length and volume of their coats. Taking regular trips to the groomer is one way to make your Golden look his best and to reduce the amount of mess and cleanup around the house. Most groomers will appreciate and look forward to seeing your dog if you can do a few simple things to prepare him for his visit there.

Handle your Golden regularly, being sure to stroke all parts, like ears, feet, and tail. Give him plenty of baths when he is young, to get him used to standing still in the tub.

Grooming professionals often groom many dogs in one day. They have a limited amount of patience or time for training your dog. The more preparation you do at home—getting your Golden accustomed to being restrained, touched and handled all over, and being placed in tubs, tables, and grooming equipment—the more skills your dog will have to cope within this new environment. Your Golden will get a better grooming if you help make the groomer's job a little easier by giving your dog some life skills to cope with this new endeavor.

Visiting the Veterinarian

The waiting area of most veterinary hospitals is a scary place for most animals. Since dogs sweat through their feet, they often leave powerful scents that convey their fear to others. Any dog, even a young puppy, will notice these scents, and if his experience is not all that pleasant he will begin to associate the veterinary environment with unpleasant experiences. The best way to be sure that your dog always has a good experience is to go prepared and make it fun. Bring your best treats or a favorite toy, and be generous with your rewards.

◀ A very cute
fifteen-week-old
female puppy
adores her owners.

Here are some tips for making sure that your dog has the most positive experience possible:

- Practice handling your dog's mouth, feet, ears, tail, and body on a daily basis.
- Teach your dog to walk on all kinds of surfaces so the slippery floors aren't so scary.
- Introduce your dog to lots of other dogs on a regular basis and make sure he has great social skills.
- Teach your dog to accept restraint without fighting you.
- Reward your dog frequently in the waiting area for anything he does right.
- Reward your dog for meeting new people by letting the new person feed him special treats.

- Be calm and relaxed yourself so your dog will feel safe.
- Make a list of problems or questions so you can concentrate on your dog and not remembering what you wanted to ask the vet.
- Tell the staff outright if your dog is nervous or has the potential to bite so they can keep everyone safe.
- Visit the vet on a regular basis and practice some obedience in the waiting room with really yummy treats.
- Drop by and have your dog weighed (let the staff do it and have them use awesome treats).

With a little training and some practice, your dog will look forward to going to the veterinarian. Visiting on a regular basis even when your dog is not scheduled for a checkup may make his future visits all that much more enjoyable. You can do a lot to prepare your Golden for all his visits to the vet by making sure that he has the coping skills and experience to get through his appointment.

Teaching Your Golden to Enjoy Being Touched

All dogs must tolerate being touched and handled, and, fortunately, Goldens usually greet touch with enthusiasm. There is a big difference, however, in being touched for petting and playing and being held still for veterinary visits and trips to the groomer. If you break down each skill into its component parts and go at your dog's pace you will have a companion that is ready for everything and will tolerate just about any amount of handling for whatever purpose.

The best time to start teaching your dog to like being handled is as a tiny puppy. In fact, it is very important that your dog was raised in an environment where he was touched on a regular basis by lots of different people. Dogs that don't get this from their early environments will be fearful of new people, new experiences, and other dogs. These puppies will require lots of early intervention and triple the amount of socialization that the average puppy receives.

As soon as you get your puppy, begin handling him and inviting lots of different friends and relatives to do the same.

Here are the shaping steps for teaching your dog to enjoy having his ears handled:

1. Prepare a supply of treats and have them nearby in an open container.
2. Put your hand on top of your dog's head, and click and treat.
3. Massage one ear gently, then click and treat.
4. Turn the ear inside out, then click and treat.
5. Put your finger in the outer part of the ear canal, then click and treat.
6. Using a tissue, wipe out any debris present, then have a helper click and treat.
7. Switch to the other ear and repeat.

If at any time your dog objects or tries to run away, slow down. Enlist the aid of a helper to keep your dog calm and keep the treats coming. Remember that your goal here is to make the experience of having his ears handled a pleasant one. It's important to move at the dog's pace. If your dog shows no objection, continue handling his ears on a regular basis. As with all handling, you can only maintain the good behavior by frequent practice.

Here are the shaping steps for teaching your dog to enjoy having his feet handled:

1. Prepare your treats and have your clicker ready.
2. Touch a front foot, then click and treat.
3. Pick up a foot, then click and treat.
4. Hold on to a foot for a few seconds and click and treat.
5. Hold the foot for longer periods of time, clicking and treating periodically for gradually increasing lengths of time.
6. Put your finger between each toe while clicking and treating.
7. Touch each nail and wiggle it a bit, then click and treat.
8. Switch to the rear feet and repeat from the beginning.
9. Repeat these steps with nail clippers in your hand but don't cut the nails yet.

10. Build up to touching each nail with the clippers, but don't actually cut the nails.

11. Trim the slightest bit off one nail and have a helper click and treat.

 **Fact**

Teaching your dog to target makes helping him get over his fears a lot easier. Whereas before you had to stand on your head to reassure him that he was safe, now you have a way to actually get him to discover for himself that life is not scary.

Feet are a very sensitive part of a dog's anatomy and most dogs do not like anyone messing with them. Preparing your dog for nail trims and foot handling is crucial to his overall comfort since throughout his life he is going to need to have his nails trimmed and feet examined. Be sure you have adequately prepared him by teaching him that tolerating foot handling is worth lots of delicious treats.

Goldens are mouth-oriented dogs—they love to pick things up in their mouths and must be prepared to have people take things away from them on a regular basis.

Here are the shaping steps for teaching your Golden to enjoy having its mouth handled:

1. Prepare your treats and have your clicker ready.
2. Put the palm of your hand on top of your dog's muzzle and click and treat.
3. Rest your hand there for longer periods of time and click and treat.
4. Lift up your dog's gum with your thumb, then click and treat.
5. With your palm over his muzzle, use the middle finger of your other hand to open his mouth, then click and treat.
6. Gradually open his mouth wider, having a helper click and treat.

7. Practice opening his mouth and putting a treat right on his tongue.

8. Open his mouth and put yummy treats in on a regular basis so he comes to expect good things.

Most people only handle their dog's mouths when they are trying to get something back from the dog or when giving medication. It is crucial to the success of your training program to break this cycle by randomly putting good things in your Golden's mouth. You can open his mouth and put treats on his tongue, or put a ball or a toy in his mouth—anything that is appropriate and that your dog will find rewarding. Since this breaks with the usual pattern, your dog will come to expect good things when people handle his mouth and come to accept and even like it. Though time-consuming to teach, every dog needs to exceed at these skills when living with people.

Walking on Slippery Floors

A slippery linoleum or hardwood floor can be frightening to a dog that has never felt such a smooth surface under his feet. Unfortunately, a dog's reaction to a slippery floor is often to walk on his nails rather than the pads of his feet, making traction impossible. After a few seconds of skidding around and not going anywhere, most dogs get scared enough to lie down and refuse to budge, even for the tastiest morsel.

The solution to this is to introduce your Golden puppy to all sorts of walking surfaces. This will help him develop the skills he needs to negotiate any surface. If your puppy is now a growing dog and hasn't had these experiences, he needs practice, patience, and some tips from you.

- Go slowly and at the dog's pace. Fear will interfere with learning and slow down the process, so make sure your dog is comfortable.
- Start by putting small bits of treat on the slippery surface and let him eat them. Repeat this three or four times.

- Sit on the slippery floor about three feet from your dog and wait.
- If he looks in your direction, click and place the treat at his feet.
- Hold your target hand out with a treat in it and wait. If he moves toward it at all, click and treat.
- Now hold out your hand without a treat and if he moves toward it, however slightly, click and treat.
- Continue to scoot back so you are always about three feet away and he is following you.
- Pay attention to any attempt on his part to cover more ground and click and treat it.
- Pay off with a jackpot (three or four small treats) if he does more than a step or two.
- The more you reward movement, the more movement you will get.
- If at any point he refuses to budge, go back a step or more until he's comfortable again.
- Keep the session short and practice frequently instead.
- Once he has mastered one surface, switch to another and repeat from the start.

 Essential

Most dogs, once they learn how to negotiate the surface at their own speed, will be much more willing to attempt another type of surface or the same surface in a different location. Remember that you are teaching a life skill to your Golden. There are great benefits to going slowly and making this a fun process.

Pay attention to any attempt on his part to cover more ground, and click and treat that behavior. Pay off with a jackpot (three or four small treats) if he does more than a step or two. The more you reward movement, the more you will get movement. If at any point he refuses to budge, go back a step or more until he's comfortable again. Keep the session short, and practice frequently instead. Once he has mastered one surface, switch to another and repeat from the start.

Mastering Stairs

Stairs are a unique challenge for many dogs. If they haven't encountered them as puppies and learned how to negotiate them through trial and error, they are usually timid about using them at a later date. Even if they have been exposed to stairs at an earlier age, many puppies find uncarpeted or open-backed stairs a special challenge. There is hope for your Golden, however, in learning to happily negotiate just about any kind of stairs.

 **Alert!**

If your stairs are uncarpeted and slippery, consider installing step grips. These are sold in most hardware stores, and they will make your staircase easier to negotiate for your puppy.

Here are the shaping steps for teaching your Golden to negotiate stairs.

- For two days in a row, feed your dog his meals at the foot of the staircase.
- On day three, put a treat on the first step and if he reaches for it, click and treat.
- Using your hand as a target, move it slowly up to the second step and if he reaches for it, click and treat.
- Stay at the first two steps for six to eight repetitions, using food in your target hand.
- Repeat the hand movements without the food in your hand. If he reaches for your hand with his nose, click and treat.

If he doesn't, go back to food in your hand for three or four times and then try it again without treats.

- Once he is readily targeting your hand without food in it, begin to toss the treat away from the stairs so he has to get down to get it.
- Gradually move your hand up the stairs so that he is climbing more steps to touch your hand for a click and treat.
- Continue to throw the treat down to the bottom of the stairs to encourage him to move away and come back.
- If at any point he seems afraid or unsure of himself, go back a step and rebuild his confidence.
- Use jackpots (more than one treat) to signify exceptional bravery (climbing more than one step, for instance).
- If your stairs are uncarpeted and slippery consider installing step grips sold in most hardware stores which will make the stairs easier to negotiate.
- Consider using your dog's meals to train this skill—nothing like working for your dinner to make the process go faster.

As with the other surfaces that you are teaching your dog to negotiate, it is important to practice in short sessions and stay at the dog's pace. You will ultimately accomplish more by doing less if you are patient and let your dog figure this out at his own speed. These life skills will go a long way toward making your Golden a more confident and enjoyable pet. 🅔

CHAPTER 8

Fears and Phobias

GOLDEN RETRIEVERS ARE NORMALLY SWEET and friendly dogs with moderate confidence levels. A healthy, active Golden Retriever will be eager to explore the world as well as the people and animals around him. Some Goldens, however, whether through an accident of genetics or poor socialization, are not so outgoing or ready for life. These Goldens can be afraid of new people, new situations, loud noises, and chaotic situations. No definite conclusions can be drawn from genetics or environment alone, but many people believe that fear-based problems result from a combination of the two.

Why Goldens Get Scared

Even before his eyes are open—at about the two-week mark—a puppy is taking in the smells and sensations of his environment through his other senses. The ideal environment is in the heart of the household, where the sights, smells, and sounds of the family are part of the puppy's early experience. Hearing and seeing the normal sounds of human interaction and other household chaos (people talking and laughing; kitchen sounds; vacuums; kids arguing, roughhousing, and playing; phones ringing) is essential for a puppy to accept these things as a normal part of his world.

Carefully orchestrated visits by friends and neighbors, including children, should also be part of this puppy's early experience.

Visiting new places within the house or yard, going for a car ride, or taking a walk apart from littermates will make a puppy more willing to explore and adapt to changes in his environment. If a puppy never has these experiences, he will experience a tremendous amount of stress when he is placed in his new home. Suddenly, all familiar sights and sounds are gone. Because he hasn't learned to adapt to change, he will cry and drive his new family crazy until he settles in. The right amount of social experience started by the breeder or caretaker of the puppy from an early age is crucial to the puppy's adaptability and sociability as a growing puppy and adult dog.

 **Fact**

People who talk to and handle puppies during the first several weeks of their lives help to develop an attachment to—rather than a fear of—people. The more diverse and varied the early social experience, the better a puppy will be able to cope with life.

The most common phobia in Golden Retrievers is a fear of loud noises. Handlers call this trait "gun shyness," but a dog that is phobic of noise is usually afraid of a lot more than gunshots. Most of these dogs are also afraid of thunder, cars, traffic, or motorcycles—anything that makes unusual or unpredictable noises. The recovery time from startle to feeling relaxed again can last anywhere from several minutes to several hours. Owners of dogs with sound phobias often report that a dog reacting to a loud noise or scary situation cannot be comforted with petting or sweet talk.

Other common phobias in Goldens include fear of new people, new situations, or unfamiliar objects. Most of these problems have their origin in a lack of enough early socialization or a less-than-desirable early puppyhood. With training, and sometimes the careful application of medication, many Goldens can be taught to be more confident and less fearful of their environment. Any improvement in this problem improves the dog's quality of life and the families' overall enjoyment of their beloved companion.

Fear Interferes with Learning

Fear is not conducive to learning. In fact, studies show that if a dog is frightened, he cannot learn anything. This means no matter how much you try to comfort him or repeat the command, regardless of whether you punish him (which is not recommended), he will not be able to learn anything at that moment. The reason a scared dog can't learn anything is a chemical one. A scared dog is flooded with adrenaline-like substances that tell him to fight or flee. This is a survival mechanism that helps the dog live another day, but it does not permit learning to occur in a training sense. In order for real learning to occur, the adrenaline-producing part of the brain must be in a relaxed state.

 **Alert!**

If you want to teach your scared dog anything, you must get him out of that highly aroused and irrational state of emotion before any real learning can begin. Sometimes the only solution in that moment is to remove him from the scary situation until he calms down.

Helping Your Fearful Golden

There is good news for scared dogs. The part of the brain that has a very basic ability to make associations is still operational, even in a full-blown panic. This means that you can use classical conditioning to pair the scary object or person with something the dog likes. This will help you make excellent progress toward your goal of a more relaxed, teachable dog.

Classical Conditioning

Classical conditioning is pretraining, if you will, a setting of the stage for real learning to occur. Even though classical conditioning is changing emotions, or the way the dog feels about something, it is still a crucial element in the overall learning process, since without it no training can be accomplished.

Though classical conditioning is not directly training the dog to do a specific behavior, it helps to set the stage for it. Some dogs are so fearful that the only progress you can make at first is to develop a very basic association between things the dog fears and things the dog enjoys. With time and patience, you can teach your dog to expect a different outcome when he experiences something he fears.

◀ Two female
Goldens, ages
four and eight.

Classical conditioning has helped many fearful dogs overcome their fears and phobias and go on to live a somewhat normal and enjoyable life. The handler must pay attention to the signals and signs the dog is exhibiting that give information about the dog's level of stress and how he is handling the environment. You cannot have your own agenda when you are working with a fearful dog. You must set realistic goals and be very flexible about how you go about accomplishing them. It is your job as your dog's trainer and handler to provide the best reinforcements, so use your very best treats when you are training a scared dog to be brave. Remember that when a dog is scared, the first thing to go is his appetite. If your dog is too stressed, he won't be able to eat. This is important in helping you keep tabs on how stimulating you make the training environment. If it's overwhelming, you won't accomplish much.

 **Esseñtial**

> If training is to be useful in rehabilitating a fearful dog, it must be well planned and organized. Each session goes at the dog's pace, not the handler's, and each session has a clearly defined goal that is broken down into tiny steps.

Negotiating Scary Situations

Fears and phobias are common behavior problems that are difficult to cure. Some dogs have a not-so-great start in life. Though you may never cure your dog completely from overreacting to loud noises or novel objects, you can still help him by managing and training him.

One thing that really helps any dog get over his fears is the ability to target an object with his nose. If a dog knows how to target, his confidence level will go way up, and you will have a great tool for getting him through a sticky situation. If he spooks upon seeing a bicycle leaning against a fence, for instance, you can have him target your hand right up to the bicycle until he is eventually touching the bicycle when you ask him to "Touch." The added benefit of receiving a yummy reward for bravery is a great confidence booster. Soon you will find that because he knows how to target, he is recovering from his fears sooner than ever. If you have a dog that tends to spook at anything novel, you have a bit of a project cut out for you in building his confidence. See Chapter 7 for a more detailed explanation of teaching targeting skills to your Golden.

 **Fact**

If your dog is feeling afraid, it does no good to punish him or try to reassure him. Punishment will have the effect of making him more afraid, while trying to reassure him may have the effect of accidentally reinforcing the fearful behavior.

Teaching your dog to be more confident is an ongoing process. Set a clear, simple goal for each session and end on a positive note. It's best to train when he is hungry and to use his favorite treats. Keep sessions very short. Pick out different objects that might be likely to make him spook—start out at a distance from these things, then move progressively closer. Don't try to force your Golden, and let him move at his own pace.

You will find that if you work at it, scared dogs will develop more confidence. They will develop better exploring skills on their own than they will if you try to force them to meet or greet new things. Giving your dog the tools he needs to cope with his environment will not only increase the quality of his life, it will make him a better companion as well.

Fear of New People

The best way to get your fearful dog to warm up to new people is to associate anyone new with really yummy treats. You can use targeting (as described in Chapter 7) to teach him to touch the new person's hand on the command "Hi." Once mastered, this behavior can be used to help your dog warm up to new people in new situations and to develop confidence in social situations. Most dogs that have learned the game well will start soliciting attention from strangers just to get clicked.

The key here is to teach your Golden how to target hands with his nose for a click and treat. Be sure, when you're teaching him to greet new people, that you arm them with his favorite treats. Helpers should sit or stand facing sideways to your dog and should avoid eye contact or sudden movements.

The more casual and relaxed the person is, and the less pushy, the more likely the dog is to want to investigate the new person. Some people find that dogs go more willingly to people who may not be dog lovers. Part of the reason for that is that people who love dogs want to touch them, and most scared dogs are absolutely terrified of being touched by a stranger. Choose your strangers well, and be sure that they follow these guidelines for optimal success.

Fear of Other Dogs

If your Golden is fearful of other dogs, you can build up his confidence with training so that the sight of other dogs does not set him off.

Building your dog's confidence to walk outside on a leash around distractions and other on-leash dogs requires the right equipment. The most useful tool for this project is a head halter, such as the Gentle Leader brand, which fits and works well. Introduce your Golden to the head halter slowly, over the course of about a week, using treats and praise to teach him to like it. The head halter allows you to control your Golden by controlling his head. The way it fits puts gentle pressure on the back of the dog's neck and just over the top of the muzzle. These are acupressure points, which help calm the dog and make him feel more secure. The original purpose of the head halter is to prevent pulling, but it also works wonders for building confidence. With your Golden safely constrained on his head collar, you can help smooth his introduction to other dogs.

Here are some tips to get you started:

- Keep your distance at first and gradually decrease it when your dog is under better control.
- Use the most delicious treats available, like liver, chicken, cheese, and roast beef.
- When other dogs are within sight, begin feeding your dog one piece at a time.
- As soon as the dog disappears, take away all the treats.
- Only feed your dog these delicious treats when dogs are present.
- If your dog is panicked or barking, move farther away from the distractions/other dog.

This is an example of classical conditioning, whose purpose is to change the way your Golden feels about other dogs. You are not training a specific behavior to your Golden at this point. Instead, you are developing an association between other dogs and good things; this will help build your Golden's confidence.

 **Alert!**

To help him gain confidence, you must be his advocate. Don't let other dogs scare him by rushing right up to him. If necessary, avoid walking him in areas where there are lots of loose dogs.

Fear of Riding in the Car

Many dog owners report that their dogs are afraid to ride in the car for one reason or another. Maybe they had a bad experience—slipped off the seat when someone stopped short or went on a particularly long ride and got nauseous. The solution to car problems is to reintroduce the car slowly and associate it with good things in very short sessions. You can start by feeding meals in the back seat of your car while it is parked in your driveway. Provide a towel or blanket so your Golden knows he has a spot to lie on. Close the leash in the door or tie it to the armrest to prevent him from leaping into the front seat. Make sure there is enough room on the leash for him to get on and off the seat without choking. You can also use treats to lure him in and out of the car. Start with very short trips, and make sure they all have happy endings— like the park or a friend's house. The key to teaching your Golden to like the car is to keep lessons short and sweet. The more you work at helping him associate the car with happy things, the more likely he will be to happily go anywhere with you.

 **Fact**

Avoid associating the car with unpleasant trips, like to the vet or the groomer. Make sure that you vary your destination to include the park, the pet store, or the beach, so that you change your dog's expectation of what the car means.

If you must travel while you are retraining your Golden, ask your vet what you can safely give your dog to calm him. Some holistic practitioners recommend giving melatonin to help a dog that is anxious. Find a holistic vet in your area to see if this is an appropriate option for your dog.

Thunderstorm Phobias

Fear of thunder is common in Goldens. At the dreaded sound, they might just cower or try to hide, or they might react more drastically by urinating, howling, or trying to escape. Some dogs are so afraid that they injure themselves trying desperately to escape any enclosure including a crate, a gated yard, or basement. Owners whose Goldens are especially frightened of thunderstorms dread the summer and always keep an eye on the forecast. Some research suggests that it isn't just the sound of the thunder that bothers some dogs—they also react to changes in atmospheric pressure and to the harsh flashes of light. Because this is often a complex problem, it is not always easy to fix.

There are some things that you can do to help your phobic Golden be more comfortable. Many holistic veterinarians recommend treating your Golden with 3 milligrams of melatonin about thirty minutes before you think the storm will start. This induces them to feel sleepy and more relaxed, helping take the edge off their anxiety.

Some behaviorists have had moderate success with systematic desensitization. In this case, you would desensitize your Golden by playing taped thunder noises at a very low level during training, feeding, or playtimes. As your dog becomes accustomed to the sound and begins to be able to ignore it, you would slowly increase the volume until he was able to tolerate it at full volume without panicking.

 Essential

Training is always part of the solution with any behavior problem, but some dogs have extreme emotional reactions to the world around them. They need chemical intervention to take the edge off their fears and help them be able to learn something new.

Getting Professional Help

Sometimes fearful dogs need more than training to help them cope with life. If you have spent some time training your fearful Golden with no real progress, you may want to consult a veterinary behaviorist. Fears and phobias are not simple problems, and there is no definite way to treat any one situation. Veterinary behaviorists specialize in the more extreme and unusual behavior problems. After evaluating your Golden, a behaviorist may decide that he would benefit from a course of behavioral drugs to help calm him down and make him more receptive to behavioral modification.

Don't be afraid of behavioral medication. Most dogs only need to be on it for a period of time during the retraining process. If conventional veterinary drugs are not an option for you, you may want to consider consulting with a veterinary homeopath. Homeopathy can offer alternatives that may not have as many side effects or be a better fit for your dog's situation. Explore all of your options before you commit to one. This way, you can be sure that the treatment you are offering your dog is right for him and will do the most good. Ⓔ

CHAPTER 9

Common Behavior Problems

GOLDEN RETRIEVERS ARE FUN-LOVING and energetic dogs with a knack for mischief. Though they can be trained to be great family companions, they are not born trained and will need a fair amount of input from you to achieve the status of well-behaved family member. You'll need a few basic house rules as well as the ability to set limits and manage his environment while you are training your Golden to be a great companion.

Leadership Basics

Dogs thrive on fair, consistent leadership. They get into trouble when the structure is too loose, especially when they are puppies. Dogs are pack animals, which means they do not live in a democratic family base. It is crucial to their survival to have someone else be in charge and make the rules. Leaders provide fair, consistent leadership as well as the opportunity to eat at consistent intervals. Leaders provide protection from predators and shelter to prolong life. They may be dictators, in a sense, but each member of the pack has a purpose that they must fulfill in order for the group to survive. As a human leader it is your job to provide food, shelter, and rules for the pack to follow. The human leader controls resources and ensures that the dog's needs are met while also providing a job for the dog to do to fulfill his role within the pack.

Golden Retrievers are intelligent dogs that are capable of carrying out many tasks. They get bored without enough stimulation or work to do. Though there are exceptions, these are not couch potatoes that are going to wait for you to show up to begin the party! Leadership provides your Golden with firm consistent rules to follow as well as allocation of resources. Valued resources for Goldens include the opportunity to play with other dogs, retrieve, swim, access to people, sleeping and resting places, access to food, access to chew toys, bones, freedom to explore, and the opportunity to interact through training.

 **Fact**

Assume that your role of leader is *not* about being forceful or physical with your dog. There is never an excuse to physically hurt or "dominate" your dog with techniques like scruff shaking, pinning down, and staring in the eye. These are old-fashioned methods. Now we know they are mostly just good ways to get bitten.

Gaining Control of Resources

Leadership is all about gaining better control of your Golden by controlling the resources he wants. By controlling what the dog wants, you make even an independent, dominant dog need you for something. You establish yourself as worthy of your Golden's rapt attention. By following these basic behaviors, you will demonstrate to your Golden that you are the leader:

- No beds or furniture until maturity and only if there are no behavior problems.
- Leaders go through doorways first.
- Leaders go up and down stairs first.
- Leaders ask for a behavior only once.
- Leaders only respond to dogs that are behaving appropriately.
- If the dog ignores the cue, no rewards are given.

- Leaders ask their dogs to do something in order to get a reward.
- Leaders only wait three seconds for their dog to respond.
- Leaders do not play or pet on demand.
- Leaders are consistent with rules.
- Leaders provide structure, training, and exercise consistently.

The best leaders are flexible when their dogs are behaving well and do not exhibit behavior problems. If your dog comes when he's called, does not jump on guests, and in general behaves well around the house, then the house rules can be relaxed. If a behavior problem develops, then strong, fair leaders tighten the reins and go back to following house rules to the letter.

Management

Management is the ability to set up your Golden for success. Management may not in and of itself be training, but it prevents your dog from making the wrong choices and thereby from rewarding himself, which encourages him to inadvertently perpetuate an undesirable behavior. Dogs do what works, and if something isn't working they abandon it as an option.

For instance, if your dog is crated when you are out, he can't eat the sofa. Crating him doesn't teach not to eat the sofa, but it prevents him from using it as his chew toy when you are not there to teach him an alternate behavior. The use of a leash is another possible management tool. You might put your foot on it to prevent your dog from jumping on someone, for instance. Think of management as prevention, and you'll be able to use it effectively in training your Golden to be the perfect pet.

Here are some management tips that will help you set limits on your dog's behavior:

- **Control space.** Use a crate when you are absent and unable to supervise. You can also use baby gates to keep your Golden from off-limit areas. Deny access to areas of your home or yard that are too hard to supervise closely. Use fenced areas for exercise so that your Golden can run and play without running away.

- **Remove opportunity.** Use a long line for exercise if your Golden doesn't come back reliably. Use a head collar if your Golden pulls on leash. Keep kitchen counters clear; store shoes and clothes safely away; keep inside doors closed.

- **Offer appropriate outlets for energy.** Provide plenty of exhausting, fun exercise. Reward good behavior with games your Golden loves and that require him to expend some mental energy, like hide-and-seek or a puzzle ball. Supply things that are good to chew, like a Kong stuffed with kibble and peanut butter.

 **Alert!**

It's unfair to punish your Golden for trouble he got into because he had too much freedom too soon. Make sure that you have set your dog up to succeed before you leave him unattended.

These are just a sampling of ways that you can use management to prevent unwanted behavior. Goldens are late to mature sometimes, but good management, combined with teaching acceptable behaviors, will help you achieve your goal of a well-behaved Golden.

Problems and Solutions

Golden Retrievers wrote the book on behavior problems. Though their problems are not usually very serious, these are big active dogs that you notice when they misbehave. You can't just pick them up or ignore them when they are bent on trouble. Even the kindest of dog owners can get angry to find a favorite rug or pair of shoes chewed beyond repair. Though it's natural to be angry with your Golden for destroying things, jumping on people, or not coming when called (to name a few favorite misbehaviors), the truth is he's only being a dog.

The Problem with Punishment

Punishment doesn't teach anything. It only puts an end to one instance of a behavior. Your Golden can't take back something he's already done. If you punish your Golden after he has chewed up your rug, he doesn't have the ability to connect the punishment with the mess. Instead, he will connect the punishment with you.

Your Golden is a master of learning by association. Once he's chewed the rug, he moves on. If you want to avoid coming home to big messes all over the house, the answer is not to yell or smack his bottom. He'll only learn to dread your return. A better technique is to help him keep out of trouble in the first place. Avoid punishment. Not only will it fail to teach your dog what you wanted, it will hurt the wonderful trust and relationship you have worked so hard to establish.

 Fact

Avoiding punishment will ensure that you maintain the trust you have worked so hard to build up. A dog can't undo a misdeed that has already been done. Move on. Next time, make sure you have set the circumstances so that it is easy for him to succeed, and reward him for it.

Teaching Desirable Behavior

So if you aren't using punishment to "fix" your badly behaving Golden, what can you do? You can teach your dog what you want him to do instead. Instead of wasting all of your energy on correcting your dog for making the wrong choices, you are going to start limiting his options and rewarding him for making the right ones.

This means that you must actively decide ahead of time what you want your dog to do. For instance, if your dog is jumping on people, you might want to teach him to sit instead. Since he can't be jumping if he is sitting, you now have a plan to get rid of jumping. You now must heavily reinforce sitting in the presence of people and prevent him from making the wrong choices by putting your foot on the leash and only allowing greeting when you are ready to train and manage him. Without a clear plan, you are destined to inadvertently give your Golden attention for undesirable behaviors. This will create a dog that gets into trouble more frequently because his bad behaviors are getting rewarded.

▲ A spectrum of gold—a seven-year-old male, a five-year-old male, and a twenty-two-month-old male.

The Joy of Digging

Goldens love to dig! As anyone with an adolescent Golden can attest, these digging escapades can seem archaeological. They are not exactly conducive to nice landscaping. The best solution is to provide your Golden with an appropriate place to dig and teach him to dig there. A digging pit is easy to construct and can keep your Golden busy for hours. Designate a spot in your yard, use garden timbers to square off a section, and fill the area with play sand. Then bury all sorts of cool stuff for your Golden to find—like toys, bones, cookies, or tennis balls—and show him that this is his place to dig.

In order to teach your Golden where to dig, you must be present and supervising. You can't expect him to figure out on his own that the digging pit is where you want him to dig. Take your Golden out to the digging pit, and let him watch you bury some really delicious treats—maybe even a stuffed Kong wrapped in tissue paper. Encourage him to find the prizes. Let him tear off the paper on the Kong—most dogs think this is awesome—and praise him for using his pit. If your dog starts to dig somewhere else in the yard, tell him "No!" Take him on leash over to his digging pit, and help him uncover something exciting.

 **Alert!**

If your Golden spends long hours unsupervised in the yard, it might be a good idea to limit his unsupervised time to twenty minutes at a time. Consider doggie day care or make play dates with other dogs to help fill in his time alone.

Jumping for Joy

Jumping up on people is a Golden favorite. Dogs jump on people to get their attention and to get close to their faces to greet them. In most households this is not acceptable, and this creates a behavior problem. What your dog considers friendly, the rest of the human world considers quite rude. The solution of course is to teach your Golden an alternate way to greet people and prevent jumping from being an option.

The easiest way to prevent jumping is to put a leash on your dog when there are people around, and step on it to prevent him from jumping on them. The second thing that needs to be accomplished is to teach the dog to sit instead. You might teach this in the absence of people and any other distractions until the dog will sit quickly and reliably. Once he has mastered this, you can then move on to adding the distraction of people at a distance and slowly working the session so that they come closer while your dog maintains his sit position.

Your clicks and treats are for maintaining the sit in the presence of the person and should be spaced very closely together until your dog visibly relaxes. An active Golden that is used to launching himself at people will need lots of clicking and treating and a firm foot on the leash for quite a while before they settle down. It may take several training sessions before the new person can even stand close to your Golden.

 **Essential**

> To make progress toward getting rid of undesirable behavior, you need to have a clear idea of what you want your dog to do instead.

As with most training sessions, the speed with which you add distractions is dependent on the dog. You must train at the dog's pace. It may be slow at first, but with practice and persistence you will eventually be successful in teaching your dog to sit for greeting and petting instead of jumping.

Here are some tips to help make your stop-jumping program successful:

- Put a leash on your dog when he is around visitors.
- Be ready to reinforce sitting instead of jumping.
- Have clicker and treats by the door or in your pocket on walks.
- If you are not willing or able to reinforce sitting, the dog does not get to greet the visitor.
- All visitors must ignore the dog—no eye contact, no petting, no talking until he sits.
- Family members must be taught to reinforce sit and ignore jumping.

- Exercise your dog regularly to help him channel his extra energy appropriately.
- Have a basket of toys by the door and have the visitor toss one to your dog.
- Have a visitor come in and sit before you release your dog to greet her.
- Put your dog in another room until the visitor has been inside and seated for at least ten minutes.
- Teach your dog to retrieve a toy when the doorbell rings— some dogs forget to jump when they are holding something in their mouths.

Jumping is not a problem that will disappear on its own, but it is a fairly easy problem to fix. Remember that your dog is only doing what comes naturally to him. Your job is to teach him an alternate behavior that is incompatible with jumping.

Using a Head Collar to Train

Behavior problems like pulling on his leash, mouthing while on the leash, and stealing can be handled safely with a head collar (we recommend the Gentle Leader). This piece of training equipment fits your Golden like a halter fits a horse. It is used to stop your Golden's forward motion. Since there are no corrections involved, the halter is self-limiting. When your Golden tries to pull forward, the halter pulls his head down. Since dogs can't walk with their heads down, they stop pulling. A head halter should always be used with a leash no longer than six feet. This prevents your Golden from jerking his neck by running to the end of the leash at top speed. You should never yank or give a leash correction when your Golden is wearing a head halter since doing so can injure his neck.

The head halter is not something that you can just put on your dog and use right away. Instead, it must be introduced slowly so that your dog can get used to how it works.

Here are the shaping steps for teaching your dog to wear a Gentle Leader head collar:

- Hold the halter in your hand and let your dog sniff it for a click and treat.
- Open the nose loop and repeat.
- Lure your dog's nose through the loop and click and treat.
- Repeat until your dog is willingly pushing his nose through the loop.
- As your dog is eating the treat, reach around and clip the neck piece.
- Leave the whole thing nice and loose so it doesn't feel confining.
- Offer treats to your dog and have him walk several steps.
- Click and treat him when he stops pawing at his face.
- If he gets the nose loop off, take the whole thing off and ignore him for ten minutes.
- Repeat from the start until he is no longer pawing his face to get it off.
- Attach your leash to the clip under his chin and click and treat for the absence of pawing.
- Take him for a short walk in a distraction-free area and repeat.
- Tighten the halter so it fits without slipping off.
- Add distractions gradually and click and treat for walking without pawing.
- Begin to use on walks but keep the walk brief.
- Gradually extend the time.

 fact

Most dogs take about two weeks to get accustomed to wearing a head halter. There are other brands available, but the Gentle Leader seems to fit the greatest variety of breeds and does not slip off easily.

The key to using a head halter effectively is to introduce it slowly and shape the dog to wear it without making him panic. It is important for the effectiveness of your training program not to rush this.

Pulling While on Leash

There is nothing more unpleasant than being dragged down the street by a Golden Retriever. Dogs pull while on leash because we inadvertently teach them that they can. Many Goldens believe that if they pull their owners wherever they want, the owner will follow.

A leash is not a natural thing to a dog. As far as your Golden is concerned, it is just an extension of your arm that he can pull on without consequence. Refer to Chapter 6 for instruction on training your Golden to walk on leash.

There are many training products on the market that claim to teach your dog not to pull while on leash. However, none of these can teach him that walking on a loose leash is what you want. If you don't make an effort to teach your dog what you expect, he will not figure it out on his own, regardless of the training device you choose.

Attach a six-foot leash to your dog's flat buckle or snap collar. Walk a few steps forward and change direction as your dog starts to pull in front of you. When your dog catches up to you, click and stop to treat. Practice where there are few distractions, like your driveway or basement, but as your dog gets the hang of it let him walk next to you for a step or two before you click and treat.

Finally, once he's trotting nicely, don't stop after the click, just treat as you are walking and keep going. Gradually add in distractions, people, noise, smells, and other dogs. Add the cue word "heel" when your dog is trotting next to you regularly without pulling.

Snooping, Scavenging, and Stealing

Your Golden practically lives by his nose. Add that to his natural curiosity and that constant rumble in his belly, and you have a dog with a distinct interest in putting his mouth where it doesn't belong. You can't always be near enough to remove the offending items. That's where the "Leave it!" command comes in.

"Leave it!" means "Stop what you are doing and look at me." "Leave it!" is a wonderful command to teach your dog to keep his mouth off things that are off limits, or to stop him from picking up things that don't belong to him. In order for this to be useful in real life, you must practice until your Golden does indeed "leave it" right away. Refer to Chapter 6 for instructions on teaching "Leave it!"

 **Essential**

If you add distractions too rapidly during training, your Golden will be overexcited and won't be paying attention to what he is getting clicked and treated for. Go more slowly, and introduce the distractions from a distance. You will find that your Golden catches on more quickly.

If Golden Retrievers were people, they would be kleptomaniacs. Goldens love to have things in their mouths. They explore their environments by picking up and chewing on just about anything they can. Whether it's taking stuff off the counter or raiding the trash, be warned: Goldens are accomplished thieves.

Whether this becomes a behavior problem for your Golden depends on your response. Dogs repeat the actions that bring them rewards and attention. How rewarding is it to have your human chase you around the house for fifteen minutes trying to get back a pair of underwear that you stole out of the hamper? Regardless of whether he gets to keep the object, for your Golden, the thrill of the chase makes stealing well worth his while.

There are many things you can do to keep stealing from becoming one of your Golden's behavior problems. You can "allow" him to steal things you don't care about, like an old towel. When he steals these items, walk away and ignore him. If he brings them to you on his own, trade him for something better. This lessens the value of the stolen object and focuses his attention on things that come from you. Practice trading him for everything on a regular basis. Offer him another ball for the one in his mouth, for instance. Trading makes him more likely to give up anything. It also teaches him to expect good things to happen when you approach him. Ⓔ

CHAPTER 10

Creating a Super Learner

TEACHING YOUR GOLDEN RETRIEVER puppy how to learn is the single most important gift you can give him. Studies of young animals show that the more stimulating the early environment, the larger the brain will grow. The synapses in the brain actually become more extensive, and the brain will be measurably larger compared to animals of the same age with a less stimulating environment. This means that you can "grow" a more intelligent adult Golden by providing lots of early stimulation and training.

What Is a Super Learner?

A super learner is a Golden that knows how to learn. By experiencing natural consequences, the forces of cause and effect, and trial-and-error learning, a puppy gains the skills he needs to know to become a dog that can think and problem-solve. It is very exciting to train a dog that can think and make choices for himself. In this style of learning, the dog takes some responsibility for his part in the learning process. This leaves the trainer free to shape and reinforce what is going right.

Super learners have the skills of learning down pat and are ready to solve whatever puzzle you dream up. These dogs are easy to train and have a long attention span. They don't tire or give up easily, which means they can be coaxed into staying in the game long after their appetite for treats has gone. Super learners can elaborate on a concept. They often jump ahead and solve the riddle before you are even done with the exercise. These dogs are amazing to watch, since they are truly communicating with their trainers and giving volumes of information back to the handler about what they need to grasp the concept.

 **Essential**

Creating a super learner involves lots of training sessions and practice in teaching your dog the skills of learning how to learn. These skills involve shaping each behavior by breaking it down into many small teachable steps that the dog performs toward the end goal.

The process of shaping is what creates a super learner. It takes lots of practice and sharp observation skills to develop good shaping skills. The ability to break things down into parts is the key to mastering this concept and becoming a great trainer. The sooner you teach your puppy about shaping, and the sooner you both become proficient at it, the quicker your puppy will become a super learner.

Super learners are dogs that are fun to be around and train. These are dogs with tons of confidence. They love to figure things out, and they are never hard to motivate. They love the joy of playing the clicker-training game and are partners in their own learning. Often labeled intelligent, willing, or high in energy or drive, they are simply dogs that know how to learn. They have the confidence that comes from knowing that they can make choices without fear of being punished—they know instead that they can expect feedback about what behavior causes desired results. Super learners know that making choices and offering behavior is the game, and they are not afraid to approach life with tails up!

Building a Training Relationship

You can become a good dog trainer by honing your observation skills and committing yourself to short, frequent training sessions. As with any physical skill, learning to become a good dog trainer takes practice. Even if your Golden Retriever is simply a family pet and will never enter the obedience ring (or do search-and-rescue, flyball, or agility), being able to train your dog how to drop on recall, find a lost person, or weave through a set of poles on an agility course will make you a great trainer and build a satisfying and rewarding relationship with your dog.

 Fact

Trying to push a stressed, overtired dog may result in a fruitless training session. If you know ahead of time that a certain type of distraction is too much, prepare yourself. Bring your very best treats, keep the session very brief, and have a single goal in mind.

Anyone can learn the skills of clicker training, but only a dedicated dog owner can truly develop the rapport necessary to truly communicate with a dog. Once you reach that level of communication with your Golden, you'll be spoiled for life and never want to train any other way. There are several ways you can build a training relationship with your Golden. Observe his reactions to treats, food, and toys, and pay attention to his favorites. Learn to read his body language so you know when he's tired or distracted. Finally, make sure you meet his basic needs—plenty of exercise, and lots of love—and you can count on him to perform for you.

Learning how your dog works is essential to any successful training relationship since you are partners in the learning process. Training is not something that is done *to* an animal; it is done *with* an animal. The more you grasp that concept and make it yours, the more successful you will be as a dog trainer.

◀ Like most Goldens, this five-year-old male is very affectionate and loves attention from people.

Organization and Consistency

Part of learning to become a good dog trainer has to do with the planning of training sessions. People who are new to dog training tend to try to cover too much all at once. Eventually, they find that neither they nor their Goldens can keep up, and the inevitable result is frustration. If you want your Golden to like training (and to make consistent progress) you need to come up with a plan that simplifies the task you are trying to teach and that teaches it one step at a time. If you try to cover too much ground at once, your dog will become bored, frustrated, and will almost always tune you out.

Break It Down

Part of the success of good trainers comes from the learned ability to break things down into steps and then methodically teach these steps to the dog. The progress you make in a given session will also depend upon the environment you are training in and the amount of distractions present. Dogs who have not been taught to pay attention and block out distractions will not be able to focus for very long. They will accomplish little without your help. Whenever you are teaching a new behavior, the most important thing you can teach your Golden is to block out all distractions and focus on you. You might think you've achieved perfection in your backyard, but if things fall apart in public, you'll see the importance of training around the distractions.

 **Alert!**

> Being successful at training means three things: planning for distractions, having a clear idea of what you want the dog to do, and being prepared to help the dog be successful.

Training is teaching. You don't have to correct your Golden for sniffing or becoming distracted. As his trainer, it is your job to teach your Golden to look away from distractions and back at you. Until you have established this pattern of behavior, you should not try to work around a distraction he cannot turn away from.

Seek Consistency

A good general rule to follow when introducing a new behavior to your dog is to get the behavior consistently (at least three out of four times in a row), and then add gradual distractions. When you add distractions, start with the least distracting and build up to the most distracting. If the behavior falls apart at any point along the way, eliminate the distractions, rebuild the behavior, and then try adding them back in. Your dog will always tell you (by his behavior) if you are moving too fast for him. It's also important to keep track of training sessions. It's easier to help your Golden meet your goals if you know what part of the behavior he has mastered and what's still giving him trouble.

Creative Thinking Skills for Dogs

Providing a stimulating environment for a Golden Retriever puppy will ensure that he grows up to be a smart dog. By experiencing the cause-and-effect nature of life, a puppy begins to learn how the world works. Puppies need to climb on things, chew on things, smell and taste different textures, and walk on slippery floors, carpet, sand, and grass. They need to learn that when they bite a littermate too hard, the other puppy will shriek and go away. They need to learn that when they go potty outside of the sleeping area, their bed stays warm and dry.

The more interesting and stimulating their early environment is, the easier it will be to train the dog that puppy will become. Rotating your dog's toys on a regular basis, going new places, seeing new people, playing with dogs of all shapes and sizes: All of these experiences will give your dog creative thinking skills. Some suggestions for making your puppy's living environment more interesting include boxes to climb over, a child's tunnel to crawl through, lots of different sizes and texture of toys, a paper bag with a cookie inside, different surfaces to walk on, toys that make noise, toys that dispense treats, or a laundry basket with a treat or toy under it.

 Fact

Dogs learn to solve problems by having a wide experience of life. The more different experiences they have, the more adaptable they are as adult dogs and the more tolerant they are of change.

Whatever you decide upon for toys, be creative and vigilant. Be sure that you supervise your dog with different toys, making sure that he doesn't tear them apart and consume the pieces. Rotate the toys frequently. Don't put so many out at one time that your Golden gets overwhelmed and ignores all of them.

The Art and Science of Shaping

Shaping is both art and science. To shape a behavior means that you break it down into its component parts, teaching the dog each step towards the end goal. Shaping can either be free or lured. Free shaping means that the dog offers behaviors without being prompted. In lure shaping, a particular action or behavior is solicited by luring the dog into the desired position. Shaping, by definition, involves selecting behaviors by clicking and treating them as the dog progresses toward our desired goal. Shaping is the process by which we move toward the end goal, by selecting behavior that is moving in the correct direction.

How Shaping Works

Some of the science of shaping comes from understanding how dogs learn and how to reach our end goal. This requires some practice, and perhaps some coaching from an experienced trainer. Being able to know what behaviors your dog has to do to reach the end behavior is crucial in order to know what to click and treat and what to ignore.

 Essential

The more opportunities your Golden has to experience life and the cause-and-effect nature of things, the more willing he'll be to try something new.

The art of shaping lies in knowing the dog well enough to be able to give accurate information. Sometimes, by withholding the click and waiting, we give the dog more information about what we want than if we kept clicking and treating the same behavior over and over again. Becoming skilled at training means knowing when to give more information and when to wait and let the dog figure it out. The more of a creative thinker the dog is, the more behavior he will offer us and the more behavior we will have to choose from. It's no fun to train a dog that just sits there waiting to be told what to do.

Dogs that are not very creative can be taught to be creative, but it definitely takes some practice. Set up training situations in which your dog has to make choices, and reward the choices you like. When your dog makes an incorrect choice, ignore it and wait for what you want. Prevent your dog from rewarding himself with the wrong choice, but don't punish wrong choices. Reinforce generously all correct choices by using a clicker to mark the right behaviors.

Use lures sparingly to keep your Golden from getting too dependent on their presence. Rely on them only to get the behavior started, and stop using them as soon as possible. Only click and treat one behavior, until the dog is offering it consistently. Once a behavior is offered consistently, delay the click so he will try something new.

▲ This sixteen-month-old male and five-year-old female, like most Goldens, love to swim.

The Rules of Shaping Behavior

Shaping a behavior involves certain rules that help the dog figure out how to get rewarded. First of all, remember that the click is a contract between you and your dog. When you click, you must treat. Even if you click the wrong behavior, it is very important to keep your contract with your dog and pay up with a treat.

Shaping a behavior is easier if you know what the individual steps are to the end goal. For instance, say your end goal is to have your Golden Retriever find his bed from anywhere in the house and lie down in it on command. You need to make a list of all the steps your dog would need to do in order to accomplish this goal. The steps can involve a combination of luring (leading the dog with a food treat) and free shaping (waiting for the dog to offer behavior), but the steps must progress toward the end goal in a logical manner.

Dogs learn more slowly and become dependent upon lures if you use them for too long. In general, you'll want to use a lure just to get the behavior started. Then stop using lures, and wait and see if your Golden will offer the behavior on his own. This can be hard for the trainer, because we all want to jump in and help a dog that is confused, but it is a crucial step in teaching your dog to think for himself. He'll be a better learner if he has to figure it out on his own. If he's thinking for himself, you'll have a Golden that does what you want because he knows the behavior—not because you have a pocketful of treats.

 **Alert!**

Clicking and treating at the wrong time may cause a residual behavior that is undesirable, like barking or jumping up, but it can be easily fixed with better timing of the click.

Another aspect of shaping that is critical for success is progress. If you click the same behavior over and over, you will never progress to the end goal. In general, once the dog is offering a behavior consistently, you'll want to stop clicking and treating it so that he will try something else. The absence of the click tells the dog that his behavior is no longer accurate, that he must try something new.

If you don't have the behavior broken down into enough steps, and the next step you are looking for is too big a leap from what he is doing, you will get a confused dog. Confused dogs do one of several things: They bark, they leave, or they do every behavior they know hoping that you will change your mind. If you find that your Golden seems to get frustrated with you when you delay the click, it is probably that you are looking for too big a leap in behavior and need to make it easier for him to succeed.

Shaping Project: 101 Things to Do with a Box

This shaping project has circulated on the Internet for years, and no one knows anymore exactly who came up with the idea. It's a brilliant exercise all the same, in part because of its simplicity. All you need is a cardboard box, a clicker, and some treats.

Put your box in the middle of your training area. Every time your dog looks at it, click and treat. Next, delay the click until he steps toward it. Then maybe he mouths it, or sticks his head inside, or picks it up, or puts a paw inside. As long as he is in some way interacting with the box, he gets clicked and treated. If he walks away and does anything else, no click, no treat.

If your dog makes an incorrect choice (like barking at you), simply don't click. By not clicking, you are giving your dog feedback that the behavior of barking is not rewardable. To make sure that barking is not rewarded at all, turn your head away from your Golden or leave the room if he is very persistent. When he is quiet, return and begin again. If you are getting a lot of barking, it probably means that your dog is frustrated with you and needs you to make it easier to earn the click and treat.

Creating Operancy: Shaping Without a Defined Goal

If you have a Golden Retriever that is new to clicker training, and does not offer much in the way of behavior on his own without luring or prompting, this is a great exercise to help him learn what the game is all about. Shaping without a defined goal means that you click and treat the dog for just about anything he chooses to do with the object. The key, though, is to only click any one behavior until he is offering it regularly, and then withhold the click until he offers some slightly different version of this behavior (or a new behavior altogether).

 **Essential**

Real learning can only take place if the dog is able to understand that his behavior caused the click to happen. Real learning is accomplished through repetition, good timing, and the absence of lures.

Remember the goal here is operancy, in behavioral science terms—which your Golden demonstrates when he tries new things in order to get clicked. To keep it interesting for the dog, you may want to keep changing the object and keep your sessions fairly short. This project is exhausting mentally for some dogs, and they need to learn this game in very short bursts or they will get frustrated and quit on you.

One really useful tool when teaching your dog to offer novel behavior is the judicial use of jackpots. A jackpot is several treats (or a very special treat or privilege) given when the dog has made a leap in understanding the game. An example: your dog may be really stuck on doing one thing over and over and, when you stop clicking for it, he may become frustrated and try the same behavior over and over, staring at you intently, wondering why you haven't clicked him. When he finally stops being repetitive and tries anything new, you would click and give a jackpot. You might use jackpots with this type of dog every time he chose to do something other than the repetitive behavior to help him understand that "other" is better.

Shaping with a Clearly Defined Goal

This is a much easier project for some people. It is a step-by-step progression that moves from where the dog is now to where you want him to be at the end of the project. For instance, you might want to teach your dog to put one foot in the box and spin around in a circle. You would need to map out exactly what you think your dog would have to offer to go from where he is now to the end goal. Here is a possible progression of steps your Golden might take toward this goal:

1. Looks at box.
2. Steps toward box.
3. Sniffs box.
4. Walks around box.
5. Puts a paw over—but not into—box.
6. Puts paw into box.
7. With paw in box, moves other front paw.
8. With paw in box, takes step to side.

You would continue this process until your Golden was spinning in a circle, either clockwise or counterclockwise, with one foot in the box. Depending on the dog and his capabilities and experience, you may skip over some steps or need to add in others in order to help him understand what you want.

Putting Behavior on Cue

Most people who are new to this training method wonder when they should attach a label to the behavior. That is, do they call the behavior by name, like "Spin on one paw" or "Stick your head in the box"? The answer lies in the consistency of the dog's response.

A behavior should be labeled when your Golden can perform it consistently, regardless of circumstances or distractions. If a particular behavior is inconsistent and the dog only does it half the time that it is prompted, chances are if you label it, you will get a variable response to the label or command. The reason for this is that it's still not clear to the dog which version of the behavior you want. When we label behavior we call it whatever word is chosen, like "Sit" or "Paw," right before the dog does the behavior. We want to be sure the dog begins to associate the action of sitting or pawing (with the label we choose) by hearing it just before he is performing the behavior. Once you have repeated it enough times, your dog will begin to offer the behavior as soon as he hears the label.

Alert!

If your Golden is having trouble around a certain kind of distraction, avoid it until you have the behavior consistently. Work on that distraction at a distance, and gradually increase your proximity to it until he can perform the behavior and ignore the distraction even up close.

It is always a good idea to test the label to see just how well the dog actually knows it. The best test is what is called the ten-for-ten rule. Ask for the behavior ten times in a row without clicking or treating your Golden, and see how many he gets right out of ten. If he is less than perfect, then you must go back and help him by varying how many repetitions of the behavior he has to do for one click and treat, until you can build the number of repetitions up to ten.

You may find that distractions are the deciding factor in this test. In that case, you would work on increasing the distraction level slowly while your Golden is learning fluency. To teach a dog to be able to perform a behavior every time you ask for it, regardless of the distraction, you must avoid letting the dog flounder or repeating yourself over and over. Ⓔ

CHAPTER 11

Teaching Your Golden to Retrieve

MOST GOLDENS ARE NATURAL RETRIEVERS, meaning that they are born knowing how to pick up things in their mouths and carry them. Some Goldens, however, are not genetically gifted when it comes to retrieving things, or they have the desire to pick up things but don't bring them back. Refining a talent for retrieving takes some training, but having a dog that you can teach to fetch his own leash or put away his toys is worth the effort it takes to polish this ability.

Natural Abilities

Golden Retrievers were originally bred as hunting dogs whose job it was to pick up downed game (mainly ducks, geese, and pheasant) and retrieve it for the hunter. Though not all Golden lovers bring their dogs hunting with them, a strong drive to retrieve can make it easier to teach your Golden other retrieve-related tasks. The Golden's original purpose as a hunting companion still creates a strong desire to retrieve in most Goldens. The best working dogs do not have to be taught to retrieve. Their natural abilities make it easy to teach them the refined art of marking and finding downed birds.

However, not all Goldens are bred as field dogs. Though most still like to carry things around in their mouths, some Goldens would prefer to eat the object or roll on it before bringing it back. These Goldens will need some training to help them learn their job in the bargain and make them more reliable in delivering the goods to hand.

Shaping the Retrieve

For those Goldens that are not naturally gifted to retrieve, there is hope. You can teach your dog step by step how to pick up and retrieve just about any object he is physically capable of carrying. Remember that the retrieve is a task with several steps, which you will have to break down into tiny pieces so that your dog can learn exactly what he is supposed to do to earn the click. As with any behavior that you are teaching, you will not always make forward progress. There will be times when you will jump a few steps ahead, but you will also have times when you will have to go back to the beginning and remind your dog of what to do. It is always a good idea to go back to a previous step and make sure that your Golden understands his job, rather than to push ahead with your dog only half-sure of what he did to earn the click.

Here are the shaping steps to teach your dog to retrieve:

- Start with a novel object that is lightweight, but not a toy or a ball.
- Arm yourself with a clicker and treats and sit in a comfortable chair.
- Hold out the object to your dog and if he sniffs it, click and treat.
- Repeat this for six to eight repetitions and then withhold the click and treat.
- If he opens his mouth to grab it, click and treat.
- Lower the object about halfway to the floor. If he lowers his head to follow, click and treat.
- Repeat until he is following the object steadily.
- Lower the object all the way to the ground and repeat the touch with his nose for a click and treat.
- Once the nose touch is well established, stop clicking for it and wait.

- Most dogs get frustrated at this point and will mouth the object. Click and treat anyway.
- Continue to click and treat for mouthing until it's well established and then stop clicking and wait.
- Again, out of frustration your dog will probably hold onto, pick up, or toss the object, but click and treat anyway.
- Continue to establish each behavior and then stop clicking for it to frustrate your dog into trying more.
- Once he is picking up the object regularly, withhold the click for a second or two and then click and treat.
- Continue to delay the click and treat so that he will hold the object for longer periods of time.
- Once your dog is regularly picking up the object, call the behavior "take it."
- Once your dog is holding the object for five to ten seconds at a time, call it "hold."
- Switch objects and then start over from the beginning.

 **Fact**

The retrieve behavior has a natural component in Golden Retrievers, but not all Goldens will pick up any object that you point out. To make your Golden a more reliable and useful retriever, consider spending some time teaching him to pick up novel objects like socks, laundry, recyclable cans, trash items, toys, car keys, or the newspaper.

No Force Necessary

Using force to teach your Golden how to retrieve is not necessary or desirable. If you want a willing partner who will work with you and do your bidding, you need to remind yourself that to your Golden, it is all a game. He has no ability to choose the training method used to teach him his role in the game, but he deserves training methods that don't cause him discomfort. You can get 100-percent reliability in retrieving behaviors in any breed of dog using clicker training and positive methods.

▲ Retrieving is in a Golden's blood. This twenty-two-month-old male loves to retrieve his bumper on land or water.

For a pet Golden, your goal is to have fun together learning something new. Using a no-force method means that you must be organized. You must break desired behaviors down into little pieces, and you must train frequently. It also means that you figure out all the different circumstances surrounding the retrieving behavior and teach your dog that his job is the same, regardless of the circumstances.

 Fact

From a positive perspective, everything is just a variable to be overcome with training. There is no deliberate disobedience on the dog's part that needs to be punished.

Despite the weather, the conditions, or whether the bird is heavy or light, your Golden must learn to pick up and bring it back every time. When the behavior falls apart under the one or two circumstances you didn't think to train for, it's back to the drawing board—time to train your dog under the new circumstances.

Retrieving Birds for Fieldwork

Golden Retriever clubs across the country hold field tests for Goldens, where they can prove their retrieving and marking abilities and earn titles. Fieldwork involves retrieving lots of fallen birds, some of which are already dead (thrown by helpers to simulate being shot). Teaching your dog to retrieve fallen birds requires that your dog have a basic knowledge of the retrieve. It is a bad idea to let his first experience with retrieving something be a dead smelly bird that he would much rather roll on than put in his mouth. You might start with a bumper (a cylindrical plastic or canvas training aid) or a rubber model of a dead duck. The benefit to this is that you don't have to keep thawing out and freezing dead birds, which tend to smell quite ripe after a while. Using the shaping steps already described, choose one of these objects as your starter. When your dog is willingly picking up and holding the bumper or rubber bird dummy, switch it for the real thing and start again.

 Essential

The benefit of shaping with a similar object is that your dog will have some idea of the basic behavior you are trying to teach him before you add in the distractions of the object being a real bird with real smells and real feathers!

Once your Golden learns how to retrieve the bird, now your job is to think up as many circumstances as possible that he will encounter in his field career. The birds he's supposed to retrieve might be hidden in tall grass or in bushes. Sometimes they will be waterlogged and hardly breaking the water surface. Your Golden will have to retrieve in all kinds of weather and despite distractions like birds flying overhead, gunshots, or other working dogs. Teach him to pick up the bird under as many of these circumstances as you can.

Teaching Tricks That Involve Retrieving

To teach tricks that involve retrieving, you have to break the behavior down into tiny pieces that will logically lead your dog to the end goal. Being able to take a behavior and break it down to its component steps is the art of trick training!

Map the Steps

Your first task with any trick is to sit down ahead of time, before you begin to train your Golden, and write out your shaping plan step by step. It is better to be overly detailed and end up skipping steps than to not write out enough steps and have to think on the fly. Another important point to remember is to not be afraid to go back to the basics if necessary to help your Golden get it right. If he forgets the basic part of the retrieve, picking up and holding the object, he will not be able to progress through the rest of the steps. This may mean backing up a bit and teaching him that retrieving this new object is not unlike any of the other objects. You do this by breaking the retrieve of this new object down into its component steps.

 **Fact**

Tricks that involve retrieving are exciting to show off to friends and family, and they're a great way to increase your Golden's skills as a retriever. Keeping an intelligent and active dog engaged in a fun activity will mean that he has less time to get into trouble around the house.

If your dog objects to a certain type of object, don't be afraid to get several of them and allow him time to become familiar with them before you ask him to retrieve them. Giving your dog a chance to overcome his uneasiness over a novel object will make him more likely to get over it more quickly and permanently. This is a much better idea than rushing ahead, only to have the whole behavior fall apart at a later date.

Back-Chaining

A great technique for teaching retrieving tricks is to figure out what your Golden has to do to perform the trick, step by step, and then teach him these steps in backward order. The purpose of using back-chaining to teach a trick is that the dog learns the hardest parts of the trick first and the easy stuff last. This means that the dog's performance will get better because he is nearing the end of the trick and therefore moving toward things he knows well. You might teach "Go get me a drink from the fridge" using back-chaining like this:

1. Retrieve bottle off bottom shelf.
2. Close refrigerator door.
3. Open refrigerator door.

Of course, teaching a behavior like this would have many more steps than just these three. Still, this is the order you would use if you use back-chaining to teach this trick. Teaching the trick backwards would mean that the behavior of retrieving the bottle would be very strong because we taught it to the dog first. By the time we were teaching the dog to open the refrigerator door, he would be moving toward the most familiar behavior and therefore more confident about what came next. If you want flashy retrieving tricks that your dog can perform on a single cue, use back-chaining to teach them!

Most Golden Retrievers live to carry things in their mouths. They can easily be taught a wide variety of tricks and useful tasks with kind, gentle methods. It is so important to offer an outlet for your Golden's need to have things in his mouth. Teaching your dog games and tricks that require him to retrieve will help meet not only his basic instinctual need to retrieve, they will also give him an appropriate outlet for all of his boundless energy.

"Go Get Your Leash"

This trick is both fun and functional. It gives your dog a job to do and makes him look pretty darned smart. The success of this trick depends not only on your dog being familiar with where the leash is kept, but also on his ability to reach it. The best solution to this is to install a designated hook upon which you always keep his leash. That way he will always know where to find it when you ask him to retrieve it. Here are the shaping steps for teaching "Go get your leash":

1. Fold your leash in half and have your Golden take and hold it for two seconds, then click/treat.
2. Increase the distance that he must travel to get to you by backing away as he approaches.
3. Shape the delivery of the leash to your hand by holding out your hand and delaying the click for gradually closer attempts to drop it into your palm.
4. Place the leash on the floor and follow the steps for shaping your dog to pick it up.
5. Once he is picking it up willingly, delay the click by two seconds so that he'll hold it.
6. Increase the time that he will hold it before clicking.
7. Hang the leash on the hook, and cue your dog to take it.
8. Once he has mastered the "Take it" reliably, cue him with "Get your leash," followed by "Take it."
9. Gradually fade out the cue "Take it" once he is reliably retrieving the leash and delivering it to your hand.

"Go Get the Phone"

This trick is a blast, but you may also have to teach your Golden to retrieve a paper towel to wipe the drool off the phone before you use it! You may want to start with an old phone that you don't currently use—some dogs are particularly clumsy and a bit rough at first. Later, when your Golden has perfected his technique, you can switch over to the real phone.

 Essential

> This trick works best if you keep the phone on a low table or on the floor in one location so that the dog can easily find it every time you ask for it. If you want a more challenging trick, you could also add in a "Find" command as well!

The shaping steps for teaching "Go get the phone" are the same as those for "Go get your leash." Remember to fade out the "Take it" cue, and always work at your Golden's pace.

"Find My Keys"

What a great solution to misplaced keys! For this trick, your dog must not only be able to pick up and deliver your keys, he must also be able to use his nose and eyes to locate them.

 Fact

> Dogs don't usually like to pick up and hold metal objects in their mouths. To make retrieving your keys easier on your Golden, you may want to attach a key ring that is attached to a soft tab of cloth material.

The shaping steps for "Find my keys" are similar to the other two retrieving tricks. However, once you've taught the behavior, you then teach your Golden to hunt your keys down, wherever they may be. Start by hiding them close by on a chair or table, for instance, and then gradually increase the distance and difficulty.

Once he is able to find them reliably, introduce the new cue "Find my keys" and fade out the "Take it" cue.

"Pull Off My Socks"

This is a wonderful trick for anyone who has trouble pulling off their own socks, or for moms hoping to speed up the undressing process while trying to herd the kids into the tub. You may want to start this trick with an old pair of socks—the more dedicated retrievers will find this trick particularly exciting, and they'll tend to rip a pair or two before they are able to perfect their technique. Here are the shaping steps for teaching "Pull off my socks":

1. Place an old sock on the floor and tell your Golden "Take it."
2. Hold the ankle part of the sock, and shape your dog to take it by the toe.
3. Repeat until he is reliably taking the sock by the toe.
4. Add some resistance, and pull back gently when he takes the toe.
5. Delay the click until your Golden is holding and pulling slightly for a second or two.
6. Gradually delay the click until he is hanging on and tugging.
7. Put the sock on your foot so that most of it is hanging off, and start from the top.
8. Gradually delay the click until your dog is pulling the sock off your foot.
9. Gradually pull the sock further up your foot until it's almost all the way on.
10. Label the behavior "Pull my sock" when it is happening reliably.

When teaching this behavior, use an adult as the sock wearer until your dog learns to use his mouth gently and not nibble your toes. Once your dog is a pro, you can gradually introduce new people, though you should always supervise young children. Ⓔ

CHAPTER 12

Choosing the Right Diet

FEED YOUR DOG WITH KNOWLEDGE, an understanding of his basic nutritional needs, and some savvy for negotiating food labels, and you'll save lots of money in veterinary bills down the road. Dogs that eat low-quality food will have health problems as a result. Feeding your dog a premium food made of the highest-quality ingredients means that you are giving his body every chance at good health.

A Quality Diet

Dogs that are fed a low-quality diet often have chronic ear infections, eye discharge, diarrhea, frequent bouts of vomiting, skin problems, allergies, and hyperactive temperaments. Not all of these ailments are caused solely by a dog's diet, but poor nutrition does not support a healthy immune system and therefore makes the dog more prone to problems. The best way to help your Golden Retriever get a balanced, high-quality diet is to educate yourself, as a consumer and a dog owner, and to buy the very best food you can.

Commercial Dog Foods

Many people are surprised to learn that commercial dog food has only been available for the past fifty years or so. Before that time, dogs lived on meat scraps and leftovers, and they were no less healthy than dogs today. In some ways, dogs that lived fifty years ago were even a bit healthier; for one thing, they had far fewer allergies and skin conditions.

The convenience of a processed food has brought with it some very undesirable side effects. The main problem with commercial dog food is the variation of the quality of the ingredients from brand to brand. Contrary to what you may have been led to believe, not all dog food is the same. As with many things in life, you get what you pay for.

Price Matters . . . But Beware

Price alone does not guarantee the quality of a good dog food, but good quality ingredients do cost more. The best dog foods are not cheap. Most of the larger companies don't invest in that market because the profit margins are just too small. The reason for this is that it is expensive to make a dog food with human-grade nutrients and proteins.

Lower-quality dog food is much easier to process because of the high grain content. The ingredients are less expensive, and therefore the profit margins are huge. A large-scale manufacturer can afford to sell its food for pennies a pound because it costs them next to nothing to produce. To avoid paying more than you should for low-quality food that is not going to benefit your dog's health, learn to read the label and decide for yourself whether or not a food is worth the price.

 **Alert!**

Beware of using price alone to determine food quality. There are many high-price brands that promote themselves as "super premium," but if you scrutinize the label you will find that the quality is not always there. More effort and money may have been put into slick advertising and marketing to get you to buy the food than into the food itself.

What's in Dog Food?

The dog food industry, though regulated, is far from strict about the quality of the ingredients that go into dog food. There are huge variations in the quality of ingredients used by even very reputable companies. As a dog owner, you will do well to read labels and compare ingredients to be sure you are getting the best quality for your money.

Manufacturers are required to list the ingredients by weight, with the heaviest appearing first. This does not necessarily indicate how much of that ingredient is present. For instance, some sort of meat may be listed as the first ingredient, followed by several meat by-products and grains. Because the meat contains a lot of water, it is heaviest and therefore listed first. However, the food probably contains far more grain and by-products than the higher-quality and more nutritious meat.

 **Fact**

A processed dog food can't be more than half meat, since any greater percentage would jam up the mechanism that processes the food and cause production problems. Production problems mean huge losses of revenue and are avoided at all costs.

Here is a list of what to look for in a quality dog food:

- A whole meat source as the first two ingredients, such as chicken and chicken meal. Avoid a food that lists a grain as two of the top three ingredients.
- The meat content should be higher than the grain content.
- Whole unprocessed grains, vegetables, and other food should appear farther down the list.
- Preserved with mixed tocopherols (vitamin E, vitamin C).
- Meat and meat meal should be labeled as coming from a

specific source. Look for "chicken" rather than "poultry" and "chicken meal" rather than "poultry meal."

Even when you have this list to guide you in choosing a high-quality food, you may still run into problems deciphering labels. For instance, a food might list a meat ingredient first but then follow that with two grain sources. Meat by weight is heavier, but if there are no other meat proteins listed in the first three ingredients, it is likely that the food contains proportionally more grain than meat.

Quality of Meat Sources

The quality of the meat source is the most important part of a food. The quality of the protein source separates the really good food from the really poor quality ones. The protein source in dog food should be from meat versus a plant source. The dog's body is not designed to process huge amounts of grains, and the canine anatomy is designed to thrive on high-quality protein from a high-quality meat source.

Meat sources also come as meat meal, which is an acceptable form of protein and still of good quality. Meal is a rendered product. It is cooked, dried, ground, or otherwise processed but still a good source of protein. Meal cannot contain blood, hair, hoof, horn, hide, manure, or stomach contents. Meat meal and bone meal have the same prohibitions except they can include bone.

 **Essential**

In general, stating the source of the protein is better than a general label. This means that chicken meal is better than poultry meal, chicken by-products better than poultry by-products, and chicken digest better than animal digest.

Meat by-products are lower-quality meat sources. A by-product departs greatly from a nutritious source of protein. By-products can include some meaty muscle, but also beaks, feet, entrails, kidney, brain, liver, bone, lungs, hair, hooves, manure, and other waste products. By-product is the trash of the protein world: mixed up, ground together, and sold as a source of protein (sometimes the sole source of protein) in a dog food.

A product called meat digest is the worst of all in quality: this is by-product treated with heat and water to form a slurry, further diluting the already low-quality source of protein.

A good general rule of thumb to follow is that anything less than meal is not fit for a high-quality diet in dog food. Avoid dog foods with less than desirable sources of protein.

The Trouble with Corn

Corn is a source of protein, but a food that uses it as its major source of protein is not a high-quality food. Corn and corn products usually make up most of a cheap food's protein content, supplying a substandard source of nutrition to any dog fed this diet.

 **Alert!**

Dog-food manufacturers often use a combination of a high-quality source of protein (like chicken or beef) mixed with a very low-quality source like corn. If corn is listed among the top three ingredients on the label, the majority of the protein likely comes from the corn source, meaning the food is not high in quality.

Corn is a cheap source of protein, and dog food manufacturers like to use it because it costs less and does not gum up their food-processing machines. This is true of corn gluten meal as well, an even cheaper source of corn protein found in many bargain dog foods to replace a higher quality source of meat protein. Not only is corn a poor protein source, but some dogs are actually allergic to corn and corn by-products.

Identifying High-Quality Foods

No single food is right for every dog, and there isn't a food out there today that is perfect. You will continue to search for the right mix of ingredients, and in the process may need to take some good with the bad. Knowing where to compromise may help you make a more informed choice when choosing among the higher quality food labels.

◀ A seven-year-old male Golden out in the field with his bumper.

A high-quality food should have a minimum of food fragments. A food fragment is the by-product of another manufacturing process. For instance, brewer's rice is actually a by-product of the alcohol industry. Wheat bran is the fibrous hull of the wheat kernel. Fragments of foods are less nutritious than the whole source. Most foods contain some filler, but you should try to avoid foods with several fragments of a single food. For instance, if the label reads lamb, rice flour, rice bran, and brewer's rice, chances are the food has a lot more rice than the meat source, driving down the quality of the food.

Meat by-products are another ingredient to avoid as much as possible. Avoid foods that use meat by-products as a protein source: This is indicative of a low-quality food. Be sure that the source of the by-product is listed. Chicken by-products are of better quality than animal by-products, for instance.

Ingredients to Avoid

A lower-quality food will advertise itself immediately if you know what to look for. Generic fats and proteins listed as animal fat or animal proteins are often the bottom of the barrel in nutrients. Some animal fat sources can actually be the recycled grease from restaurants. A preferable alternative would be beef fat or chicken fat. Again, it's the name of the source that makes this a better alternative than the generic label "animal fat." In addition, be mindful of terms like animal protein or poultry protein. These are inferior to beef or chicken protein.

 **Essential**

Avoid buying a bargain dog food at your local discount store. Chances are the source of protein is mostly corn, and the sources of meat are of very low quality. The price tag may seem like a bargain, but the health problems to follow won't seem nearly as cheap when you are making those frequent trips to the vet.

Steer clear of artificial colors and preservatives. There isn't a dog alive that cares whether its food is brown, green, or red. Colors are added to enhance the way a food looks to the owner. They do nothing to contribute to the quality of the food for the dog.

Artificial preservatives have received a lot of hype over the years, and, regardless of which studies prove what, they are best avoided. Artificial preservatives are listed as BHA, BHT, or ethoxyquin. These are all chemical preservatives used to make the food last longer and to survive the occasionally extreme heat and cold involved in trucking the food to the local pet supply store.

Probably the most offensive ingredient in the lower quality foods is, by far, propylene glycol. The same ingredient found in antifreeze, this chemical is added to chewy foods to help them stay moist. High levels of propylene glycol can shut down the kidneys and kill a dog. Avoid foods with this ingredient.

Sweeteners make dog food more palatable. These include corn syrup and sucrose and are often added to foods to increase their appeal. A high-quality food shouldn't need anything to make it taste better, not even so-called natural chicken or beef flavor.

Natural Diets

After poring over dog food labels, you may well be so fed up with commercial dog-food manufacturers that you start searching for a better way. Dog-food manufacturers aren't the only ones who can create a food that dogs thrive on. People have been feeding dogs the same foods that they eat for decades without half the problems the dog-food industry has created.

 Fact

The more available the nutrients in a food are without having to be broken down by digestive enzymes, the more likely the dog is to gain the most benefit from the food.

If this information has you rethinking your choices, you might consider a homemade or raw diet. Many great resources can be found on the Internet (along with all the really great canine nutrition books out there) that describe how to prepare nutritious, wholesome food for your dog. Investigate how these diets are put together, and determine whether or not they are right for you and your Golden. People switch to a homemade or raw food diet for their Goldens for all kinds of reasons. Most have to do with the dog's improved overall health and increased longevity. This is also a good way to address basic problems like allergies, dull coat, intestinal upset, frequent ear infections, or skin and coat problems.

The ability to hand-pick what goes into your dog's food by making your own makes reading dog food labels a nonissue. By making nutrients available in a usable form, your Golden can use his food a lot more efficiently. This means he gets all the benefits of good-quality and carefully selected ingredients.

Bones and Raw Food Diet

The bones and raw food diet (commonly known as BARF) was popularized by an Australian veterinarian named Ian Billinghurst. He believes that dogs require raw meaty bones and meat as the basis of their diet, with fresh vegetables from a variety of sources and very minimal grains. Dr. Billinghurst has written several books on what he calls the natural diet (listed in Appendix A).

 **Alert!**

The volume of stool output is a good indication of how well the dog's body is able to absorb the nutrients in the food it is eating. People who feed a raw diet claim that stool output is minimal, meaning that their dogs are gaining maximum benefit from the food they are eating and creating very little waste.

This diet calls for giving raw bones to dogs in the form of chicken, turkey, beef, and lamb. "Raw" is the key here. Cooked bones are dangerous to dogs because they splinter and can perforate the stomach and intestines. They should be avoided completely.

Some folks who are squeamish about giving whole raw bones grind them or chop them up into smaller pieces.

There have emerged several resources for people who want the benefits of feeding raw but don't have time for the labor of preparing meals. Several companies make a raw diet, which consists of ground bones and vegetables, and package the resultant mix in frozen patties or sleeves. Trying this out requires a little room in the freezer and a bit of preplanning. The basics of this diet are simple, and though you can supplement the bones and raw meat and vegetables with vitamins, the simpler you keep it the better. Supplementing with essential fatty acids (like cod liver oil or fish body oil) may be beneficial to some dogs depending on their current overall state of health. The type of vegetables used should be varied, so that they come from both an underground and an above ground source.

You don't have to make every meal balanced, so long as your Golden gets the variety of foods he needs to be healthy. Dr. Billinghurst recommends thinking about your dog's diet the same way you think about your own diet. Every meal that you eat is not complete and balanced; you get the nutrition you need over the course of a week's time, not at every meal.

Homemade Diets

There are several sources out there that recommend their own version of a homemade diet. Check the person's credentials before following their word as gospel. Most homemade diets are at least partially cooked, and most don't include bones.

Some of these diets are what is commonly referred to as the "kitchen sink approach." They include a little bit of everything, all tossed together in one big porridge-like mixture. Most of the homemade diets include some grain, meat, and vegetables along with supplements like alfalfa and kelp, with vitamin E, vitamin C, and essential oils.

Homemade diets are definitely more time-consuming for the dog owner, but some people prefer them to the convenience of kibble. One benefit of a homemade diet is that you can fine-tune it to your own individual dog's needs. In fact, many people who have come up with these homemade diets started out doing so out of necessity. One of their beloved pets could not eat storebought food because of a medical condition or allergy, and so they developed their own diet that lacked the ingredients that aggravated the problem. People who feed a home-prepared diet swear they would never go back to commercial food, and they are always looking for ways to make their home-prepared mixture better and more nutritious for their very lucky pets.

 **Essential**

Thoroughly research any diet, and make sure you understand how it works before feeding it to your Golden. If your dog has any allergies to certain proteins like chicken or beef, or to grains like wheat, you'll want to provide meals that steer clear of those ingredients but still meet his dietary requirements.

Dietary Supplements

Depending on which diet you feed, you will need to follow the author of that diet's recommended guidelines for supplements. There are tons of prepackaged feeding supplements on the market today. Make yourself familiar with them to help simplify the process. Read the ingredients label to see exactly what is in each supplement, and be sure that you are not overdosing on any one vitamin. You can also go to any health-food store and purchase each supplement separately and add them to your dog's food at each meal. Some common supplements are kelp, alfalfa, vitamin E, vitamin C, cod liver oil, fish body oil, eggs, flaxseed oil, and yogurt.

One supplement that most Golden Retrievers can benefit from is the proper balance of essential fatty acids. EFAs, as they are commonly called, are often present in commercial dog food, but evaporate out of the kibble before you have a chance to feed it to your dog. The essential fatty acids for dogs are a combination of omega acids 3, 6, and 9. Every dog is a little different in the way he uses these fatty acids, but their absence can result in the chronic skin problems so common in the Golden Retriever.

Finding the right balance of fatty acids is essential for healthy skin and coat. These supplements can be found in a prepackaged form in dog supply catalogs and pet stores, or you can go to the local health-food store and purchase them separately. EFAs are extremely heat- and light-sensitive and should be stored in the refrigerator after they are opened. It is important that you do a bit of research by reading a good canine nutrition book (as listed in Appendix A) for the dosage recommendations, and finding the right source of essential fatty acids for your situation.

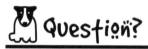 Question?

My dog is overweight. What should I do?
If your dog is overweight, assume the responsibility of taking the weight off of him. A Golden Retriever will literally eat himself to death. Goldens have absolutely no ability to regulate how much food they eat—if left to their own devices, they would literally eat until they exploded. It is entirely up to you as your Golden's guardian to reduce his calorie intake and help him stay lean.

How Much Should I Feed My Golden?

Keeping your Golden Retriever lean and fit is probably the best thing you can do to ensure his good health and longevity. Fat dogs are much more susceptible to health problems, including diabetes, cancer, heart problems, skin problems, bone and joint malformations, and injuries. If you feed your dog commercial food in the form of kibble or canned, do not use the label as a guide on how much to feed your dog. Most labels on the major brands recommend feeding way too much of their food compared to the weight of the dog. Is this because your dog has to eat huge amounts of the food in order to meet the dietary requirements for a dog his size? Or do they simply want to sell you more of their food? Whichever is the case, the result is a fat dog that is not going to enjoy a problem-free life if you don't reduce his caloric intake and trim him down to a leaner form.

Observe Closely

First of all, you'll want to be sure you are feeding a very high-quality dog food. The higher the quality of the food, the more calorie-dense the food. High-quality dog food has very little if any filler, which makes the food less bulky and more compact. This means your dog needs less of it to be healthy and fit. A cup of high-quality dog food per 60 pounds of dog is a good general rule of thumb for feeding your Golden Retriever. If your dog weighs slightly more or less, you can adjust it accordingly.

Feed your dog this amount for about four to six weeks, and then observe his weight. If he looks too thin, then gradually increase the amount by a quarter of a cup at each meal until he is at his ideal weight. If he's looking heavier than when you started, back off on the amount at each meal by a quarter of a cup and re-evaluate his weight in a month's time to see if you are moving in the right direction.

Dogs on a Diet

The quickest way to get extra pounds off an obese dog is to decrease the amount of food he is consuming and to provide more exercise. A very overweight dog should not be exercised vigorously. A short game of fetch or a short walk in the neighborhood is better than nothing.

Of all activities that dogs participate in, swimming is by far the safest. Most Goldens love to swim, and even an overweight dog can get in and paddle around a little to burn a few calories. Swimming is actually a pretty safe way to exercise an obese dog because there is virtually no impact on the joints. It goes without saying that you should provide exercise in moderation, and always observe your overweight Golden for signs of fatigue. If you observe him carefully and go at his pace, you will find that in time your Golden will be able to last longer than you will at his newfound activity.

To avoid adding calories to your dog's daily intake, use his dog food for training sessions or cut back the amount you give at mealtimes to make up for a busy day of training.

We owe it to our dogs to make sure they live the longest, healthiest lives possible, and they cannot do that if they are overweight. With a little help from you, your Golden will soon be lean, healthy, and be able to look forward to a long and happy life. Ⓔ

CHAPTER

Visiting the Veterinarian

ESTABLISHING A GOOD RELATIONSHIP with a qualified veterinary professional is essential to the overall well-being and enjoyment of your Golden Retriever as a healthy family pet. Being comfortable with and well informed about veterinary issues will ensure that your Golden gets the very best care available. It will also help you make the best choices about your Golden's overall health. It's every pet owner's dream to have a dog that lives to be a ripe old age. With the help of excellent veterinary care, you can make sure that dream becomes a reality.

Searching for the Right Vet

Choosing the services of the right veterinary clinic or hospital will benefit both you and your dog and ensure that you both have many happy years together. The time you take to search for just the right practice will mean peace of mind later, should your animal become ill or you need advice about a chronic health problem.

Veterinary Options

Most veterinary hospitals also come with a staff of veterinary technicians and management professionals that must also be proficient at their jobs. When you are searching out a new veterinary hospital, be sure to ask other dog owners where they go and why. It is essential to be sure that a practice has what you need to take the very best care of your pet. Remember, you'll be using this practice for the next decade or longer.

A full-service veterinary hospital will not only offer yearly check-ups and vaccinations, but also offer diagnostic testing, X-rays, and surgeries. The more services they offer as far as health care is concerned, the more likely they will be able to serve your Golden's needs throughout his entire lifetime. Being able to communicate effectively with the staff is important, but being comfortable with their veterinarians is also crucial. Though a group practice may have several veterinarians, you can get to know two or more of them and request one of your favorites when you make an appointment.

 Essential

It is perfectly appropriate to bring along small, novel, and delicious treats to feed your Golden during the exam, so long as it does not interfere with the exam itself. This alone may help relax your Golden if it's his first time on the exam table.

Choosing the right veterinary professional is a lot like choosing a doctor. The ideal person will be friendly, sociable, knowledgeable, and capable. The right vet will ideally belong to a practice that is not too large or too small and that can accommodate the needs of your pet without a lot of extra fuss. Once you find this person, stick with them. A good relationship with the professional who is going to be taking care of your beloved companion for the next ten to fifteen years is worth its weight in gold. Choose well.

What to Expect at Your First Visit

Most veterinary practices have a puppy visit or a well-dog visit that includes a physical exam and vaccine boosters, if necessary. The physical exam can vary from vet to vet, but in general most veterinarians will check your Golden's ears and eyes, open his mouth, and look at his teeth, tongue, and gums. They will palpate the belly, look at the feet, lift up the tail, check the genitals, and listen to the heart rate and lungs. Some will take your Golden's temperature, especially if he has been acting a little off. Most of the time, the vet will also take a stool sample to check for intestinal parasites. Some vets will trim the nails and empty the anal sacs as well, while some only do this if you ask them to.

Preparation for a Good Experience

There are lots of things you can teach your dog to make sure he gets excellent veterinary care throughout his life. Whether he likes it or not, being touched, held still, and handled will be a big part of his future around veterinary hospitals. The sooner he learns that these are good things, the better for both of you. You can begin to prepare your dog for experiences at the vet by working with him daily in calm, nonconfrontational sessions. Find a low table, and cover it with a towel or mat. Practice putting your puppy or adult dog up on the table and feeding him treats. Keep one hand on him at all times so that he does not fall off the table, and make sure he doesn't jump off on his own. Pat him and talk to him as you slowly go over every inch of his body.

 Fact

The more time you invest in getting your puppy used to being handled, the better treatment he will get at the veterinarian and the happier he will be receiving that treatment. It is unreasonable to expect a dog that was never taught to be handled to allow complete strangers to handle him at will.

Start with his head. Turn his ears inside out, while feeding him tiny pieces of a treat. Go really slowly if he seems not to like this, and stop if he struggles. Wait for him to calm down, and when he does begin again. Work your way down his body. Open his mouth, look at his teeth, put a treat on his tongue. Move the gums on either side of his mouth and count his teeth, then give a treat. Hold his mouth shut gently, and give a treat.

Clean the corners of your dog's eyes with a piece of gauze or a tissue while you give a treat. Touch under his chin. Feel his trachea, and trace it down to his collar while you feed him. Talk to him quietly. Tell him what a wonderful puppy he is and how much you love him. Move on to his neck.

Grab the loose skin over his shoulders and feed him treats while you play with it. Practice grabbing the loose skin all over his body, all the while feeding him treats and talking in a happy voice. Examine his tail, and feed him a treat. Lift it up, push it side to side, and tug on it a little while you praise and talk to him and tell him what a wonderful dog he is.

Next comes the belly. Touch it while he is standing, sitting, and lying down. Roll him over, and give it a rub. Keep his mouth busy with treats and a toy to chew on. A toy will help for those dogs that have to have their mouths on something. Work on the legs and feet next. Put the puppy in your lap. Gently run your hand over each toe and up and down the leg. Feed him treats for putting up with this—most dogs do not like having their feet touched. The more he associates touch with good things, the more he will like it.

As your puppy begins to tolerate the once-over, gradually extend the time you take to examine each part. If yours is the Golden that is full of energy, be sure to do this in very short thirty-second sessions at first. Your goal will be to gradually increase the amount of time to a minute and then later to longer and longer periods of time.

Good Health Maintenance Basics

The better job of health maintenance you provide for your Golden, the more certain you can be of preventing problems from becoming big issues. Golden Retrievers are a relatively healthy breed, but they are prone to some chronic problems.

Prevent Ear Infections

Ear infections are one common problem in Goldens. Golden ears are floppy. Because this breed also loves to swim and roll in mud puddles, Goldens are more prone to ear infections than other breeds of dogs. As a maintenance basic, you should wipe out your Golden's ears with a tissue or piece of gauze once a week. The inside of the ear should be healthy pink, with very little black dirt or wax. The black dirt is often wax that should easily wipe out. Buy an ear cleaner at the veterinary office that has a drying agent, and put a squirt of it in each ear. Let your dog shake his head, and then wipe out the excess.

 **Essential**

The ear canal is deep and at a right angle, so don't be worried that you will puncture the ear drum—you won't be able to reach it with your finger wrapped in gauze.

If the ear is not pink and healthy but is red and irritated-looking instead, or if there is a lot of black crud, take him to the vet for a check. Ears that are red and irritated-looking might mean an ear infection. Some dogs hold their heads to one side or shake frequently when they are beginning to get an ear infection, but others show no obvious signs.

Tooth Care

The Golden's teeth are easy to maintain and keep healthy. As a breed, they are not all that prone to a lot of tartar buildup, though this may depend upon the quality of their diet. Maintaining healthy teeth requires a gauze pad and a small amount of dog toothpaste. The human kind irritates the doggie stomach and should not be used. Put a small amount of paste on the gauze, and rub it on the teeth. Do this daily if possible for maximum results. Most dogs don't really mind this much. If yours does, break the process down into simple steps, and use treats to reward your dog for holding still.

Look at the Eyes

Goldens don't usually have a lot of trouble with excessive eye discharge. Still, it's a good idea to wipe your dog's eyes with a tissue every morning. This way you can be sure that the discharge doesn't build up and irritate the eye. Goldens are prone to scratches on their eyes from rolling in grass and dirt. If your dog is squinting or has a yellow or green discharge from one or both eyes, it's a good idea to bring him in for a check. Dogs can get conjunctivitis just as people do. The form they get is not transmissible to humans, but it is extremely contagious to other dogs. Your veterinarian will check for scratches on the lenses of the eyes and give you the appropriate ointment.

◀ An eleven-year-old female Golden.

The Paw Pads

Cut paw pads are a given with any active breed, and Goldens are no exception. A cut pad cannot be stitched—the skin on the pad is dead and callused and heals from the inside out. Cut pads should be seen by a veterinarian and washed and bandaged carefully. The bandage will have to be changed several times over the course of a week or two before the tissue granulates in enough for your Golden to walk around without a bandage. It is crucial that the bandage is not too tight and that it is kept clean and dry.

 Question?

How can I keep the bandage on my dog's paw dry?
A great trick for keeping a bandaged paw dry is to put an inside-out latex glove on the paw and secure it with masking tape.

Spaying and Neutering

It is highly recommended that all dogs that are not going to be used for breeding and showing purposes be spayed and neutered. An unspayed female is at risk of unwanted pregnancy and a serious infection of the uterus called pyometra. An unneutered male dog is also at risk of breeding other dogs and contributing to the problem of puppy overpopulation as well as developing testicular cancer and prostate problems as he ages.

Avoiding the magnification of certain behavioral problems is also another reason to spay or neuter your Golden. Common problems associated with being intact include marking territory inside and outside, aggression, territorial guarding, resource guarding, fighting with other dogs, and running away. These problems are not solely relegated to unneutered animals, but the fact that they are unneutered isn't helping the problem.

The medical problems associated with being intact include mammary tumors and cancer, pyometra (an infection of the uterus), testicular cancer (rarer but a threat), anal tumors in male dogs, and prostate problems. Yes, there are people who leave their dogs intact and don't have problems, but leaving your Golden intact is a huge responsibility for the average pet owner.

Vaccination Schedules

Vaccinations help the dog's body make antibodies against the disease it is being vaccinated for. When they work correctly, they prevent the dog from developing the disease by teaching the immune system how to recognize and eliminate the disease should he encounter it. Most veterinarians recommend that dogs receive the Da2PPL and rabies vaccinations. The Da2PPL stands for the combination vaccine, which covers distemper, adenovirus type 2, parvovirus, parinfluenza, and leptosporosis. Puppies are vaccinated differently than adult dogs because the ideal timing of vaccine administration is not known.

 Fact

You will find that the vaccination schedule varies from region to region, but only slightly. Depending on the region you live in and what diseases are prevalent in your area, your veterinarian may make recommendations for additional vaccinations. These might include Lyme disease or coronavirus.

Ideally the vaccinations should be given when the mother's immunity wears off, but no one knows exactly when that happens. Therefore, puppies are vaccinated monthly until they are sixteen weeks old. Once an adult dog has received his initial puppy vaccinations, he is normally vaccinated yearly or every other year for the distemper series, and every three years for rabies. In most states, in order for the rabies vaccinations to be good for three years, your dog must have received two vaccinations nine to twelve months apart. If you miss the cutoff by even one day, the rabies vaccine is considered good for only one year.

Vaccinating the puppy helps him develop immunity against the more common diseases that he might be exposed to during this critical time in his immune system's development. Most conventional veterinarians recommend two to three doses of Da2PPL combination vaccine. This is usually administered somewhere around eight, twelve, and sixteen weeks. A rabies vaccine is given somewhere between sixteen weeks and six months. The most life-threatening diseases for your dog are distemper, parvovirus, and rabies. Any additional vaccinations will vary depending on the region where you live.

Vaccine Titers

No one knows exactly how long the effect of a vaccination lasts. The vaccine companies make recommendations to veterinarians as to how frequently they think that vaccines should be given, and most veterinarians pass this information on to their clients in good faith. The vaccine company—which profits from the administration of vaccines—is probably not the best source of that information. However, there has been very little study of how often vaccines are really needed.

Homeopathic veterinarians believe in vaccines for pets, but they do not recommend they be given quite so frequently. They also recommend the use of titers to determine just how much immunity a given animal has toward a disease. A vaccine titer is a blood test that is used to determine a ratio of immunity. The lab that performs the test usually comes up with a value that tells how much of a response the dog's body has had to that particular part of the vaccine. This provides the vet with information about whether revaccination is warranted or not.

Titers are usually checked every two years to determine whether the dog is still carrying immunity to that particular disease. Arguments among conventional and holistic veterinarians abound because no one can decide just how much immunity is enough. Most homeopathic vets say that any immunity is immunity and is enough to justify not revaccinating. Most conventional vets, on the other hand, say that the risk of contracting these diseases is real and probable without frequent (yearly or every other year) vaccination. Deciding the right approach for your Golden is tricky. Everyone wants to do the right thing and protect their Goldens from these awful diseases. No one can give you absolute answers, and no one wants to face the consequences of making the wrong decision.

 **Alert!**

Strong arguments exist for using vaccines sparingly. Many homeopathic veterinarians believe that the overvaccination of pets is the source of many of their chronic problems and development of cancers.

Do your homework. Read, research, and search for answers before you make a decision on how often to vaccinate. It is very important to be an informed consumer in today's world; the health and well-being of your beloved Golden depends upon it.

The Hazards of Overvaccination

Many homeopathic veterinarians believe that we are killing our pets and destroying their health by overvaccinating them. If your dog's body is constantly bombarded with a barrage of vaccines that it doesn't need, the results can manifest themselves in many ways. Too much of a good thing does have consequences, and those consequences often present themselves in ways that are detrimental to the health and well-being of your pet.

Problems that some people believe are related to overvaccination include chronic skin problems; hair loss; hot spots; excessive licking, scratching, and biting of feet, rump, and tail; ear infections and allergies; and temperament and behavior problems. No formal conclusive testing has been done to conclude that vaccinating pets too frequently causes these problems, and that is the problem.

Until there are conclusive studies, veterinarians will continue to recommend vaccinating dogs yearly or every other year. If you begin to read the research, a lot of evidence does suggest that these chronic problems are related to overvaccination and a poor diet. There is a lot of overlap between the quality of food we provide and the excessive use of vaccinations, medications, and steroids. Everything we do for our dogs has a consequence. The best you can do for your Golden is to arm yourself with knowledge, search for answers, and make the best decision you can.

Remember that what you find in your original research may lead you to the decisions you make now, but don't leave it at that. Medical technology is advancing rapidly. The more you keep on top of things, the better you will be able to make the right decision for your Golden. When it comes right down to it, no one is trying to harm your pet—it's just that everyone thinks they are right. It is up to you as your dog's caretaker and provider to make the best decision with as much information as you can gather. Ⓔ

Common Health Problems

EVERY BREED HAS ITS SHARE OF health problems, and the Golden Retriever is no exception. Many dogs carry the genes for hereditary problems without showing expressions of the disease themselves. These dogs can pass those problems on to future offspring, however, and this is why it is so important to be an informed buyer when you are purchasing a puppy. Making sure that the puppy's parents have been cleared for certain genetic diseases will give you the best chance at a healthy puppy that grows up to be a healthy adult dog.

Hot Spots and Skin Issues

Skin problems are unfortunately very common in Golden Retrievers, and some dogs are much more prone to them than others. These problems can begin with an allergic reaction to a flea bite. This causes the dog to bite and scratch at the spot until it is raw and bloody. Depending upon your region, this may be a seasonal problem or a problem that constantly plagues your Golden. If flea season lasts year-round where you live, you probably need some sort of insecticide to keep these pests from feasting upon your Golden. If you live in an area where fleas are seasonal, you might be able to get away with frequent vacuuming of rugs and furniture, with plenty of dog baths and brushing.

Topical flea preparations are not to be taken lightly—these chemicals can be quite powerful. Though they will kill or repel fleas, you want to make sure that they don't also harm your Golden. There are numerous flea and tick products on the market today, and each proclaims its superiority at repelling and killing these pesky pests. This is another subject that you have to research so you can find the best product for your dog. You'll want to find out about the chemicals in the flea repellents as well as the methods of administration.

There are powders, spray, topicals, and flea collars. Each of these may be useful, depending on your situation and your dog's overall health. Be wary of waterproof flea and tick products, as these have a longer staying power on your pet. This might be desirable if you want the product to withstand frequent swimming escapades, but it's not so great if your dog has a sudden allergic reaction and you need to wash it off right away. Remember that insecticides are poisons that we are putting on our dogs to keep pests at bay. Use them sparingly, follow package instructions, and bathe your dog before reapplying them.

 Essential

You may take a wait-and-see approach and apply a product only if fleas or ticks become a problem for your Golden that year. Or you might choose to apply the product every eight weeks instead of every four weeks. Minimize the chemicals you expose your dog to, and you will benefit his health in the long run.

Be a smart consumer, and read up on the latest products. This is a good way to avoid getting talked into using something that is more toxic and powerful than you need. Your dog is depending upon you to make the right decisions for his health and long life, so do your homework!

Digestive Problems

Golden Retrievers are the ultimate scavengers. They absolutely love to eat just about anything they can fit their mouths around. This causes problems with their intestinal tracts, which often can't quite keep up with the barrage of new and delicious delicacies. Be it acorns, grass, leaves, mulch, tissues, paper, wrappers, leftovers, or stuff that they find on their walks, a Golden will just about eat anything. The dog's digestive system is designed to take a lot of punishment, but sometimes it has had enough. It lets the rest of the body know it by presenting itself as diarrhea, vomiting, and sometimes lethargy. If you have a Golden whose frequent raiding rampages land him with a sick tummy, there are lots of things you can do to help him get his belly back on track. Try these tricks:

- Withhold food for twelve hours to help him empty out his system.
- Give an adult dog one adult dose of an antidiarrhea pill (such as Imodium); give a child's dose for puppies sixteen weeks and up.
- Allow access to plenty of fresh water.
- Give plain boiled (not instant) rice with plain boiled chicken or hamburger for the next meal.
- Continue this until the stool is firm again and there is no vomiting.
- Gradually wean back to dog food by mixing it in with each meal.

Watch your dog closely for signs that the problem is more serious, in which case it might require veterinary attention. If your dog vomits after eating, is extremely lethargic with a painful belly, or vomits or has diarrhea more than a few times in a row, have your vet take a look.

Intestinal blockages are very common in dogs that tend to eat things that they shouldn't, and Goldens are likely candidates. Keep track of what your dog is eating, and train him to leave it when he has something he shouldn't. Dogs that are blocked usually vomit after eating and become very lethargic. This situation requires immediate attention, including X-rays and possibly surgery, so don't delay getting your dog to the vet if you think he has eaten something that is stuck.

 **Fact**

There are lots of causes of diarrhea and vomiting. If you own a dog—like a Golden—that likes to scavenge, it's easy to get a little blasé about it. You should still be careful. There are many serious problems that can manifest themselves with diarrhea and vomiting in the initial stages, and these should be ruled out if there is any question.

Socks, plastic bags, and cellophane are common culprits of intestinal blockages. These are more dangerous because they are difficult to detect on an X-ray.

Pancreatitis is another condition that requires prompt veterinary attention. It can be the result of eating very greasy, rich food, like the drippings from the turkey or garbage that has been sitting around a while. Because there is often no way to tell if the diarrhea and vomiting in your dog is just something small or the symptom of a more serious problem, it is important to stay alert and monitor your dog closely.

If you have any question at all about whether you should take your dog for medical attention, call your vet and describe your problem. The staff will be able to tell you how long it is safe to wait before having your dog seen.

Genetic Screening

Some common problems in Golden Retrievers appear to have a hereditary component. Hereditary defects mean a predisposition to develop the disease, not the actual presence of the disease. In some cases the genetic link has not been proven, but compelling data suggests that certain defective traits run in families of dogs. To avoid perpetuating the problems caused by the defective genes, it is important that affected animals never be used as part of a breeding program. Some dogs can be carriers of a certain defect. They never develop the disease themselves, but they can pass it on to their offspring.

 **Alert!**

Many backyard breeders or puppy brokers are only looking to make a profit on the dogs they breed. They are not interested in genetic screening or careful selection of mates for their dogs. Buyer beware! If the price sounds too good to be true, it probably is.

Genetic screening is meant to help weed out animals that carry defects and stop their perpetuation. It is not always possible to know ahead of time if an animal is going to develop a defect, but screening can detect problems before they manifest themselves. This helps breeders make good decisions about which animals to include in their breeding programs. Some genetic screening is done one time only, but other tests are done every year or every couple of years. All screening provides information about the genetic potential of the animal to develop problems. You'll want to choose a breeder who is knowledgeable about this process, with the ability to explain each type of screening and what it means. Reputable breeders keep current on the latest genetic screening processes. They can provide written proof that the tests have been performed by board-certified veterinarians.

Eye Problems

Golden Retrievers are prone to certain eye defects that are thought to be genetically based and passed on. One common eye problem in the Golden Retriever is entropion—a turning in of the eyelashes that causes rubbing and damage to the cornea. This condition can usually be corrected with surgery. It does not have to be a debilitating problem. Cataracts are another common defect in Goldens that can affect one or both eyes. Some cataracts are hereditary, while others are not. Though most do not cause vision loss, some types can progress to severe loss of sight or total blindness. Progressive retinal atrophy is a degeneration of the retina that does leave a dog blind. This can be detected by yearly genetic screening. Retinal dysplasia is an inherited defect of the lining of the retina. It can cause a reduction of vision but usually does not progress or result in blindness. Overall, it is important to be sure that the breeder you choose is familiar with these possible eye problems and has done his or her best to screen the dogs so as to avoid passing along these undesirable defects to future puppies.

 **Fact**

Certain environmental factors may make the appearance of the defect more likely in animals with a predisposition to it—for instance, sudden rapid growth, or excessive intake of calories. The environmental factors can trigger the disease but only in an animal that was predisposed to developing it anyway.

Entropion

This is the most common eye problem in the Golden Retriever. The lower lid rolls in, bringing the skin hairs and/or lashes in contact with the cornea of the eye. This rubbing of the lashes or hair across the surface of the cornea causes discomfort, irritation, squinting, and, over time, damage to the cornea. There are a number of variables that manifest entropion in a dog that is predisposed to the condition. Most animals are not born with the defect. Instead, they acquire it between one and four months of age. Some of the variables that can cause the defect to develop into a problem are the growth rate of the skull; conjunctivitis, an inflammation of the membrane that lines the inside of the lids; distichiasis, which is extra lashes growing on the lid that rub against the cornea; loose skin around the eye, possibly caused by a loose ligament at a corner of the eye; and ectopic cilia, misplaced eyelashes on an upper lid.

Overall, entropion is a fixable problem if it is caught early enough. There must be surgical intervention before the cornea becomes too damaged. Affected animals and their parents should not be bred.

Cataracts

Depending upon their severity, cataracts can cause blindness in Goldens. A cataract is defined as partial or total opacity of the lens of the eye. It appears as a triangular white spot, usually on both eyes, but occasionally on just one. Most cataracts do not interfere with the dog's vision. Examination by a board-certified veterinary ophthalmologist is necessary to determine whether the cataract has genetic origins. Dogs with hereditary cataracts should not be bred, nor should their parents.

 **Esseñtial**

Most cataracts are not present at birth. Usually, they begin to develop within the first year. Most cataracts can be removed surgically with great success—they need not cause a permanently debilitating condition in the dog.

Progressive Retinal Atrophy and Retinal Dysplasia

Progressive retinal atrophy is a disease that leads to the degeneration of the retina, leading to complete blindness. This is screened for annually in breeding animals, and any animal who has not been completely cleared should not be bred. Golden Retrievers considered for breeding should be examined every year by a board-certified veterinary ophthalmologist until the age of eight. A written evaluation of the exam, as well as registration with the Canine Eye Registry Foundation (or CERF), will make the dog eligible for a clearance number. Do not buy a puppy from anyone whose dogs have not been examined and cleared.

Retinal dysplasia is an inherited defect of the lining of the retina and is more common in Goldens than progressive retinal atrophy. This disease reduces vision seriously, but the disease does not progress and does not result in total blindness. The same guidelines still apply, and all Goldens should be cleared of all eye defects on a regular basis in order to participate in a breeding program.

Hip Dysplasia

This is by far the most common of defects in large-breed dogs. The more common the breed, the more commonly you will come across this defect. A dysplastic dog is one whose hip joint is not properly formed. The hip joint consists of a ball and socket. In normal, healthy hips, the ball is seated tightly in the socket of the hip. In a dog with hip dysplasia, the hip joint does not fit together well due to poor placement of the aligning structures or shallowness of the socket. The poor placement causes uncomfortable movement and often friction from constant bone-to-bone contact or because the joint is too loose.

Effects on the Dog

The resulting effects on the dog can often be devastating. Dogs with bad hips often experience bouts of lameness, have trouble getting up after lying down, and have trouble maneuvering stairs and jumping. As these dogs age, the problem can progress to the point where they are in severe pain and euthanasia is the kindest option. Because the joint does not work correctly, it is prone to develop arthritis and worsens with age and excessive weight gain. In the past, it was advised that dysplastic dogs not be exercised a lot and not be allowed to run or do anything strenuous. Though their activity level may be severely impaired, it is actually *better* for dogs with hip dysplasia to be as active as possible so they can develop the proper muscle compensation they will need to remain mobile.

Though hip dysplasia has a main genetic component, there are several environmental factors that can exacerbate the problem in dogs with a predisposition. Obesity is a serious one. Dogs that carry around extra weight put stress on all of their joints. They are much more prone to injury than dogs that are fit. Dogs with hips that are not well formed are even more prone to problems from excessive weight, which puts way too much stress and strain on a joint that is already compromised. Rapid growth spurts, often seen around adolescence, can also be a problem, as can physical stress from sports involving repetitive jumping or jarring, like disk catching or flyball. These factors would not trigger problems in a dog with normal hips, but in a dog that is predisposed to hip dysplasia it can cause major problems. It is always best to have your dog examined by a veterinarian before starting any new sport or activity that involves a lot of jumping and twisting.

 **Fact**

It is believed that many different genes affect the expression of hip dysplasia. Because of that, researchers are unable to isolate any one single cause of the disease.

Genetic Screening for Hip Dysplasia

The most common diagnostic tool for evaluating a dog's hips are X-rays. These must be taken and then read by a board-certified veterinary orthopedist. The Orthopedic Foundation for Animals (OFA) operates as a voluntary diagnostic service and registry of hip status for all breeds of dogs. Based on evaluations of hip X-rays, dogs over two years old are rated as follows: excellent, good, fair, borderline, mild dysplastic, or severely dysplastic.

Most informed breeders will not breed any dog with less than a fair rating. Doing so would almost certainly pass along at least some traits of malfunctioning hips to at least some of the offspring, thus making the incidence of hip dysplasia far more likely in future dogs.

 **Essential**

> Ask lots of questions of your breeder, and make sure that both of your puppy's parents have received a fair rating or better from the OFA. This alone will not guarantee your puppy will not develop a problem, but it is your best gamble.

Another way to evaluate hips has been developed recently. A procedure called Penn Hip evaluates a dog's hips by the laxity as well as the tightness of their fit. The values are given in percentages within each breed. After the evaluation, you get a value that tells you where this particular dog falls within his breed. If, for instance, your dog fell in the 30 percentile, his hips would be considered better than 30 percent of the Goldens who have had Penn Hip measurements taken, but worse than 70 percent of the overall dogs tested. Each breed has an average range that careful, knowledgeable breeders try to stay within to prevent the occurrence of hip dysplasia from rearing its ugly head in their breeding programs.

Elbow Dysplasia

Elbow dysplasia is a malformation of the elbow joint. The OFA has developed an elbow registry to provide a standardized evaluation of the elbow joint and help breeders choose healthy dogs for their breeding programs. Elbow dysplasia is a common cause of lameness in large-breed dogs.

Most elbow dysplasia occurs before the bones have fully developed, with clinical signs beginning to show between four and seven months of age. The symptoms can vary, ranging from recurring bouts of lameness to moving awkwardly while at a trot. Commonly, a young dog develops a sudden limp, which goes from intermittent to severe to slight without any apparent outside cause. Elbow dys-plasia can be diagnosed only through X-rays. Like hip dysplasia, it is believed that elbow dysplasia is mainly an inherited problem, with environmental factors influencing its development.

Epilepsy

Epilepsy is a neurological disorder that manifests itself in recurring seizures that are caused by abnormal electrical patterns in the brain. Epilepsy in dogs can be inherited from affected parents; acquired due to environmental factors such as viral infections, nutritional disorders, toxic reactions, or head injury; or idiopathic, with no known cause.

▲ This five-year-old female leaps into the water. Goldens love to swim and it's great exercise.

The length and severity of epileptic seizures can vary. Some dogs have one mild seizure occasionally with no ill side effects, while others have frequent, thrashing, severe muscle spasms along with a loss of consciousness and often involuntary urination and defecation. The onset of heritable epilepsy is six months to three years old, with attacks occuring more commonly at night than during the day. Some dogs experience lingering side effects of seizures, including disorientation and disturbances in vision and cognitive ability.

Subvalvular Aortic Stenosis (SAS)

This inherited heart defect is caused by a stricture in the left ventricle of the heart, which results in a murmur that ranges from slight to severe. Diagnosis can be made as early as eight weeks, but the preferred age is sixteen weeks old. Screening should be done by a board-certified veterinary cardiologist, and any dogs used in a breeding program should be re-evaluated every twelve to twenty-four months to be sure they stay clear.

 Fact

A breeder who considers the whole dog—not just one aspect of a dog—is worth pursuing. Health, temperament, and conformation must all be considered together, not one at the expense of another. All the parts make up the whole. The very best breeders make sure they take all these elements into consideration before choosing to breed a particular dog.

No dog with any sort of heart murmur should be used in a breeding program. Prospective buyers will do well to be sure both parents have been cleared for this heart defect. You can sometimes obtain a great deal of information from discussing the breeder's family of dogs and finding out which problems occurred and what the breeder has done to stay clear of them. No dog is perfect, and no breeder makes the perfect choices all the time. The important point to determine is whether the breeder made an effort to avoid problems in the lines. He or she should be constantly searching for the healthiest and most problem-free dogs possible.

Get to know your breeder. Find out his or her breeding philosophy. Make sure you are comfortable with the reasons for those choices. You may be living with those choices for a very long time.

Hypothyroidism

Hypothyroidism is a malfunction of the thyroid gland. It shows up in problems related to obesity, lethargy, coat problems, skin problems, reproduction problems, irregular heat cycles, and sterility. Though hypothyroidism is not life-threatening, it disrupts the rhythm of the whole body. The thyroid gland is one of the major sources of hormone production. If it is not operating properly, the whole body is affected.

The skin and coat problems alone are very disruptive to the animal. They cause him an extreme amount of discomfort and a fair amount of lost sleep. When the thyroid is not functioning properly, the animal will often gain an excessive amount of weight without increasing the amount of caloric intake, and his energy level will be very low. The treatment for hypothyroidism is fairly simple. Daily medication and periodic blood tests are used to determine whether the hormone level is correct or if the dosage must be adjusted. The main diagnostic tool to rule out hypothyroidism is a blood test that measures the T3 and T4 levels in the blood. Not all skin and coat problems are a result of hypothyroidism, but it is worth ruling out as a cause.

Cancer

The rate of cancers in Goldens has reached an alarming number and no one knows for certain why this is true. Many young Goldens are succumbing to cancer at early ages, often dying well before their average ten-year life span. Some people believe that the reason is genetic—that we are selecting dogs that carry genes that make them more susceptible to cancer—but others believe the cause is environmental.

There isn't a simple answer; the problem of cancer is multifaceted. More than likely it is a combination of genetic and environmental factors that is causing the increase in the rate of cancers. One thing being considered is that individuals that develop cancer have a compromised immune system. No one can agree on just what is taxing that immune system so much that it is allowing cancers to predominate and perpetuate themselves. Some argue it is the constant barrage of vaccines we subject our dogs to. Other factors might include overmedication or exposure to toxic substances, like flea-and-tick products, lawn fertilizers, and other chemicals.

You can help your Golden live longer by keeping him out of contact with these and other toxins. Some things that you can do that may help your dog live longer are:

- Vaccinate sparingly and use blood titers to check immunity.
- Avoid flea and tick products except under extreme circumstances.
- Avoid using chemical fertilizers and pesticides on your lawn.
- Avoid smoking around your dog.
- Bathe your dog every month to six weeks to remove toxins from the skin and coat.
- Feed him a good-quality diet and steer clear of chemical preservatives.
- Offer filtered water rather than tap water.
- Check your dog weekly for lumps or abnormal growths.
- Visit your veterinarian yearly for checkups.

There is some treatment available for cancer caught early enough. Some of the larger veterinary hospitals have the means to treat dogs with chemotherapy to help reduce tumor size and give the dog a little longer life. Treatment does not come cheap, however. Despite heroic measures, dogs often succumb to the disease well before we think they should. Treatment is a personal decision that is best made with expert veterinary advice and a hard look at the dog's quality of life. Each dog owner is different, and each case is different. A solution that was perfect for one family may not be right for another. **Ⓔ**

CHAPTER 15

Alternative Medicine

HOLISTIC PRACTITIONERS BELIEVE that the body has the ability to heal itself if it is given the proper support in the form of alternative therapies. Many chronic diseases are the result of compromised immunity. They are the body's way of signaling an imbalance. Unlike conventional veterinarians, who treat symptoms of disease, the holistic veterinarian treats the whole animal.

A Holistic View

Alternative medicine is the use of a combination of therapies to treat the whole animal and restore balance so that the body can heal itself. The three most common therapies used by holistic veterinarians are acupuncture, chiropractic care, and homeopathy. A holistic approach to healing involves a consideration of the entire animal, not just the symptoms of its disease. This approach considers that the physical and psychological health of the animal are equally important. An animal's diet, lifestyle, relationships, and stress levels affect its health, and all these aspects need to be considered when treating illness.

The Holistic Approach

Many chronic diseases are the result of a compromised immune system. Compromises to immunity include poor diet, exposure to chemicals and toxins, overmedication, poor water and air quality, and overvaccination. Holistic practitioners aim to balance the body's internal mechanisms so that the body can regain health, an approach that is quite different from the conventional practitioner, who looks at and treats only the symptoms of disease.

The holistic approach considers the underlying causes of disease, not just the symptoms that are present. In a holistic approach, it is believed that each organ system affects the others. If there is illness in one system and it is treated, it shifts the position of all the other systems. The whole body is dynamic. It is the interaction among the different metabolic systems that gives the body balance and the ability to heal itself.

 **Essential**

Conventional veterinarians treat symptoms of disease, while holistic veterinarians treat the entire animal with the aim of supporting the body to heal itself. The views of both types of veterinarians are very different and their approach to healing entirely unique.

Tools of the Trade

Alternative practitioners use a wide variety of tools to help the animal reclaim health. Most holistic veterinarians are quick to point out that what they do to the animal is less important to its overall recovery than what they try to balance. Common tools for holistic veterinarians are diet and nutrition counseling, acupuncture, chiropractic adjustment, homeopathy, enzymes and dietary supplements, and flower essences.

There are times when antibiotics are given or surgery is performed but unlike the Western approach, alternatives are explored in combination with or instead of the application of antibiotics or other medications. Being able to address the whole animal is very important to permanent healing and an overall return to good

health. Some of the best tools of the trade involve the holistic veterinarian's experience, knowledge, and skill at applying the alternative therapies, as well as an understanding of when a combination
of therapies will give the dog the best chance of being able to return
to full health.

◀ A two-year-
old male Golden
watching field
practice.

Continually bombarding a compromised immune system with
antibiotics or vaccinations may work to temporarily alleviate a
symptom or ward off a particular disease. But if there is a
greater underlying problem that is not being addressed, the
animal will revert back to illness, and this time its body will be
even more compromised and out of balance. Regardless of the
method used to treat the illness, careful consideration of the
entire animal must be made in order to push the healing in the
right direction.

How Can It Help?

The purpose of alternative therapies is to fill in the gaps left by Western medicine. They are not intended to take the place of Western medicine when it is clearly called for. If an animal has a broken leg or an infection, it needs surgery or antibiotics. No amount of homeopathy or acupuncture is going to replace that need. However, alternative therapies can be used to help support the body as it heals. The goal is to restore the body's balance, so that health can be maintained once it is achieved. For instance, that animal with a broken leg might benefit from acupuncture or a chiropractic adjustment as it heals, since its body will have had to compensate for the lack of use of that limb causing stress on other joints and muscles.

 Essential

Alternative treatments are only beneficial if the overall goal is holistic. The key is consideration of the entire animal and ensuring that the body remains in a good state of health.

Alternative therapies can further support Western medicine or eliminate the need for long-term treatment. Diabetes is a good example. This disease is often treated with insulin, but alternative therapies can restore the balance of health to the point where insulin dosages are decreased or even eliminated over time. A knowledgeable holistic veterinarian will know when to use a certain alternative therapy and when an entirely different approach is needed. Healing and restoring animals to health is an art as well as a science—the approach and the decisions made have an effect upon a being that cannot make its own decisions. Your Golden is entirely reliant upon your ability to choose well for him and on your holistic veterinarian's ability to treat his ailments and diseases. Consider all options, and make good decisions about the professionals you entrust with your beloved Golden companion. His good health depends on it.

Finding a Qualified Holistic Veterinarian

Not all practitioners are the same, and finding a talented holistic veterinarian may be a bit of a challenge. There are several qualities to look for when considering hiring a holistic veterinarian to treat your pet. The first, of course, is the educational background of the individual. All holistic training is in addition to the completion of four years of regular veterinary school. To be minimally competent, the person should have had 100 to 200 contact hours, with several dozen of those hours spent working in an instructor-supervised, hands-on practice. An in-depth level of competence requires two to three years of full-time study, with hours of practical experience. Experience is very important when choosing the right person to doctor your Golden, but results speak for themselves. Most honest holistic vets will be straightforward about their success rates with different problems and diseases. They should give you a very clear prognosis for your Golden's particular ailment (and their ability to treat it).

There are three major alternative medicine courses offered to veterinarians that should be completed before the holistic practitioner can claim that he or she is certified. The three courses are chiropractic, acupuncture, and homeopathy. Board certification is achieved after completing a two- to three-year program—which comes *after* completing veterinary school—and hands-on practical experience in a supervised setting in each area. Since most people don't have the time to be competent in all three areas, they usually choose one as their specialty and readily refer clients to other competent professionals as needed.

The last consideration is continuing education. All veterinarians should read journals and attend conferences and meetings. It is the only way to know what is happening and keep current in a particular field.

Acupuncture

The practice of acupuncture comes from traditional Chinese medicine. Practitioners believe there are channels of energy, called meridians, that run in regular patterns throughout the body and over its surface. The energy, or chi, flows in these meridians like water in a river. The body maintains its health when the chi is not interrupted. When the flow of energy *is* interrupted, it backs up, and disease results as a manifestation of the disturbance or imbalance of energy.

 **Fact**

Acupuncture is used worldwide and has become more widely accepted because of the amazing results achieved through its healing practices. It is currently used on people and animals, including exotic species kept in zoos and aquariums the world over.

How Acupuncture Works

The actual process of acupuncture therapy involves the use of very thin stainless steel needles placed at specific points, called the acupoints. These needles are used to unblock obstructions in meridians and re-establish the flow of energy so that the body can heal itself. When energy is restored within the body, the energy circulation is free to help the body work to its potential. The body's internal organs correct imbalances in digestion, absorption, and energy production if they are working to their full capacity.

The body is then able to use its own healing powers to cure itself from chronic acute diseases or injuries that are the result of imbalances. Veterinarians who practice acupuncture follow a very precise chart of acupoints. Each acupoint is used specifically for a certain function or ailment. The needles are solid but flexible, with a rounded tip, and are not painful when inserted into the skin. Acupuncture is a common treatment for pain, but it can be used to treat all kinds of ailments, including lameness or even paralysis; noninfectious inflammation or allergies; spinal cord injury, disk and musculoskeletal problems; asthma and arthritis; and gastrointestinal problems, certain reproductive disorders, and epilepsy.

Choosing an Acupuncture Professional

The International Veterinary Acupuncture Society (IVCS) in Longmont, Colorado, takes the stand that only a veterinary acupuncturist can diagnose and treat the whole animal. A veterinary acupuncturist is your best choice in your search for the right practitioner. As with other alternative medical professionals, you'll want to be sure that this person has attended a certification program. He or she should also have had the necessary hands-on supervised practice to become a competent practitioner. Avoid anyone who is dabbling or has only attended a weekend or conference seminar. Most professionals agree that in order to practice acupuncture competently, a person must put in the necessary hours of study and practice. If you feel that your Golden would benefit from acupuncture, seek a referral from a holistic veterinary practitioner. You can also contact IVCS for a referral in your area.

Chiropractic Therapy

Modern chiropractic therapy was developed in the later part of the nineteenth century. The term "chiropractic" refers to the process of hands-on adjustment. The goal of chiropractic care is to improve health by strengthening nerve function through the manipulation of the joints, especially the spinal column. The benefits of chiropractic adjustment include an enhanced range of motion, restored joint function in older or injured animals, increased vitality, and energy. Chiropractic professionals see these as added benefits that come from seeking the true goal of overall improved general health.

Not all animals will benefit from chiropractic adjustment, and it does not work as a cure. As with the other alternative therapies, it helps the body regain its natural balance so that it can heal itself. Because chiropractic adjustment affects the nervous system and the function of all organ systems connected within the network, it has the effect of improving the body's response to disease. For instance, many animals with thyroid disease or diabetes actually need a smaller dosage of medication once they have been properly adjusted. The adjustment does not cure the disease, but by helping the body to function to its full capacity it allows the body to heal itself as much as possible.

 **Alert!**

If the nervous system is working properly, it can fight chronic and debilitating conditions that resulted when it was out of balance. Disease is always a sign of an imbalance in the body. It's nature's way of sending up a warning flag that a certain area is under siege and needs help.

Treatable Problems

Chiropractic care can be administered on dogs both young and old for a variety of problems. Most practitioners agree that not just old dogs benefit. In fact, some go so far as to say that if more young dogs started receiving chiropractic adjustments sooner, they would not develop some of the crippling arthritic problems associated with aging. Arthritis and getting older don't have to go hand in hand. Good candidates for chiropractic adjustment include dogs with lameness or abnormal gait, middle-aged dogs that haven't yet developed arthritic problems, older dogs with arthritis, and canine athletes.

Treatment, especially of arthritic conditions, does not always cure the problem, but it can slow or stop its progression. For instance, in the case of a dog with very bad hip dysplasia, chiropractic adjustment cannot cure the fact that the dog has bad hips. What it can do is make sure that as the dog automatically compensates for the unstable joint, his body does not harm itself irreparably.

If one hip joint is bad, the dog will put more weight on the other hip and other associated muscles. This causes stress and, in some cases, overwork in different areas. Left untreated, these can develop into more serious problems that threaten the dog's quality of life. By taking your Golden to the chiropractor from a young age, debilitating damage can be minimized or prevented, and health can be maintained to its highest degree.

 **Essential**

You can overdo things or cause the body to react negatively if you do not know when to apply treatment and when to back off. Contraindications to chiropractic adjustment include fractures, tumors, acute inflammation, and acute infection. An inexperienced chiropractor could actually make your dog worse by adjusting the wrong area.

The Chiropractic Adjustment

A chiropractor's job consists of identifying the specific site of subluxation, identifying the direction in which the joint is stuck or loose, and finding the contact point where the adjustment will be performed. The actual adjustment is performed by moving the hand in a short, quick movement that is aimed to return the joint to its normal function.

Most dogs benefit from numerous regular adjustments until improvement is seen. After that, they will probably need periodic visits to maintain the balance. After the dog is adjusted, the practitioner looks for pain and motion in the affected area by watching the dog walk. He or she will make suggestions for home care and also schedule a return visit to be sure that the adjusted area stays in place. A veterinary chiropractor may also make recommendations for diet, exercise, or nutritional supplements that he or she feels would benefit the animal's overall condition.

Finding a Qualified Practitioner

There are two types of chiropractic practitioners who are permitted by law to work on animals. The first type is a doctor of chiropractic (or DC) who has received adequate training in animal anatomy and physiology; the second type is a veterinarian who has received the adequate training in chiropractic adjustment and technique. Currently the educational program for vets and chiropractors who want to practice on animals consists of 150 hours of postgraduate study in animal chiropractic. The American Veterinary Chiropractic Association (AVCA) admits only doctors of chiropractic and doctors of veterinary medicine.

Ask about your chiropractor's qualifications, and steer clear of anyone who has not been certified through the AVCA course. They do not have the training to benefit the patients they are treating and can do more harm than good.

 **Fact**

One of the benefits of using a veterinary chiropractor is that they also are well versed in the general care and maintenance of animals. They can make recommendations for overall health and may be able to catch problems that could be overlooked by a nonveterinary chiropractor.

Homeopathy

Sometimes the terms "homeopathic" and "holistic" are used interchangeably, but in fact they are two entirely different things. A holistic veterinarian is a veterinarian who uses homeopathy as one of his alternative treatment methods. Homeopathy is an alternative therapy whose underlying premise of treatment is "like cures like."

Homeopathy defies common sense. Though it has been practiced for nearly 200 years with great success, no one has been able to prove by modern medical standards exactly how it works. The founding father of homeopathy, Samuel Hahnemann, was a physician and chemist. He found after years of experimenting and testing that the same substances that created the symptoms of a particular disease could also cure that disease. This is the basis of homeopathic remedies.

Homeopathic remedies are very diluted versions of the particular ailment they are thought to cure. Hahnemann believed that the more diluted the remedy, the more powerful it became. The key to using homeopathic remedies effectively is to match the entire patient to the remedy, including the animal's physical and emotional makeup to determine which remedy to use.

Holistic veterinarians work from a list of remedies. They try to match the remedy as best they can to the patient's ailment and individual personality. The remedy is usually given orally, in a pill or liquid form, though some holistic practitioners are able to use injections. The remedy may be given as a one-shot treatment, or it may be administered daily for several weeks. This depends upon the condition and what the case calls for. Classic veterinary homeopaths tend to give remedies in single doses, but others combine remedies from a number of ingredients and administer them together at a very low potency.

 Fact

A homeopathic veterinarian uses mainly homeopathic remedies to cure disease except in the most extreme of circumstances.

Homeopathy has been gaining in popularity and many holistic veterinarians are beginning to use homeopathy as one of their tools for regaining the body's natural balance and returning it to health. As with other alternative therapies, extensive classroom and hands-on practical experience are needed for a homeopathic vet to be effective in treating patients. As your Golden's caretaker, you would be wise to find a practitioner with both the knowledge and experience to give your Golden the best treatment and care possible.

Bach's Flower Essences

Dr. Edward Bach was an English homeopathic doctor who discovered that diluted versions of flowers and tree buds could be used to address certain mental and emotional conditions in humans and animals. The therapy, known as flower essence therapy, has since become quite popular among holistic practitioners. They are quick to warn that flower essence therapy doesn't necessarily cure anything; instead, it has been known to improve the emotional states of both people and animals. The thinking behind the therapy is that the mind and body are intimately connected. If an animal is in a negative emotional state, fearful or aggressive, the body's ability to heal itself is blocked, which allows disease processes to take over.

Flower essences can be purchased from any health-food store along with a guide explaining how they are used. The remedies come in small dark brown bottles. They must be kept out of direct sunlight and should not be exposed to extreme temperatures. The dosage is usually four to five drops in the dog's drinking water or one to two drops directly in the mouth.

 **Essential**

The essences themselves are prepared by soaking the flower in pure water in sunlight for an extended period of time. The resulting mix is stabilized and preserved with brandy. Since most animals do not like the taste of alcohol, you may seek advice about making a mixture with pure water and refrigerating it or finding an alternative natural preservative.

How to Use the Essence

The effect of the essence is not to take away a problem but to improve the emotional state of the animal and help him cope with his problem. Often, the Goldens we love are deeply tied to us emotionally. If we are suffering a difficult time, they suffer right along with us. Goldens are especially sensitive to our moods and the more in tune with us they are, the more they can benefit from appropriate use of flower essences. The guide provided with your essences contains information on how to use them. For instance, crabapple is used for detoxification after vaccinations, snapdragon for biting or chewing, and Star of Bethlehem for grief or trauma. The remedies are benign and do no harm if you choose the wrong one and there are also no side effects. You can use up to four different essences at a time without negating the effect of the others.

Rescue Remedy

Rescue Remedy is the most popular and widely used of all the flower essences. It is made from a combination of five different flowers and comes as a diluted liquid or a cream. The liquid form can be put in the dog's drinking water, and the cream can be used topically for accidents and emergencies. Here are some instances in which Rescue Remedy may be warranted:

- Stressful situations, such as a move to a new home or other trauma or turmoil
- Travel
- Trips to the vet
- Change of schedule
- Competitions, such as field trials, agility, or obedience
- Physical injury
- Grief over loss of another pet or owner

The use of Rescue Remedy in stressful situations may alleviate a state of anxiety. It is worth a try if you or your dog is experiencing a rough time. Ⓔ

CHAPTER 16

Goldens as Athletes

GOLDENS ARE ACTIVE DOGS that take direction well and love to work for their owners, which makes them perfect candidates for dog sports of all kinds. Whether your interest is disk catching, flyball, competition obedience, agility, tracking, or rally obedience, your Golden will gladly accompany you to play whatever game you want.

Keeping Fit and Staying Lean

The key to a long and successful career in any sport is staying in good physical shape and keeping lean. Dogs are no different. The more regular exercise a dog gets and the less extra weight he carries, the better athlete he will be and fewer injuries he will incur.

There is a huge increase in the number of dog owners taking an interest in dog sports of all kinds. It's a wonderful way to spend time with your Golden pal and at the same time learn how to work as a team. Sharing your life with a Golden means being active and outgoing, for these are not dogs that like to spend long hours on the couch. The more active your dog is, and the higher his energy level, the more rigorous the sport you will want to participate in. Being able to play in the sport you decide is right for the two of you means making sure that your dog remains in good shape day in and day out.

This may mean taking him on regular hikes in the woods where he can run and jump and swim on a regular basis. It may mean getting him to the local dog park to play and wrestle with other dogs so that his body remains in tip-top shape. Feeding your dog only what his body needs is also important and is the key to keeping him lean and fit.

 **Fact**

A dog that is overweight even by just a few pounds is far more susceptible to injury than a dog that is an ideal weight.

Flyball Competition

The sport of flyball is a fast-action fun sport with great spectator appeal. The North American Flyball Association (or NAFA) organizes and oversees tournaments in North America. All dogs, both purebred and mixed breed, are eligible to compete. Even dogs that are not totally crazed by tennis balls can be taught using positive reinforcement to hit the box, grab the ball, and jump the jumps.

How the Game Is Played

Flyball races consist of two relay teams, with four dogs on each team. Jumps are set to be four inches lower than the shoulder height of the shortest dog on the team. The minimum height is eight inches, while the maximum is sixteen inches. The hurdles are spaced about ten feet apart, with the handler standing behind the start line while the dog works. The first jump is six feet from the start/finish line while the flyball box is set a distance of fifteen feet from the last jump. The total length of the course is fifty-one feet.

The handler stands behind the start line and holds the dog by the collar. When the go is given, the handler releases the dog, which jumps over all four hurdles to the flyball box. The dog must hit a pedal on the box to release the ball, catch the ball, and then turn around and race back over the same four jumps to the finish line. The next handler in line releases the next dog as the previous dog crosses the finish. If the dog loses the ball or misses a jump he must run again after the rest of the team has gone. The first team to finish without errors wins. This all happens in twenty seconds or less, with the winning team winning by a split second.

 **Alert!**

This fast-paced fun sport is not without risk of injury. Jumping, bouncing off the box, and turning sharply on the return all take their toll on the dog's body. Depending upon the dog's level of fitness and physical shape, a handler can minimize injuries by practicing regularly and stopping the action if the dog seems out of control.

Flyball Awards and Titles

At NAFA-sanctioned events, teams are divided so that they compete against teams of equal ability. This way each team has a chance at winning an individual race. Dogs earn points toward flyball titles by completing the race within a certain amount of time. The team does not have to win the race, only complete it.

Points are awarded by how quickly the race is run. If teams finish in under thirty-two seconds, each dog on the team gets one point. If the team runs in less than twenty-eight seconds, each dog earns five points. If the team comes in under twenty-four seconds, each dog earns twenty-five points toward his title. Titles are awarded for varying point levels, from twenty all the way to 30,000 points. Not all events are for competition. Some teams get together to run their dogs just for the fun of it or to give demonstrations at dog shows or other events.

▲ A female Golden pounces on the flyball box, releasing the tennis ball. Flyball is one of the fastest growing dog sports.

The best way to get started in flyball is to contact local trainers. Find out if anyone is offering it as a class or workshop or if there is a local team you could practice with and learn from. Try to find a team with a like-minded philosophy for training, as you will be working closely with them as you train your Golden to compete.

Competition Obedience

Goldens excel at obedience trials for the sole reason that they love to be with and work for their handlers. There are few things more enjoyable than watching a dog-and-handler team work in perfect unison. Competitive obedience trials were designed by the American Kennel Club to demonstrate the dog's ability to perfectly follow a predetermined set of exercises. Handlers and dogs compete to earn titles at three different levels: novice, open, and utility. Each level is increasingly difficult, and the dog must demonstrate higher and higher degrees of training in order to qualify. To qualify at each level, the dog and handler must accumulate at least 170 out of a possible 200 points. Each exercise must be completed to a designated standard of competency. Complete rules, which are available through the AKC, explain the exercises and the scoring process in greater detail.

Novice Level, Companion Dog Title

This is the first and most basic level of competency. At this level, the dog must heel while on and off leash, do a stand for examination by the judge, recall to the handler at a distance of thirty feet to sit in front, and participate in two group exercises. The first group exercise is the long sit, which is performed for one minute with the handlers standing on the opposite side of the ring from the dogs. The dog must hold the sit for the entire minute and remain in place until the handler returns and releases him.

 **Essential**

Golden Retrievers are natural athletes, and running, jumping, and retrieving are natural abilities to be honed rather than taught in most cases.

The second group exercise is the long down, performed for three minutes with the handlers standing on the opposite side of the ring from the dogs. The dog must hold the down for the entire three minutes and remain in place until the handler returns and releases him. Moving or changing positions during this exercise means automatic disqualification. At this level, the dog must receive a score of 170 or better in order to earn a leg toward his companion dog title. A dog and handler must earn three qualifying scores (or "legs") from three different judges in order to earn the title Companion Dog and the right to add the initials CD after his registered name.

Open Obedience, Companion Dog Excellent

This level is significantly more difficult than the novice level and was designed to show a higher degree of training. The open level exercises involve heeling off leash, a drop on recall, retrieving the dumbbell on the flat, retrieving the dumbbell over the high jump, and clearing the broad jump. The group exercises also involve sits and downs, but the time is longer—three minutes and five minutes respectively—and the handlers are out of sight. The drop on recall exercise involves calling the dog and dropping him into a down about halfway to the handler. The handler and dog must qualify with at least 170 out of 200 possible points and get three qualifying scores from three different judges in order to earn the title Companion Dog Excellent, or CDX.

Utility Dog

This third level of obedience competition is elite. Not many dogs make it to this level of competition without a substantial amount of practice and training. The exercises that set this level apart involve scent discrimination, the directed retrieve, the moving stand, and directed jumping. During the scent discrimination exercise, a small pile of nine leather-and-metal dumbbells is placed on the ground, and the dog must find the one which has been scented by the handler. This exercise is done twice.

In the directed retrieve, the handler indicates one of three gloves dropped about eighteen feet away that the dog must retrieve on command. The dog must take direction from the handler in retrieving the glove designated by the judge.

The moving stand exercise involves the handler walking the dog into a standing position during heeling. The dog must remain in place while the judge examines the dog. The dog must return to heel by the handler's side when the judge gives the release cue to the handler.

Directed jumping involves a forty-foot go-out, which means the handler cues the dog to run across the ring between the panel and bar jumps and sit facing the handler. The dog must then jump the hurdle indicated by the handler and return to front position. This exercise is done twice, once with the bar jump and once with the panel jump. Qualifying three times under three different judges earns dog and handler the title Utility Dog, or UD.

Utility Dog Excellent

Requirements for earning the Utility Dog Excellent title or UDX are that the handler and dog have earned both the Open and Utility Dog titles. The dog needs to qualify ten times at ten different shows in both the Open B and Utility B Classes. Each level is divided into A and B, designating the difference between inexperienced (A) handlers and experienced handlers (B).

Obedience Trial Champion OTCH

While the dog is earning the UDX title, he can also be earning points toward his obedience trial championship, or OTCH. Points toward this title are accumulated depending upon how many dogs are competing within the class and on whether the dog and handler earn a placement. A total of 100 points is needed as well as three first places. These can be a first place in Utility (only if there are three other dogs competing), a first place in Open B class (only if there are at least six competing), and one additional first place in either of the above categories. All three firsts must be under three different judges.

 Fact

Dogs that achieve the Obedience Trial Champion title may use the designation OTCH after their names to show the world just how talented they really are.

The Sport of Agility

Dog agility is a fast-growing sport known for its upbeat pace and spectator appeal. A favorite among dog-lovers, this sport involves dogs running an obstacle course with jumps, tunnels, weave poles,

A-frames, see-saws, a dog walk, and a table. The courses are timed and designed by the judge to challenge the dog and handler at different levels of difficulty. The handler is allowed to walk the course before running it, but the dog is not. Handlers use this opportunity to develop handling strategies. Learning to develop a handling strategy is part of the challenge of being able to run a course well. The object of the sport is to run the course fast and clean (meaning no faults or errors). Faults are incurred for knocking into bars, going off course, not performing the obstacles correctly, or handler error. There are several different organizations that offer sanctioned trials in which handlers and dogs can compete to earn titles for their performances. The rules for each organization vary, and all but the AKC allow mixed breed dogs to run.

Health Considerations

Agility is a very athletic sport in which the dog is jumping, running, twisting, and racing at top speeds, with his handler panting to catch up. The more fit the dog and the less extra weight he is carrying, the longer his career will be. Repetitive jumping and twisting can take its toll on a dog that is not in good shape or has poor conformation. Dogs with long careers in agility have healthy hips, elbows, and knees, and their owners are constantly vigilant for unsafe circumstances like slippery conditions on the field or a less-than-ideal surface to jump on. Being your dog's partner in this sport also means being his advocate. It's your job to make sure that the course is safe for him and that he is in top physical shape.

 Essential

If you are interested in competing in agility and are in the market to purchase a puppy, have an experienced person help you choose the dog with the best conformation and personality for this sport. You will want the most physically sound dog with the greatest desire to be with people.

AKC Agility Classes

In AKC agility, levels are divided into three categories: novice, open, and excellent. Each level has a set requirement for the number and type of obstacles allowed on course as well as allowable faults. As the level of difficulty increases, fewer faults are allowed. At the excellent level, the run has to be just about perfect to qualify. A new division, the performance class, was recently added to accommodate older dogs.

◀ This 6½-year-old female Golden blasts out of the weave poles during an agility trial.

The performance class dogs run at all the same levels but at a lower jump height. Jump heights depend upon the dog's height at the shoulder. Dogs must be measured by an AKC-licensed measurer and be issued a jump height card. When a handler signs a dog up for a trial, he or she must send along a copy of the height card with the premium in order to run.

Dogs without height cards must be measured on the morning of the trial before the show starts. The jump heights range from eight to twenty-four inches. Dogs of the same height run at the same time, then the height is changed and the next group runs. Within each height, the dogs are ranked according to dogs of the same height and class. For instance, a sixteen-inch dog in the performance class may have the fastest time of all the other performance class dogs in his height division, while the sixteen-inch dog in regular classes may place first among the dogs in his division.

 **Fact**

The standard course times for regular classes are often much faster than for performance classes. The performance dogs don't have to compete against the faster, more able-bodied dogs in the regular classes.

Agility Titles

Dogs can earn titles from all of the different organizations, and most divide the classes up into categories. The AKC has three divisions—novice, open, and excellent—and dogs must earn three qualifying scores within each category in order to earn their title. There are two different types of courses, standard courses and jumpers courses, and titles can be earned at each level in both of these categories. At the excellent level, handlers can go on to compete for a master agility excellent title as well as a master agility championship.

These titles are elite, and only handlers and dogs with lots of motivation and drive are persistent enough to pursue them. The main purpose of agility, whatever the title, is to have fun showing off and demonstrating the dogs' incredible athleticism. Goldens love this sport. If they are not overweight, they can compete with ease and little risk of injury.

Tracking for Sport

Golden Retrievers have great noses that can detect smell just about anywhere. Tracking enthusiasts insist that the sport of tracking with a Golden is a sport of trust in your dog's ability to follow and find the appropriate scent. The AKC devised a tracking test at two different levels in which dogs can earn titles and show off their wonderful abilities.

The first level test is for the title Tracking Dog, or TD. This test's basic goal is to determine the dog's ability to follow a track or path walked by someone who is a stranger to the dog under a variety of weather and terrain conditions. At this level the terrain is moderate, and the dog must either retrieve a glove or wallet left by the track-layer at the end of the track. The dog wears a harness and a twenty- to forty-foot lead. The handler's job is to follow his dog at least twenty feet behind and give vocal encouragement. The handler may not use commands or body language to guide the dog. Each test must be on virgin ground, 400 to 500 yards in length, and have three to five turns. Two of the turns must be at right angles. The scent of the track must be thirty minutes to two hours old under moderate terrain and varying weather conditions.

 Fact

The purpose of the test is to demonstrate the dog's ability to recognize and follow human scent and to show the dog's willingness to work for his handler. Goldens excel at this sport since it combines two of their favorite pastimes: being with and finding people, and sniffing!

The second level is designated by the title Tracking Dog Excellent, or TDX. Dogs at this level are tested for stamina, perseverance, courage, and their ability to discriminate scent under a variety of conditions. The track at this level must be 800 to 1,000 yards long, with five to seven turns, at least three being at right angles, and the scent must be three to five hours old. The TDX test also has two cross tracks laid one hour and fifteen minutes to one hour and forty-five minutes after the original track at specified points. This of course acts as a distraction and further challenges the dog's ability to discriminate scent. The terrain at this test is more complex, often involving streams, gullies, woods, and so on. The dog that earns the TDX title must find indicate and retrieve four personal and dissimilar articles left by the track-layer, such as a sock, scarf, shoe, hat, glove, or wallet.

Rally Obedience

The sport of Rally obedience was designed by a man named Charles "Bud" Kramer. Bud is a dog-sport enthusiast who has been instrumental in using positive training methods with dogs in the sport of agility and now Rally obedience. He pitched Rally to the AKC for review, and it is expected that they will design a title system and allow breed clubs to host trials throughout the country. The AKC would require that only purebred dogs compete, but other organizations, such as the Association of Pet Dog Trainers (or APDT), allow all dogs both purebred and mixed to compete.

The sport of Rally obedience has gained in popularity in recent years. It borrows its name from the sport of road rally for cars. Designed to test the dog-and-handler team's ability to work together, this sport is similar to competitive obedience without the formality. This is great news for people put off by the strictness of competitive obedience who still want to get out and have fun with their dogs. Courses are designed to test the handler and dog's ability to follow signs, which are spread out on the testing field.

 Essential

In Rally obedience, the handler is not directed by the judge. Instead, the dog and handler must perform the exercise indicated on signs spread out along the course.

The handler and dog must perform the exercises according to the rules, but the handler may talk to the dog, cue him with gestures, encourage him, and praise him. Unlike competitive obedience, where only one command is allowed, the sport of Rally encourages handlers to talk to and praise their dogs during performance. No food or toys are allowed on the course, as the course is designed to test the dog's level of competence at each level. The course designer selects from forty-five different approved Rally exercises and designs a course with about twenty-five to twenty-eight different exercises that the handler must perform successfully. As in agility competition, the handler is allowed to walk the course ahead of time to plan out a strategy. Seven of the Rally exercises can be used more than once, but the rest cannot be repeated. Each directional sign gives instructions for that exercise. When the handler and dog complete it they move on to the next exercise.

Sample Rally Exercises

Rally exercises are designed to demonstrate and test a dog's response to obedience but with an element of fun. Here are some exercises you might find on a Rally course:

- Figure eight
- 90-degree turn
- 180-degree turn
- 360-degree turn
- Halt: Stop, with dog sitting parallel
- Spirals: Circle cones while dog heels by doing the outside three, then two, then one.

Judging Rally Obedience

There are currently two levels of Rally performance, but more levels could easily be added with more complicated exercises. Level 1 is the entry level and is performed on leash. Level 2 is off-leash and more challenging. Each dog-and-handler team starts with 200 points, and points are deducted for various errors made by the handler or dog. The handler may repeat verbal and hand signals without losing points and may praise the dog after an exercise has been completed correctly. The dog's attitude, attention, and response are emphasized over his precision. Verbal reassurance and reminders are allowed, as in the case of a stay exercise or while heeling. The judge follows the handler around the course and may deduct points for errors made in executing each exercise. Point deductions range from one-half to three points. If a dog loses five or more points on one exercise, he cannot qualify. This might happen if a dog does not remain in a stay, fails to come on the recall, balks at a jump, or if he knocks over a cone.

The sport of Rally obedience has been well received among the dog-owning community. It's dog- and person-friendly and a great sport to try with your Golden, young or old. Many clubs and groups offer matches for the fun of it, and handlers show up in great numbers to work their dogs for the same reason. If you are a hesitant competitor or a person who just wants to get out and enjoy being with your best friend, this may be a great sport to start with. The lack of intense competition makes it more relaxed and fun than other sports, and it's often a favorite among people looking for a fun game to play with their older or retired dogs.

The Golden Retriever as Therapist

N RECENT YEARS, THERAPY DOGS HAVE become popular visitors at local hospitals, nursing homes, and rehabilitation centers. The Golden Retriever is the ultimate therapy dog. He is unrivaled in his ability to comfort and give hope to the many lonely folks who eagerly count the days until his next visit. Not every dog can be a good therapy dog. A therapy dog must not only possess the right temperament, he must also have extensive training and social skills with other dogs and people to be a useful partner in the visiting therapy team.

What Is a Therapy Dog?

Therapy dogs are highly trained dogs that visit nursing homes, rehabilitation centers, and other facilities. They offer comfort in the form of hands-on visits to those that seek their company. Animal-facilitated therapy work has become more widely accepted thanks to a tremendous amount of education and highly trained dogs to lead the way. Thanks to the many handlers who put lots of time and training into their dogs and who have worked to be sure their dogs are ready for anything, the profession of animal-facilitated therapy has become available to many people all over the country. In some facilities, especially rehabilitation hospitals, animal-facilitated therapy is highly recommended by doctors.

Animal therapy is used in all kinds of areas of rehabilitation. Therapists use it to increase attention, concentration, and range of motion, as well as to improve dexterity, balance, memory, and clarity of speech.

In these interactions, the dog may retrieve objects under the patient's direction, delivering them to the person's hand or lap. The dog may accompany the person who is learning to walk again, come to a person learning to use her voice again, or simply lie down next to someone who is undergoing uncomfortable physical therapy. In these cases the dog must be highly trained, sensitive to each patient's needs and under excellent control. Dogs used in animal-facilitated therapy are the ultimate in therapy dogs. They sometimes work with the most critically damaged and discouraged patients, helping them to get through a difficult time. The patients most likely to benefit from working with this type of dog have usually suffered a head injury or a stroke and are severally limited in their ability to interact with those around them. The overall goal here is to increase the patient's participation and cooperation so that they can derive the maximum benefit from their treatment.

Getting Certified

Not all Goldens are blessed with the qualities of an exceptional therapy dog. It is important when considering whether a dog is appropriate for therapy work to take into account all his qualities, both good and bad.

The Right Temperament

A good candidate for therapy work possesses a stable temperament with a moderate energy level. Nothing ruffles this dog. He is not the nervous or clingy sort and will go to anyone, regardless of the way they look or what equipment they may be hooked up to. An ideal candidate is forgiving of rough handling—many debilitated patients may not know how to interact with a dog or may have a disability that prevents them from patting your dog gently. Therapy dogs are people-oriented, and if there is a choice between being with a group of people or another dog, they choose the people paws down. Goldens who like to nudge you for attention or rest their head in your lap are wonderful at bringing the shyer patients out of their shells. A brave constitution is essential since many patients are hooked up to unusual equipment or use walkers, wheelchairs, or oxygen machines.

 **Question?**

Is therapy work right for my Golden?
The perfect therapy dog is adaptable to almost any situation and will not be stressed by unusual sights, sounds, jerky or unusual movements, or loud speech. Most certification programs will conduct a temperament test to determine whether or not your Golden is a suitable candidate for therapy work.

Certification Programs

Do a search in your area to find what local visiting programs exist, and contact them to find out what they require to get started in their program. These programs are a great way to learn the ropes from folks who have been visiting with their dogs. They will be glad to teach you how to get the most from this experience. Most local programs have a certification test that you must pass in order to visit through their program, and they will happily mentor you and your dog through your first visits. The major programs for therapy dog certification are Therapy Dogs, Inc., Therapy Dogs International, Delta Society/Pet Partners, and Alpha Affiliates.

Smaller programs exist locally, but they are usually connected to the larger programs in some way. Many offer their own temperament tests and evaluation before certifying your dog through one of the larger programs. Certification allows your dog access to the insurance coverage required by most facilities.

Most of the major programs offer a temperament test. This is usually conducted by an approved member of their program, who evaluates your dog's abilities and temperament as a therapy dog. Not all requirements are the same for all programs, but there are a few particular qualities they all look for. A dog must be able to do the following:

- Walk nicely on a leash without pulling
- Be able to be handled without objection
- Be able to greet a stranger without jumping, barking, or pawing
- Be good with children and accept rough handling
- Be dog-friendly on and off leash
- Be under control around other dogs
- Be able to ignore other dogs in close proximity
- Be able to tolerate being petted by a group of people
- Know how to sit, down, stay, and leave it
- Not show any aggression or fearfulness to other dogs or people

 **Alert!**

It is useless to have the perfect dog for therapy work if you can't control him in busy and distracting situations, especially those involving other dogs. Every training session you have with your dog will bring you closer to your goal and make your visits all the more beneficial.

Each program varies in what it requires your dog to do to pass its certification test. As you can see, the general requirements involve both temperament qualities and training requirements. If your dog has the right temperament for therapy work, you can improve the quality of his visits by working on his obedience as well. There are many training businesses and obedience clubs that offer a therapy dog class that will help you increase your dog's obedience skills and teach you what is required of you as the handler. Learning how to interact with patients, including what you can and can't do for them, is important for the safety of all involved.

Training a Therapy Dog

Take a few obedience classes to teach your dog the basic skills of sit, down, come, stay, leave it, and walking without pulling. This is crucial to the overall success of your therapy work. Find a trainer in your area who offers a varied program that involves lots of work around distractions, and practice these skills everywhere you go. The more varied the environment in which you train your dog, the more likely those behaviors will hold together under the pressure of a new place with new smells and distractions.

If there is one behavior a Golden Retriever must learn, it is "Leave it." Goldens are scavengers by nature, constantly on the hunt for food and things they can hold in their mouths. It is important that your dog not be searching for every tidbit on the floor when visiting. In a therapeutic situation, there may be all kinds of things that could harm him, including dropped medication.

 Fact

You and your dog are ambassadors for all other visiting therapy teams, and it is important to keep in mind that you represent every other dog that will walk into that facility. You need to be sure that your visit inspires the facility and its patients to request more visits—not ban all dogs because yours behaved inappropriately.

Another factor to remember is that your dog must be able to ignore food distractions. Many patients get food gifts or may have leftover crumbs or stray cookies littering their room. Your job as the handler to is to make sure that you keep your dog safe and that you have control over your dog's behavior before you set foot in any facility. Training your dog to be ready for anything is an important part of your success as a visiting team.

The most important thing that many of these programs will teach you is how to recognize stress in your dog and minimize it. In some cases, especially when a dog is just getting started, a reasonable visit might only last a half hour before the dog gets stressed and needs to leave. Signs of stress for you to watch for in your visiting dog include excessive panting, whining, disinterest in surroundings or the people, becoming clingy, pulling to get away, dilated pupils, and leaving wet footprints on the floor.

Basic Obedience Skills

Most dogs that do therapy visits have to sit or lie down and stay for extended periods of time while you visit with the patient or staff. Being able to hold the sit or down for as long as you need them to is important since you don't want to have to keep nagging your dog to stay with the patient.

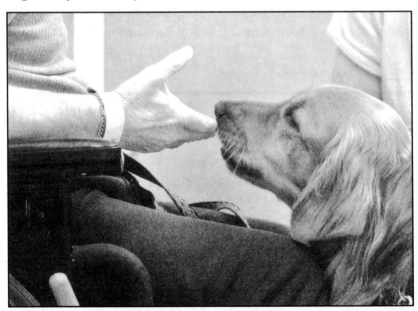

▲ Goldens make great therapy dogs. Here, a four-year-old male participates in pet-assisted therapy at a local hospital.

You should be able to get your dog to sit or lie in any position around a wheelchair, regular chair, bed, or walker. Remember that a patient's reach may be limited. If yours is a smaller Golden, you may want to teach a "Paws-up" command so that you can help the patient reach your dog to pat him. Teaching your dog to put his front paws on a chair next to the patient is a great solution for someone confined to a bed or wheelchair.

Walking without pulling is also a necessity since many facilities have slippery tile floors and lots of foot traffic. Teaching your dog to walk nicely next to you is important for overall safety of patients, dogs, and staff as well as the impression you make with your dog.

Appropriate greeting behavior is also necessary if your dog is going to succeed in this endeavor. Your dog should not jump on anyone. Nor should he paw or lick except on command. In many facilities the patients are quite fragile and cannot tolerate any impact of a paw or toenail that may bruise or scratch their fragile skin. An acceptable greeting involves sitting or lying down and staying until told otherwise.

Being able to direct your dog to interact with a patient will make your visits more meaningful. If your dog knows how to go under a table, or to the left or right of a chair or bed, you will be able to more easily direct him to maximize the contact between patient and dog.

 Essential

Handlers who allow their dogs to pull them wildly do not inspire much confidence from the staff in their ability to control their dog around fragile patients. If necessary consider using a Gentle Leader head collar (see Chapter 9) to help prevent pulling so that you can reward your dog for more appropriate behavior.

For advanced therapy work involving participation in treatment sessions, you might consider teaching or refining your dog's abilities to retrieve objects. Being able to hold the object until the patient can take it from them and being able to deliver it directly to the person's hand or lap are polished qualities. Facilities need these skills to make their program more successful. Teaching your dog the commands up, under, left, and right will make his retrieving skills more useful in therapy sessions.

Social Skills for Therapy Work

A therapy dog has had superior exposure to people, dogs, kids, sights, sounds, smells, the unusual, and the mundane. If your Golden puppy is to become a useful therapy dog, he must be exposed to just about anything and everyone you can think of. The more opportunities you have to expose your dog to new situations, and the more he learns that his obedience skills work everywhere, the better success you will have with him as a therapy dog.

Take your dog with you on walks. Stop and let him meet all kinds of people, young and old; of different races; in different dress and with various occupations. Socialize your dog to lots of other dogs, both big and small, and of every breed you can find. Let your dog play off-leash with all different types of dogs so that he learns how to play and interact with his own kind. Teach your dog to leave it when on leash around other dogs, and make sure he knows that he is not allowed to interact with other dogs when he is working.

Here are some ideas for getting your dog ready for anything:

- Take your dog downtown and train him in foot traffic.
- Stand outside a grocery store and let people pat him as they go in and out.
- Take your pup for a ride on public transportation.
- Stand outside a school when the kids are being let out.
- Go to the local park when the kids are playing ball and visit.
- Invite friends over on a regular basis to help you train appropriate greetings.
- Take your dog with you when you go to the post office or bank.

- Walk your dog on a busy street now and then to accustom him to cars and trucks.
- Hang out at a construction site and let your dog watch from a distance.
- Sign your dog up for doggie day care to help him improve his social skills.
- Visit parks and beaches where there are other dogs, and practice leave it and come.
- Work on being able to call your dog out of a group of dogs that are playing.
- Work on teaching your dog to leave other dogs on leash.
- Teach your dog an appropriate on-leash greeting of sniff and sit.
- Take your dog with you wherever you go, and work on his obedience and manners.

 **Alert!**

Working on your obedience commands around real-life distractions will help make your dog's response more reliable and his attention to you all that much greater. As a general rule, once you have established a behavior reliably, add distractions of varying difficulties right away.

By training your dog in all kinds of different environments, you will be teaching him to ignore distractions and pay attention to you. Remember that you cannot expect your dog to magically know what you want or how to behave in an environment you have not taught him to behave in. So get out there, and get busy teaching him what to expect wherever you go.

Grooming and Appearance

A therapy dog should always be well groomed. Nothing is more unpleasant than handling a dog that is smelly and unkempt, especially for someone who doesn't come in contact with dogs all that often. It is important for health and sanitary reasons as well as aesthetics to make sure your dog is clean and presentable.

If you visit on a monthly basis, plan to give your dog a bath right before your visit, perhaps using a conditioner to help soften his coat. At the very least, be sure to trim your dog's nails and brush him thoroughly to remove any mats or tangles. Be sure to wipe any excess goop from his eyes and ears, and be sure he is wearing a collar and tags as well as your therapy identification badge.

A bandanna is a nice addition and can be related to the season or an upcoming holiday. If the weather is inclement on the day you visit, be sure to bring a towel to dry your dog's feet and body. This will not only make him more pleasant to touch, it will also prevent him from slipping on wet floors.

The Visiting Experience

Training and handling a therapy dog is a wonderful experience. Being able to share a special dog with other people is a tremendous responsibility and a great honor. Working with your dog in partnership, experiencing breakthroughs in a patient's recovery, perhaps visiting a patient and offering comfort in her last days of life—these are irreplaceable experiences. Being a ray of sunshine, a bright spot in someone's day is an incredible feeling. Some patients count the days until the next time they get to visit with your dog.

Facilities and Programs Vary

Some programs will offer group visits in which you will visit one facility together, perhaps splitting up to cover different floors. Other programs may allow you to visit with a large group of patients in a common room.

Inquire about the facility's policies for visits, and see if you can talk to the staff. Ask whether there are patients who aren't able to come out of their rooms whom you could plan to visit. Planning to cover large numbers of patients in one visit is a bad idea. It is far better to plan to cover one small section. Visit with three to five patients on one visit, and let the rest of your team split up and visit as many others as they can. The more volunteers a program has, the easier it is to cover more ground and be able to see more patients in one day. The frequency of visits is often dependent on the volunteers' individual schedules, but many therapy dogs visit facilities every other week, while others visit once a month. The closer the facility is to where you live, the more likely you are to get there. This is especially true if you work a full-time job and plan to visit on your day off or a weekend.

 Fact

Visiting with patients in a common area is the least desirable type of therapy work. The people who can't come to the common area are often the most depressed and lonely, those who would benefit most from a visit from you and your Golden.

The Handler's Role

Some people may feel entirely comfortable with the dog part of therapy work, but they may be very uncomfortable talking to patients. Maybe you're a shy person at heart, or maybe you just don't know what to talk about. In general it is always good to ask the staff about the person you are visiting. Find out about their likes, interests, hobbies, and family. This will give you fuel for conversation and openers to get the person talking. Most elderly people love to reminisce and they will often talk your ear off about their childhood experiences, their children, or their pets.

When in doubt, talk about your gorgeous dog. You could tell the person all about where you got him, what his favorite things are, his antics as a puppy, and so on. Think about putting together a photo album of your dog, from puppyhood to adulthood. Or how about pictures of all the great places he has been? Ⓔ

CHAPTER 18

Teaching Tricks

TRAINING YOUR GOLDEN RETRIEVER to perform tricks is a fun way to develop your skills as a trainer and to build his enthusiasm for learning new things. Most Goldens love to learn and perform tricks, and even novice trainers can learn the skills they need to help their dogs to be successful. The bottom line here is to keep it fun. Make sure you train in short, goal-oriented sessions.

Natural-Born Performers

Golden Retrievers were born to show off and clown around to make people laugh. Their sweet and friendly dispositions and outgoing personalities make them well-suited for teaching tricks. Keep in mind your dog's overall health and well-being, and if he is overweight, perhaps skip over a trick that requires lots of dexterity until he loses a few pounds. As with all training, it will help your cause greatly if you pay attention to your own dog's unique needs and motivations.

If you want your dog to work with you, you need to make sure you are offering him what he wants as far as reinforcers go. Be sure that your training plan makes sense to him. Offering boring dry dog food as a treat will not make him want to learn how to sit up and beg. In order to ensure that the behaviors you have taught do not fall apart, remember that once you have begun a behavior and your dog is starting to get it, be sure to start introducing distractions right away. This is the best way to make sure that the behaviors you worked so hard to establish do not fall apart at the first strange sight or sound. It isn't necessary to work very closely to a distraction at first. If your dog has a hard time performing with kids or other dogs present, by all means work at a distance until he can handle having them close by. Above all, have fun playing and training, and your dog will love learning tricks!

Elements of a Great Trick

Some tricks, though simple, can be made elegant by the fluency of their performance. If there is one mistake that novice dog trainers make, it is labeling a trick before the dog is really performing it reliably. Using clicker training to teach your dog to perform a trick is easy and fun.

It is important to the overall flow of the performance to be sure that your dog understands what is expected of him *before* you ask him to offer the behavior around distractions and on cue. Tricks that are simple and executed with a single cue are more impressive than more complicated ones performed with lots of added cues and lures from you.

Keep the basics in mind when teaching tricks to your Golden. Use tasty treats, train in short sessions with a clear goal in mind, and break the behavior down into small, teachable steps. If at any point the behavior falls apart, go back and review the steps rather than repeating yourself.

 Alert!

If you find you and your dog are doing a lot of standing around and staring at each other, it means you need to further break the trick down into more steps so that it is easier for him to be successful.

Skills Needed for Trick Training

Though you can teach tricks using a cookie lure, the overall performance of your trick will be more reliable and less choppy if you teach your dog some simple skills that allow you more of a hands-off approach.

Free shaping is a skill of waiting and watching. This method uses the clicker to change a behavior from what it is now into what you want by clicking and treating approximations of the behavior. This means that you wait for the dog to offer a behavior that is on its way to the end behavior. You reward the dog for moving the behavior in the right direction. Using free shaping for teaching your dog to spin in a circle might involve clicking and treating him for gradually turning his head further and further to the right or left until he moves his whole body with it into a spin. Free shaping is a crucial skill to becoming a really good trick trainer and one that you will likely master with enough time and practice.

 Fact

It is important to keep in mind that targeting is a form of luring. Once the dog is on the right track the target should be gradually faded so that the dog will perform the behavior without that assistance.

The other skill that is useful in trick training is targeting (see Chapter 7 for detailed information). Targeting is the skill of teaching your dog to touch his nose to a target, be it a hand or a yogurt lid. This skill is taught by luring with a treat at first until the dog is reliably touching the target. Then, you wean the treat away so that the dog is freely touching the target and receiving his treat separately. Targeting is used to move an animal away from you and to specify to him where you want his head to be. Targeting is a useful tool in not only building your dog's understanding of the task at hand but also building your dog's confidence.

Kindergarten Tricks

Starting off with teaching a simple trick will help boost your confidence as a trainer and raise your Golden's enthusiasm for working with you. Even if you consider a trick simple, your dog may not understand what you want and will need a more detailed shaping plan.

Goldens in particular are easy to teach since they are so willing to please and perform for the attention of it all. You will still have to break things down into simple steps. Feel free to embellish the steps listed to make it easier for your dog to be successful. Dogs are not mind readers. Most are willing to do your bidding if they understand what it is you expect from them. Set your goals low, and reward your dog with treats, toys, games, and affection. The more fun he has, the more willing he will be to work with you.

 Essential

Remember to go back and teach the trick skills of shaping and targeting. There will be times when you can use them to help explain to your dog what it is you want him to do.

Teaching "Spin"

Your can teach spin with free shaping or a lure. For a beginner, it is probably easier to teach with a lure. You can see the results more quickly and will be more motivated to want to train more often. Feel free to add more steps to the shaping plan if you feel your dog needs more help in understanding what you want him to do.

Here are the shaping steps for teaching spin:

- Use a cookie to lure your dog's nose about a quarter turn to the left or right.
- Click and treat when his head is in the quarter-turn position.

- Use a treat in your hand for six repetitions, clicking and treating each quarter-turn.
- After the sixth repetition, try it without a treat in your hand.
- Use your hand to make the same motion and click and treat if your dog offers the same turn.
- If your dog doesn't follow your hand, go back to using food in your hand for three to four times and repeat.
- Go back and forth between luring and not luring until your dog offers the quarter turn reliably without a food lure.
- Once your dog will offer the quarter turn, go back to a food lure and try to get him to go halfway.
- Click and treat right at the halfway mark for six or so repetitions.
- Once your dog is moving reliably, try without the lure.
- When turning halfway is not a problem, click the halfway mark but deliver the treat from your pocket.
- Delivering the treat a second or two later but clicking at the halfway mark will help speed up the spin because the dog will be trying to get around faster to get his reward.
- Label the behavior "spin" as the dog hits the halfway mark for many training sessions.
- Once the dog is beginning to spin, as you start to move your hand, you can add a verbal cue to your hand signal by saying "spin" first and then offering the signal.

Alert!

If you are recording your training progress, don't make it too complicated. If you do, you won't record your sessions or you won't want to train at all. It is no good to keep a notebook if half the time you don't write in it and the other half you just scribble anything just to be done with it.

If at any point the behavior of spinning becomes slow or begins to fall apart, drop the verbal cue (don't ask for the behavior) and go back to luring your dog for a few repetitions. Then fade the lure until he is performing the spin reliably and fast. Add the cue back in when your dog's behavior is the way you want it.

Teaching "Bow"

The general behavior we want is for your Golden to bend his front end to the ground while leaving his butt end in the air and hold it. This is a natural behavior for dogs and is called a play bow. Most dogs don't offer it reliably enough for you to try to catch your dog doing it and click and treat him. If yours is a Golden that does offer play bows frequently, you can certainly take advantage of it by clicking and treating as he is bowing. However, for those dogs that aren't offering it on their own here are the shaping steps.

- Start with your dog in a standing position.
- Using targeting, teach your dog to touch your hand for a click and treat.
- Put your hand about halfway to the floor, and say "touch."
- Click and treat your dog for bending his head to touch your hand.
- Repeat this for six to eight repetitions.
- Gradually lower your hand to the ground so that your dog has to bend his elbows to touch.
- If his back end flops down, too, simply don't click and try again.
- You may find it useful to click the front-end dip and then toss the treat away for the dog to chase.
- This tossing away will help restart the behavior for your next repetition.
- Once your dog is reliably bending his front end down, delay the click by a second or two.
- If the dog holds the position without lying down, click and treat.
- If he lies down, don't click and try again.
- Once your dog can bow and hold it for a few seconds, label it "bow" as he is doing it.

- After several training sessions, you can begin to say "bow" right before the hand signal.
- Later, you can fade the hand signal by gradually offering less exaggerated hand motions.

 **Essential**

Don't be afraid to keep your training session short or to add more steps to shaping the lowering of the front end if necessary. In no time at all, your Golden will be bowing at everyone he meets.

First-Grade Tricks

These tricks, though not all that complicated, do require a little better planning and shaping on your part. You may find that your dog picks these up right away, but he may need several short training sessions to get him started in the right direction. Remember that the easier it is for the dog to be right, the more willing he will be to work with you.

Keep your shaping plan clear, and make it easy for the dog to be right. Don't be afraid to jump ahead if your dog is catching on more quickly or slow it down and review if he seems confused or frustrated. As with the easier tricks, you'll want to get these started in a quiet environment but move your training sessions around distractions as soon as your Golden shows that he understands what you want.

 **Fact**

Practicing around distractions almost from the beginning will teach your dog to perform his tricks wherever you ask for them. If you wait until later to add in distractions, you will have to start from the beginning and rebuild the whole behavior to fluency.

Sit Up and Beg

This is a trick that requires some balance and muscle development on the dog's part. Though Goldens are athletic dogs, they are not always in good enough shape to balance on their haunches for long periods of time. Practicing this trick in small frequent sessions is ideal since your dog will need time to learn the skill of balancing and using muscles he doesn't normally use.

Here are the shaping steps for teaching sit up and beg:

- Start with your dog in a sit.
- Use a treat to lure your dog's nose in an upward direction.
- If he tips his nose up, click and treat.
- Keep several treats in your hand and let your dog nibble at them.
- When you have your dog's interest, raise your hand slightly.
- As your dog raises up from a sit, click and treat.
- Leave your hand stationary so he has to hold the stretch, then click and treat.
- Repeat this until your dog can successfully hold the sit and stretch his nose skyward.
- Gradually increase the height of the stretch so that his front feet are off the ground.
- If he rears up completely out of the sit, lower the treat and begin again.
- If he holds onto your arm with his front paws, lower the treat until he regains his balance.
- Once he can sit up without holding on, fade the food so it is not in your hand every time.
- If the behavior falls apart, go back to using food for a time or two and begin again.
- Click when the dog is sitting up with his front feet close to his chest, and deliver the treat.
- Once the dog is sitting up, as you move your hand over his head begin to label it "Sit Up." Remember, you want to label the behavior as the dog is doing it.
- When your dog begins to anticipate your hand motion, go ahead and ask for "Sit Up."

▲ This four-year-old male Golden is practicing the Honor exercise for Rally obedience competition. This exercise requires the dog to perform a sit or down on leash.

The skill of being able to remain in a sit with the front feet off the ground is a learned skill for most dogs. Each dog must be given time to build up the muscles in his lower back so that he can hold this position without falling over. It is important to use the food lure to accomplish this ability. At the same time, remember to fade it as quickly as possible so that the dog does not become dependent upon having it present in order to perform the trick. It may take a while to accomplish this, so be patient and accurate with your clicks.

Roll Over

Believe it or not, this can be a fairly difficult trick to teach your dog. One reason may be that some dogs do not like being on their backs. Another may be that many dogs don't like the sensation of being slightly out of control. Regardless, all dogs can learn this trick with the proper amount of patience and the right kind of tools.

Here are the shaping steps for teaching your dog to roll over.

- Start with your dog in a down.

- Use a treat to coax your dog so that his hip is out to the side, then click and treat.
- Repeat this until he lies down and rolls onto one hip with a single motion, then click and treat.
- Now move the treat a bit toward his neck and shoulder.
- If he lowers his shoulder to the floor, click and treat.
- Repeat this until he will easily lower his shoulder to the floor.
- Once he is completely on his side, go ahead and coax him a little farther, then click and treat.
- Gradually use the lure to have him reach farther and farther until he is on his back, then click and treat.
- Gradually have him reach until he rolls all the way over, then click and treat.
- Repeat from the start having him go a little further each time before you click and treat.
- Eventually work it so that he will lie down and roll most of the way for one click and treat.
- Fade the lure by having him start the behavior without it, then click and treat.
- If you lose the behavior, go back to using a lure for a few times and then try it again without.
- Once your dog is rolling over easily, label the behavior "roll over."

 **Alert!**

Some dogs are more reluctant than others about wanting to get on their backs, but most dogs will do it in time if you give them a chance. It may be a good idea to practice on a soft surface, like a rug, so that your dog isn't uncomfortable when he rolls onto his back.

Roll over is a great trick to teach an active dog that loves to show off. It is important to fade out the use of the lure as soon as possible so that your dog doesn't become dependent upon it. Once he masters rolling, he may be so good at it that you'll want to teach him to roll multiple times or have him learn to roll in both directions.

Junior-High Level Tricks

These tricks are a little more complicated than the others but still doable for most dogs. The sky is the limit for what you want to teach your dog so long as the task is physically possible for the dog to accomplish. Breaking things down into tiny increments is essential, as is some knowledge of free shaping. Remember when using free shaping to teach a behavior that you are using the clicker exclusively to give the dog information about what it is doing correctly.

 Essential

Well-timed clicks done at the exact moment your dog gets the trick right will produce progress toward your end goal. Stingy or sloppy clicking will produce a confused Golden that doesn't want to play anymore. Take your time with these, and you will reap the rewards of a dog that loves to perform tricks!

Bang! You're Dead

Playing dead is a favorite, and gets a chuckle out of just about any dog lover you meet. For this trick, the dog must lie completely flat on his side without so much as a tail wag. The difficulty in this trick is not so much the position the dog must be in, but the fact that he must be absolutely still.

Here are the shaping steps for teaching your dog to play dead:

- Start with your dog in a down.
- Use a treat to get him to roll onto his side, then click and treat.
- Hold the treat close to his shoulder to coax him closer to the ground, then click and treat.

- Repeat this until he will get onto his side from a standing position easily.
- Once he is in position, delay the click by a second or two so he will hold it.
- Gradually build up the time he will stay by delaying the click by a few more seconds.
- Now start from the beginning without a lure and click any attempt to get into a down.
- Gradually require that your dog get closer to the right position before clicking and treating.
- Once he is easily flopping onto his side, click and treat.
- Label the behavior "Bang" as he is in position, then click and treat.
- Replace your hand signal with a thumb and finger gun right before you say "Bang."

Teaching your dog to play dead isn't difficult, but it may require you to work it in short frequent sessions. This is especially true if you have a young active Golden that hates sitting still. A good time to practice this might be after your dog has had exercise and is ready to take things a little more slowly.

Say You're Sorry

This is an adorable trick taught entirely by free shaping. Free shaping involves using clicker and treats to capture behavior that is on the way to an end goal. Free shaping is a great tool and skill to have as a trainer, and it can produce the most amazing results. This trick involves the dog lying down and lowering his head to the ground, eyes up and looking at you. It is the ultimate heartbreaker; those soulful eyes will get your audience every time.

Here are the shaping steps for teaching "Say you're sorry":

- Start with your dog in a down.
- Watch him closely for any head motion down, then click and treat.

- Continue to click and treat for gradually more downward head motion.
- Once your dog is bobbing his head up and down, stop clicking and wait.
- If he makes an effort to lower his head to the ground, click and treat.
- Withhold the click until he rests his chin on the ground, then click and treat.
- Once he gets his chin on the floor reliably, delay the click by a second or two.
- Gradually increase the time you delay the click until he is holding it for several seconds.
- Build up to the desired amount of time.
- When you have the duration you are looking for, label the behavior "Sorry," then click and treat.

 **Fact**

You must make sure that your dog has connected the behavior to being clicked before withholding the click, or he won't understand what you are aiming for with the delay. The more closely you watch for subtle head positions or minor details, the better you will be at teaching this trick.

This is a fun trick to teach and a great skill for you to learn. With free shaping, you are basically only clicking one aspect of a behavior until your Golden is doing it regularly. Once he is offering it regularly, you then withhold the click so that the dog will offer something more dramatic or will hold the position for a longer period of time. Ⓔ

CHAPTER  **19**

Golden Retriever Grooming Basics

GROOMING YOUR GOLDEN RETRIEVER can be a wonderful way to bond to him and get to know his body. Goldens vary in their coat length depending on their genetics, but all Goldens require brushing on at least a weekly basis. Grooming your Golden Retriever regularly can help you maintain his health in a variety of ways. You can identify parasites before they become a problem, keep track of lumps and bumps, and teach your Golden to trust you to handle his body. The time you spend brushing, bathing, trimming nails, and tending to feet can be a wonderfully quiet and special time if you take the time now to train your dog to accept and enjoy it.

Training for Grooming

Golden Retrievers will, at a minimum, need to be brushed, bathed, and cleaned when they get muddy. By acclimating your Golden to all this handling, you can help this be a pleasant experience instead of one that requires the whole family to pin down the dog. It is best to avoid using force to groom any dog, as harsh treatment will never make your Golden Retriever a big fan of being brushed and cared for. You may get the job done this time, but you will soon discover that the process becomes more and more difficult as time goes on and your Golden gets bigger and better at evading you.

There will be many times when your Golden Retriever must be held still, not just for grooming issues but for veterinary checks and quick home checks to ensure that he is healthy and stays that way. Many people never even give it a second thought, but throughout your dog's life, he will need to be held or restrained for various procedures and routine checks.

The most common restraint technique used by most veterinary staff involves hugging the dog to your chest. The right arm goes over the dog's back, and the other goes across his chest with the left hand pressing his neck into your shoulder. This hold not only prevents the dog from escaping, it also prevents him from biting should the procedure be painful or if he is uncomfortable from an injury.

 **Essential**

Training for grooming is a very practical way to help your Golden Retriever become a welcomed member of your family wherever he goes. If you are planning on sending your dog to the groomer for his bathing and brushing, all the more reason to train him to tolerate it and maybe even like it.

Teaching Your Dog to Tolerate Restraint

Teaching your Golden to accept this restraint involves breaking it down into small pieces. Unlike clicker training (which is operant conditioning, meaning the dog must do something to earn his click and treat), this shaping exercise involves developing an association between the restraint step and the treat. This is commonly called temperament training, and its main goal is to develop an association between being held and good things versus the dog learning to do a specific behavior. The shaping steps are as follows:

1. Find a helper who can feed the dog delicious treats as you practice the steps of this hold.

2. Call your dog to you, and feed him a delicious tidbit for coming.

3. Have several treats in your hand, and, as you feed him with your left hand, run your right hand over his back lightly from neck to rump.

4. Repeat this several times while he is nibbling at the treats, until he ignores your right hand movement.

5. Have your helper feed him tidbits as you move your hand down his right side, so that your bicep is touching his side.

6. Gradually increase the pressure until the weight of your arm is resting on his back.

7. Gently pat him down his side as your helper feeds him treats and talks to him.

8. With your left hand, gently stroke his chest until he accepts this without moving away.

9. Gradually work your left hand so that you are patting him from throat to chest.

10. Slowly work your left hand so that you are touching his right shoulder, and pat slowly.

11. Work your way up to the side of his neck, and stroke him gently.

12. Increase the pressure of your touch until you eventually have him hugged in tight to your body.

Teaching Stand

The "Stand" command involves your dog standing on all four legs without moving his feet or cranking his head around to see what you are doing. This is probably one of the most useful behaviors you can teach your Golden Retriever for grooming. It works well for brushing, nail trims, ear cleaning, bathing, paw wiping on muddy days, and overall body checks for lumps and bumps.

The shaping steps for teaching your dog to stand are as follows:

1. Use a treat to lure your dog out of a sit; click and treat.

2. Repeat this until the dog will easily follow your hand to move into a standing position.

3. Repeat this without a food lure in your hand, then click and treat for following your hand into a standing position.
4. Use your empty fist to get your dog to stand then count to two before you click and treat.
5. Slowly build up the time so that your dog is standing for longer and longer periods of time.
6. Fade your fist as the cue by saying "Stay" and quickly taking your fist away. Click and treat if your dog holds his position.
7. Practice taking your fist away for longer periods of time, click and treat your dog for holding the stay.
8. Once your dog is standing and staying for twenty seconds or more, add distractions.
9. Practice running your hand down your dog's back while he stays, and click and treat him for holding the stay.
10. Replace your hand with a brush, and click and treat for staying.
11. Practice turning his ears inside out.
12. Practice lifting each foot while he holds the stay.

 **Alert!**

If at any point your dog objects to being handled, teach that piece first before adding it to the stand. Trying to combine a whole new behavior with a just-learned behavior will only make the dog feel frightened and panicky to get away. It pays to go slow and be sure you have taught all the pieces before combining them into one exercise.

Basic Grooming Equipment

A grooming table can greatly simplify the grooming process, especially if your Golden Retriever has a lot of coat that tends to get matted. Grooming tables are fairly inexpensive, and they usually fold flat for storage, making them portable to the basement or outdoors in good weather. Most dogs don't like the grooming table at first, it's quite a precarious perch as far as they are concerned. With a little training, most dogs will learn to jump up on it and stay put until you have made them beautiful. There are several behaviors that are required to use a grooming table safely. Your Golden must be able to jump on and off the table, to stay on the table until you release him, and to stand, sit, and lie down on the table.

Table Manners

To teach your Golden Retriever these behaviors, you will want to start with the table flat on the floor. Click and treat him for stepping on and off of it. Be sure you are timing your click for when his feet are on the table, and throw the treat so that he steps off to get it.

◀ A four-month-old female Golden puppy.

As your Golden becomes more comfortable with this, raise the table slightly so that it rests a foot or so off the ground, and repeat the exercise. As you raise it to its full height, deliver the treats on the table to prevent the dog from leaping off and hurting himself. Once your Golden Retriever is comfortable getting on and off, start requiring that he stay up there longer by delaying the clicks and treats by at first a few seconds and later several seconds. You are basically teaching him a sit or down stay on a table. See Chapter 6 for more on the shaping steps of teaching sit or down/stay.

The Right Tools for the Job

Using the right equipment to get the job done is essential when grooming your Golden Retriever. You can order all of the supplies you need from any of the numerous pet supply catalogs or over the Internet (see Appendix B for references). To groom your Golden, you will need a flat slicker brush, a straight pair of scissors, a pair of thinning shears, an English comb with coarse and medium teeth (sometimes referred to as a greyhound comb), a pin brush, and a excellent pair of nail clippers or a grinder to do his nails.

 Fact

As with all things, you get what you pay for. It is far better to pay a little extra and get well-made equipment that will get the job done than to skimp on less-expensive equipment that you will continually have to replace.

Grooming equipment can be a bit expensive, but you do get what you pay for. If you own a Golden and are planning on doing any grooming or maintenance at home, you will do well to make the investment in decent equipment that will make your job quick and easy. Don't be afraid to ask the advice of the catalog folks (many of whom are dog lovers themselves) for advice on the right product for the Golden you are grooming. You might also want to invest in a grooming table. An inexpensive back saver, these usually have legs that fold and a rubber surface to prevent your dog from slipping off while you are grooming him.

Trimming Nails

This is probably the hardest of all the grooming areas to master. If you are squeamish and unsure of what you are doing, or your Golden has had a bad experience in the past, pay a professional to trim his nails for you. The fee is nominal and well worth it to know that your dog's nails are a healthy length and that he was not traumatized in the process. You can then concentrate on teaching your Golden Retriever to accept and like having his feet handled and held, ultimately making his experience better down the road.

The shaping steps for teaching your dog to like having his feet handled for grooming are outlined in Chapter 7. If you are attempting to trim your dog's nails yourself, hold the paw under the light so that you can view the nail from the side. You'll want to trim just the pointy part of the nail. Avoid the area where the nail gets thicker, and you will avoid making the nail bleed. Always have some sort of styptic powder handy to stop a nicked nail from bleeding and avoid a mess.

Keeping the nails trimmed is important to your dog's overall gait and comfort. Goldens with long nails can get them caught and torn off on brush outside or snagged in carpets around the house. Walking on feet with nails that are too long can distort the foot, making it difficult and painful to walk or run. If your Golden Retriever walks on pavement on a regular basis, you may find that you do not have to trim his nails quite so often.

 Essential

An alternative to using a nail clipper is to use a grinder or dremel. These are battery operated and are an excellent alternative to using clippers. One word of caution: A grinder can heat up and burn the nail if you hold it in one spot too long. Try to keep it moving over the edge of the nail until it is the desired length.

Trimming Feet

The hair between a Golden's toes can prevent him from gaining enough traction on a slippery floor and may cause him injury and discomfort. Keeping the hair on his feet trimmed back will ensure that he can grip the floor without slipping and hurting himself. You'll also be helping to prevent ice and snow buildup on his feet during the winter and mud and dirt from being tracked in the rest of the year.

Trimming your Golden's feet is an easy process if he is used to having his feet handled. Have your dog lie down, and have a helper feed him treats while you trim the excess fur around each foot. Use your straight scissors to trim the excess hair on the bottom of his feet, but to avoid accidentally cutting the foot pad, rest your scissors on the foot pad and point them away from the rest of the foot. Stand your dog up and cut around the outline of each foot, then pull the hair up from between his toes and trim off the excess with the thinning shears. Use the thinning shears to blend the fur so it looks less choppy and gives more of a sleek outline to the foot.

The more often you do it, the better you will get at it. If you find it a difficult task because your Golden will not hold still and allow his feet to be touched, see Chapter 7 for a detailed recipe for teaching him to have his feet handled.

Protecting Foot Pads

The bottom of a dog's feet are very sensitive. It is important to check your Golden Retriever's paws weekly to be sure that the pads are not cracked and bleeding. In wintertime, a Golden's feet are especially susceptible to cracking and soreness because of the heavy use of rock salt. Some people find that coating their dog's feet with Vaseline before venturing out helps prevent the development of sore feet. If your Golden Retriever likes to dig, he is likely at some point to cut a foot pad on a rock or other sharp object. The skin on the bottom of your dog's foot is callused and dead and cannot heal by being sutured. This part of the body heals from the inside out. It must be bandaged and given time to mend.

 **Essential**

Consider using a dog bootie to cover the bandage if your dog cuts the pad of his foot. This accessory will allow him to move about freely outdoors without getting his bandage wet and needing to have it changed every time he goes out. Using dog booties in winter may also be an option if you live in the city and can't avoid walking on sidewalks loaded with rock salt.

Cleaning Teeth

Brushing your Golden Retriever's teeth may seem a bit extreme to you but it can save you a bundle down the road in veterinary care. Goldens don't usually develop a lot of plaque and tartar on their teeth, but preventative dental care can help keep the quality of their lives at a healthy high. There are many dog toothpastes on the market today that should be applied to the teeth with a soft brush or gauze pad. Most dogs like the taste, as they are flavored, and will tolerate a quick wipe better than a full-blown brushing.

Using a dental instrument to remove plaque and tartar isn't recommended, since using it to scrape the teeth often leaves grooves in the enamel, which will attract more plaque in the future. If you can't wipe or brush the plaque off easily, consider having your dog's teeth cleaned professionally.

Cleaning and Trimming Ears

Golden Retrievers can be prone to frequent ear infections mainly due to their floppy ears, and lack of air circulation to the ear canal. Many homeopathic veterinarians believe that frequent ear infections are a sign of an overworked immune system and are a symptom of a larger issue. If your Golden has frequent ear infections and doesn't swim or get his ears wet often, consider consulting a qualified homeopathic veterinary professional for advice and evaluation of his overall health.

A Golden Retriever's ears should be cleaned on a weekly basis with an over-the-counter ear cleaner (purchased through your veterinarian or pet supply catalog). Turn the ear inside out, and squirt a small amount of ear-cleaning solution into the canal. Close the ear canal, and massage the base of the ear until you hear it make squishy sounds. Let your dog shake his head a few times to loosen any waxy junk, then use a gauze pad or soft tissue wrapped around your finger to wipe out excess junk. Dry the ear as best you can with a dry gauze pad or tissue.

 fact

Ear infections manifest themselves in frequent head shaking, black, waxy-looking junk in the ears, and a bad odor. You should bring your dog to your veterinarian if you notice these symptoms as your dog probably needs to be treated for an ear infection.

Brushing Basics

Most Golden Retrievers like to be brushed if you familiarize them with the brush slowly and gently, and don't get hung up on getting too much done all at once. If there is a way to turn a dog off from grooming, it is to make the process long and uncomfortable. Make sure that your Golden's first encounters with the brush are pleasant ones, and you are sure to teach your dog that being groomed is a pleasant experience.

The basic brush that you will need to get out the most dead hair is a regular flat slicker brush. There are all different kinds of brushes available on the market, and each is used for a different coat type or to groom a certain part of the dog: the feathering on the legs, the tail, or the whole body. The slicker brush will remove the undercoat and dead hair next to your dog's skin. This brush will allow you to remove the most dead hair from his body and feathering on his legs.

Shedding

Golden Retrievers shed a lot, all year round, but they tend to lose the most coat in the spring and fall. At these times of year, you may want to brush your Golden Retriever twice weekly or more to ensure that you remove as much of the dead fur as possible so that his new coat will come in quickly. Frequent brushing is recommended to keep the volume of fur to a minimum.

There are many products on the market that will help cut down on the mess. Decorative covers for your car seats, couches, and the lining of your van or SUV are also available, making it easier to contain the shed hair. Most die-hard Golden Retriever lovers have also given up wearing black, or have simply learned to just close their eyes to the golden locks that adhere to their dress-up clothes.

 **Essential**

Brushing your dog outdoors will prevent you from spreading the mess all over your house and may make cleanup a bit easier. As a bonus, the birds and squirrels will love the loose fur for nest lining.

Mats, Burrs, and Tangles

Depending upon the length of your Golden Retriever's coat, you may find that he has a talent for picking up all kinds of plant material in his coat, or that his coat gets matted around the ears, groin, or feathering on the rear legs. Removing mats and tangles should be done carefully as a dog's skin is quite elastic and the danger of cutting the skin is high. A great technique for removing mats and tangles is to use a comb under the mat held close to the skin (so that you remove the danger of cutting it) and then trim the mat out with the scissors. Thinning shears can then be used to even out the fur so that the cut does not leave a hole in the coat.

Checking your Golden Retriever for tangles and mats on a weekly basis will help prevent this from becoming a huge problem in the future. Always brush and remove all mats before bathing your Golden or letting him swim, as water will tend to make the mat even more difficult to remove.

Giving Your Golden Retriever a Bath

Goldens don't need to be bathed all that often, maybe every eight to ten weeks (unless they roll in something smelly). Most mud and dirt is easily brushed out of their coat if you allow it to dry first. You can bathe your Golden indoors or out, depending on the season, but either way you will probably want to do so with your dog on leash to prevent escape.

 **Alert!**

Don't give your Golden a bath too often! Frequent bathing can destroy the natural oils in their skin making it dry and itchy.

To give your Golden a bath, you may want the assistance of a helper to hold your dog while you wet him down and scrub. The helper may feed the dog to help keep him in the tub and otherwise comfort him. Thoroughly wet the coat to the skin, then apply a shampoo designed for dogs. Starting with the head, work it into the coat. Lather the shampoo and cover him from head to toe, including between his toes. Thoroughly rinse the coat with warm water, and then let your dog shake off the excess water. Use a towel to wipe off the remaining water, but use a patting motion to dry rather than rubbing one to avoid matting the fur.

Gently brush the wet coat, and put your dog somewhere to dry. When dry, brush the coat completely, including under the belly, tail, and feathering.

Professional Grooming

Even if you normally groom your Golden Retriever yourself, there may be times when you would like to have him groomed professionally by an experienced groomer. There are many excellent groomers everywhere that are capable dog professionals, but finding just the right person can be a daunting task when there are so many to choose from.

To find the right person, start by asking other dog owners or your veterinarian who they use. Try to go with someone who comes recommended. In order to find the groomer who can be the most helpful to you, it is a good idea to be clear about what you want them to do as far as trimming goes. Be sure to inform them of any skin or health conditions. Be prepared to present an updated copy of your dog's vaccinations, and be sure you clarify all fees ahead of time—remember, cheaper isn't necessarily better.

Grooming dogs is hard work. Often, people can be finicky about how they want their dog to look, but they don't mention it to the groomer until after they have completed the grooming. It's not fair to be unclear about your expectations and then disappointed in the results. Being a considerate consumer will help your dog to get the best grooming experience possible. You can earn your groomer's admiration by following a few simple tips.

- Pick up your dog on time; don't leave him at the shop longer than necessary.
- Brush your dog frequently at home and remove mats promptly—don't send a mess to a groomer and then expect miracles.
- Ask the groomer how your dog behaved. Offer to work on foot handling, standing, or any other areas in which your dog was more difficult to handle.

- Be understanding of your groomer's time, and try not to linger when you pick up your dog
- Realize that many groomers work alone; try to be understanding if they are running behind.
- Let your dog take a potty break before you bring him into the shop.
- If you can't keep your appointment, cancel with as much notice as possible.
- If you love your groomer, refer friends to them!

The Golden Retriever is a gorgeous dog with a style and flair all its own. There is nothing as beautiful as a healthy robust Golden that has been groomed to perfection. Learning to groom your Golden isn't a difficult task, but it may be more time consuming than you initially anticipated. You might consider having your dog professionally groomed every eight to ten weeks and simply doing maintenance brushing, ear and teeth cleaning, and mat checks in between. Keeping your Golden looking his best can be a shared effort. The benefits for you will be more time to relax and play with your Golden buddy. Ⓔ

CHAPTER 20

Goldens at Work

THE GOLDEN RETRIEVER IS a spectacular working dog. Combining beauty and brains in one dog is no mean feat, but the Golden Retriever does it all. As a hunting partner, the Golden is a steady working dog able to work long days in the field with enthusiasm. As search-and-rescue dogs, Golden's are enthusiastic and biddable, often working long hours for a game of fetch or tug. As service dogs, Goldens bring independence and freedom to their human partners day in and day out.

Beauty and Brains

The Golden Retriever is like no other breed of dog. Goldens bring great comfort and joy to the people they meet, and their intelligence is exemplary. Don't get a Golden if you are a shy person because with a Golden on the end of the leash, you are sure to draw attention wherever you go. People can't resist touching such a gorgeous, friendly dog, and thankfully most Goldens thrive on excessive attention. This is not just a pretty face, however—Goldens are sweet intelligent dogs that are easy to train and incredibly sensitive to the needs of the individuals they are bonded to.

Properly socialized and exercised, these are dogs that will run all day in the field and sleep at your feet in the evening. Goldens prefer to be with their owners more than anything. They will gladly accompany you on the most mundane of duties around the house or in the car. No matter what the task, the Golden will excel at it given the proper training and socialization. Whether you want to take your Golden along as a hunting partner or train him to be a search-and-rescue dog, this breed is extremely versatile and used the world over for a variety of specialized jobs.

Sociability

A good working dog must be highly sociable and able to tolerate being around all kinds of people and other dogs on a regular basis without overreacting to anything. A Golden that is going to be a good working dog must be socialized to everything the handler thinks they will ever encounter in their work. They should meet hundreds of people of all shapes and sizes, play with dozens of dogs off leash, and go to every different place the handler can take them to. There is no limit to the amount of exposure you can give a good working dog. The more places they go, the more people and dogs they meet, the better they will be at the task they are taught to do. Working dogs should be friendly with all different kinds of people and other dogs; the handler never knows where they might end up and whom they will meet. The best way to prepare a dog for a successful working career is to take him everywhere, from puppyhood on through adulthood. You cannot oversocialize a working dog.

 **Fact**

Research shows that the more exposure a dog has as a young puppy, the more he will include those experiences as part of his world. The wider his experiences while he is young, the more easily he will accept just about any experience he encounters as an adult.

It is quickest and most successful to begin to socialize a dog when he is between eight and eighteen weeks of age. Continuing socialization past this point is crucial to normal development, but starting within this range is critical to a well-adjusted adaptable adult dog.

Trainability

Golden Retrievers are highly trainable dogs. With their built-in desire to please and work for a handler, along with their sweet, biddable nature, Goldens are the Einsteins of the dog world. No harsh training methods are necessary to train this willing dog to handle just about any task. Ease of trainability varies from dog to dog, and the job you want the dog to do will determine the personality of the dog you choose. It would not be a good idea, for instance, to choose a Golden that has an independent streak and prefers to work at a distance from his handler if the job you are training it for is a service, guide, or hearing dog. Conversely, it would be a frustrating task to train a very dependent Golden personality to be an independent, problem-solving hunting companion or search-and-rescue dog. How easily a dog will be trained depends on several factors, including these:

- The task you will be training the dog to do
- Whether the dog will be working close to the handler or at a distance
- Whether the dog will need to make decisions independent of the handler
- How much energy the dog needs for the task being taught
- Whether the dog wants to be with people or off exploring its environment

Choosing the wrong dog for the task you wish to teach can be an exercise in frustration. Knowing something about temperament testing and developing a list of required criteria is important in making sure you choose the right dog for the task that must be done.

Hunting Partners

The original purpose of the Golden Retriever breed was to retrieve upland game birds for the hunter. The Goldens of yesteryear did this with great enthusiasm and style, accompanying their owners on daylong excursions and persevering through all kinds of weather to fulfill their job. Golden enthusiasts enjoy exercising their dog's ability to retrieve and hunt, and so they have designed tests that allow anyone to participate in preserving this ability in their companions.

 Fact

Some enthusiasts have never hunted a day in their lives, but they train their dogs to retrieve as a sport. If you take up the sport of hunting trials with your Golden, you will meet people from all walks of life, most of whom have never held—much less fired—a gun.

There are three major divisions of the sport of hunting in which your dog can earn titles from the American Kennel Club or the Golden Retriever Club of America. They are field trials, hunt tests, and working certificates. Each division has a set number of requirements that the dog and handler must pass in order to qualify and earn titles. Handlers range from the very serious and driven competitor to the laid-back, out-for-fun dog owner who enjoys being with their dog learning something new.

Field Trials

Competing with Goldens in field trials is a serious sport. Field trials are extremely competitive and difficult. It takes hours and hours of training and practice to create a dog that can hold its own in competition. The purpose of field trials is to test the natural instincts and trainabilities of Goldens in the field in order to preserve the original purpose for which the breed was developed.

The tests are designed to simulate a day in the field. They test both land and water skills of marking, retrieving, and delivery of the game. The dogs are tested to determine whether they will find, retrieve, and deliver the goods in any condition and under any circumstance. The skill of marking is an important one. Marking is defined as the ability to determine where the fallen bird has landed and, in some cases, remember it after retrieving several other downed birds. The dogs in field trials are judged for natural abilities in the areas of memory, intelligence, attention, nose, courage, perseverance, and style. They are also judged on the abilities they have acquired through training, especially steadiness, control, response to direction, delivery, and ability to retrieve any type of bird under any condition. In addition, the dog should not injure the game in any way, retrieve decoys, or pursue game without being sent.

◄ Goldens were bred to retrieve ducks and other game birds while hunting, as demonstrated by this twenty-month-old male.

Retriever Hunt Tests

The retriever hunt tests were created as an alternative to field trials. Hunt tests are less intense and not competitive. They were designed to give average Golden owners the opportunity to prove and enjoy their dog's natural retrieving ability in the field, without the elimination process associated with competitive field trials. In hunt tests, the dogs are judged against a set standard of performance guidelines—they don't need to perform better than other dogs in order to qualify. The purpose of the hunt test is to evaluate the qualities of the Golden as a hunting dog in a simulated hunt situation.

 **Essential**

The hunt test was proposed and begun by the North American Hunting Retriever Association and later co-created by the American Kennel Club. Now both organizations have their own version of the hunting test trials that owners can compete in and title their dogs.

The hunt test evaluates the Golden at three levels: junior, senior, and master hunter. The junior level is very basic. The senior level is more challenging, and the master level is very difficult. Scoring is based on the AKC's established standards, which evaluate marking, style, perseverance, and trainability. Dogs are given a score ranging from one to ten in each category by two different judges.

To qualify, a dog must receive an average score of seven, based on the scores from both judges, with no score lower than five for each category. The junior hunter title requires four qualifying scores or legs to earn the title Junior Hunter, JH. The senior level requires five qualifying scores, or legs, to earn the title Senior Hunter, or SH. Six qualifying scores are necessary to earn the title Master Hunter, or MH. Once these titles are earned, the suffix appears after the dog's name on all certificates issued by the AKC.

Working Certificates

The Golden Retriever Club of America developed the working certificate tests to determine the natural abilities for which the Golden Retriever was originally bred. These tests, offered at two levels of difficulty, give the average Golden owner the opportunity to exercise the dog's natural retrieving abilities in a fun and informal manner. In general, the working certificate is earned in a more casual and noncompetitive venue, hosted by member clubs across the country. The working certificate was designed to demonstrate the Golden's natural abilities of memory, marking ability, style, intelligence, nose, perseverance, trainability, and desire to retrieve. The test was not designed so much to test a dog's degree of training but to determine a more natural, inborn level of performance.

 Fact

In order to compete in a working certificate test, dogs must be at least six months old and have an AKC, foreign, or ILP registration number.

The rules of the working certificate (basic level) state that no decoys are allowed. The dog must be brought to line on leash and not sent until his number is called. Hand delivery of the bird is not necessary, but the dog must deliver to the area of the line. The requirements to pass the test include the retrieval of two previously killed upland game birds on land in moderate cover, with birds forty to fifty yards from the line and at a ninety-degree angle to each other. This part of the test determines the dog's ability to mark, remember, and retrieve a double fall.

The second part of the test is the retrieving of two freshly killed ducks in swimming water as two separate single retrieves, twenty-five to thirty yards from the line. This test will demonstrate the dog's ability to swim and retrieve waterfowl and willingness to re-enter the water. No voice or hand signals can be given while the dog is working.

The title Working Certificate Excellent (WCX) is a step up from the basic working certificate. This test is designed for dogs trained beyond the WC but not to the competitive level of the AKC field trial dog. The requirements are the retrieval of three upland game birds on land in moderate cover, two previously killed and one live flyer. The second part of the test is the retrieval of two freshly killed ducks in water as a double retrieve with an honor. A double retrieve means that the dog must watch both ducks go down before attempting to retrieve either one. Honoring means that the dog must remain in a sit/stay while it watches another dog work without breaking position. Decoys can be used at this level and should be completely ignored by the dog. The dog must go to line off leash and under control, be steady until sent by handler, and deliver to hand.

Search-and-Rescue Goldens

There are three major types of search-and-rescue dogs used to recover lost people. Air-scenting dogs are used mainly to search large outdoor expanses, such as woods and forests. These dogs use their noses to detect human scent on the wind current. These dogs do not need an article with the scent on it.

The handler of an air-scenting dog must position the dog to sniff in the direction of the wind and detect the presence of any human out there. The air-scenting dog can detect human scent from at least 150 yards away. Their job is to go to the source and come back and take the handler to the person. This task is performed completely off leash in the wilderness or woods. One of the benefits to an air-scenting dog is that he can work at night.

 Essential

In water, a search dog detects human remains by scent given off from the oils in the skin. The gases of the decomposing body rise to the surface and can be detected by the dogs from the shore or from a boat.

There are also the tracking and trailing dogs. The tracking dog performs on a leash or long line. He uses a scent article and follows the exact footsteps of the lost person by following the scent particles left behind. The trailing dog also performs his job on leash or long line, but he follows a ten- to fifteen-foot wide path along which the person traveled. This dog's nose follows the human's scent in a zigzag pattern until he finds the source.

Search dogs use their noses to follow the scent of a human being. They must also be agile and persistent enough to follow it through extreme circumstances. Each of us has our own unique scent, which is made up of discarded skin cells called rafts. This personal scent is mixed with shampoo, soap, detergent, and even gum or bug spray. All of these things make scent, including our exhaled breath. Air-scenting dogs can detect human scent under water, in snow, or in rubble piles. They can be trained to focus on the living or the dead. There are subgroups within each category that can concentrate on forensics or human remains, depending upon the specialty.

Qualities of a Search Dog

A Golden has to have the right stuff to be a good search-and-rescue dog. The ideal candidate will have a strong play drive, high endurance, and a strong desire to be with people. Goldens make great search dogs because they have great noses. They love to be with people and display incredible endurance and perseverance for very little reward. Most search-and-rescue dogs work for the opportunity to play with their handlers upon the completion of a job well done. Some handlers might use a tug toy, others a ball or a quick game of fetch.

A good candidate for search and rescue has a high degree of trainability. This means some problem-solving ability and the willingness to take direction. A dog with a balance of confidence and independence but who accepts direction easily is ideal. Lastly, the best candidate for a search dog should be able to be called off or able to ignore game birds and other wildlife and concentrate on finding only human scent.

Training the Search Dogs and Handlers

Search dogs are very versatile animals that are constantly in new situations. They are around new people, places, and circumstances that require them to be extremely adaptable. Socialization to all kinds of people, dogs, places, and things to climb on, through, and over are the keys to a successful candidate. Training in agility and obedience are helpful as they prepare the dog somewhat for the conditioning he will require.

 **Alert!**

Expenses for search-and-rescue training and travel are entirely up to the handler and are not subsidized by any government agency. These expenses include veterinary care, travel, equipment, gear, and training expenses for both the dog and handler.

Some typical things that a search dog must be familiar with are boats, helicopters, elevators, escalators, and unstable surfaces. Search training involves hide-and-seek games, in which the person hiding runs away and the dog must search to find them. It takes about two years to train a search-and-rescue dog to competency. By far the majority of the training is for the handler in the search-and-rescue dog partnership. The handler must be physically fit, with survival awareness, first-aid, and CPR training. He or she should be able to use a map and compass and be familiar with search strategies.

Hours of practice go into teaching and maintaining the skills acquired by both the dog and the handler, and handlers must practice on a regular basis to maintain the dog's sharpness and abilities. Endurance on both the dog's and handler's part is essential, since searches range anywhere from three- to eight-hour shifts at a time. In searching for lost or missing persons, time is of the essence. The longer the search takes, the less likely the outcome will be a happy one.

Assistance Dogs

There is no breed better than the Golden to serve as a service or assistance dog to a disabled handler. Goldens serve as service dogs and hearing and guide dogs throughout the world, assisting their human partners with everyday tasks and bringing them the independence they desire. Golden Retrievers excel as assistance dogs because of their desire to be with their people and their retrieving abilities.

Assistance dogs are usually raised by foster families, who generously raise them for the first eighteen months of their lives. The foster family housebreaks, socializes, and trains the puppy basic obedience exercises until he is ready to be tested and to begin training as an assistance dog. Policies among assistance dog organizations vary concerning the qualities they are looking for in a future guide, service, or hearing dog. In general, they are looking for a dog with a stable temperament that will work under a variety of conditions and remain reliable, regardless of the handler's skill.

 Fact

Foster-puppy raisers focus on socializing their foster puppies to anything and everything. Then when these little guys grow up and begin their jobs as assistance dogs, they can do their job with confidence and reliability.

Dogs that pass the initial temperament test are generally started in training, which varies in length, depending upon the tasks involved. The dogs are then usually placed with their new handlers by the time they are two-and-a-half to three years old. Some organizations require the handler to come out to the facility for training, while others have instructors and field representatives who train on location. Handlers must learn how to work with their assistance dog and form a working partnership with them. Assistance dogs often fail because of physical limitations, including hip and elbow problems, but they can also fail because of a lack of confidence, drive, or temperament issues.

Service Dogs

A service dog is a dog that is trained to help a disabled person become and remain more independent. These dogs often pull wheelchairs, help the person dress and undress, turn light switches on and off, retrieve fallen objects, and open and close doors. The tasks can be varied depending on an individual's disability. Candidates are usually put through a rigorous information-gathering process and interview to determine their needs and to specialize a dog's training.

Service dogs accompany people with all sorts of disabilities. They belong to the more general category of assistance dogs. Some service dogs may be trained to alert to seizures in a person with such a disorder. Though the dog cannot be taught to predict an oncoming seizure, seizure-alert dogs often become predictive after living only a short time with their new partners. No one knows by quite what mechanism a dog detects a seizure. Some believe it is a change in the person's scent, while others believe that it is the person's behavioral changes. Service dogs are invaluable to people with disabilities, giving independence to those who were previously dependent upon human caretakers for every aspect of their care and enabling them to be self-sufficient members of society.

Hearing Dogs

A hearing dog is a dog that is trained to alert to sound and cue the owner, who is deaf or hearing impaired. The hearing dog's tasks depend entirely upon what the individual handler needs in his day-to-day interactions. Hearing dogs can be taught to alert to the doorbell, the smoke detector, a baby crying, the microwave timer, a person calling the handler's name, a telephone ringing, or almost any other sound.

Hearing dogs help people with hearing disabilities to live a more independent and self-sufficient life. A person with a hearing dog must maintain the dog's training in order for the placement to work. This may mean acknowledging the dog, even when there are hearing housemates present to cue the person to the sound.

 **Essential**

Hearing dogs must be well socialized and alert to their environment. They must often distinguish between several sounds and cue only the one they have been trained to alert for.

Guide Dogs

Guide dogs are by far the most common type of assistance dog and the one that the average person is most familiar with. Guide dogs are trained to assist blind or visually impaired persons. Guide dogs are highly trained, highly skilled animals. They must be able to safely negotiate city streets, office buildings, and the great outdoors with their partner's safety foremost in their minds. Guide dogs can be taught to judge height, alert to danger, and determine when it is safe to cross the street.

Of all the types of assistance dogs, the guide dog probably requires the most stable temperament and the sharpest intellect. A guide dog's job changes daily, depending upon where the person wants to go and where his handler's job and life take him. A guide dog needs perseverance to work long hours by his handler's side without tiring of the tasks at hand. The Golden Retriever seems perfectly suited for this task, since he loves to be with people and has a high tolerance for change. Guide dogs the world over bring independence to their human handlers, and many a person has admitted that without their beloved companion they just could not function.

Work Dogs Work

The Golden Retriever is by far the biggest overachiever in the world of working dogs. Never has there been a dog with quite the same desire to please or such an exceptional ability to perform the task presented to them. These are dogs that love to be with people in any capacity. They will accompany their humans to the ends of the earth, doing whatever crazy job we have dreamed up for them to do. The Golden likes to work, and many who are left without anything to do will show their displeasure by getting into trouble and otherwise wreaking havoc. If you've chosen this wonderful breed to live with, and you find yourself with more dog than you bargained for, consider what your dog was bred for, and find some meaningful work for him to do. How terrible it must be for a dog to have so much talent, drive, and dedication to work for people but so little opportunity to exercise it. If you are the owner of an unemployed Golden, find some gainful employment for your dog, and reap the rewards of a well-adjusted and contented companion. 🐾

APPENDIX A

Bibliography

Books

After You Get Your Puppy, by Ian Dunbar (Berkeley, CA: James and Kenneth Publishers, 2001).

Bach Flower Essences for the Family, by Judy Howard, et al. (London, U.K.: Wigmore Publications Ltd., 1993).

The BARF Diet, by Ian Billinghurst (N.S.W. Australia: Ian Billinghurst, 2001).

Before You Get Your Puppy, by Ian Dunbar (Berkeley, CA: James and Kenneth Publishers, 2001).

Behavior Problems in Dogs, by William E. Campbell (BehavioRx Systems: 1999).

Click for Joy!, by Melissa C. Alexander (Waltham, MA: Sunshine Books Inc., 2003).

The Culture Clash, by Jean Donaldson (Berkeley, CA: James and Kenneth Publishers, 1996).

Dog Behavior: Why Dogs Do What They Do, by Ian Dunbar (Neptune, NJ: TFH Publications Inc., 1979).

The Dog's Mind: Understanding Your Dog's Behavior, by Bruce Fogle (New York, NY: Howell Book House, 1990).

Dogsteps—A New Look, by Rachel Page Elliott (Sun City, AZ: Doral Publishing Inc., 2001).

Dr. Pitcairn's Complete Guide to Natural Health for Dogs and Cats, by Richard H. Pitcairn (Emmaus, PA: Rodale Books, 1995).

Excel-Erated Learning, by Pamela J. Reid (Oakland, CA: James and Kenneth Publishers, 1996).

Flyball Racing: The Dog Sport for Everyone, by Lonnie Olson (New York, NY: Howell Book House, 1997).

The Golden Retriever, by Jeffrey Pepper (Neptune, NJ: TFH Publications, Inc., 1984).

Help for Your Shy Dog: Turning Your Terrified Dog Into a Terrific Pet, by Deborah Wood (New York, NY: Howell Book House, 1999).

The Holistic Guide for a Healthy Dog, by Wendy Volhard and Kerry Brown (New York, NY: Howell Book House, 1995).

K9 Kitchen: Your Dog's Diet: The Truth Behind the Hype, by Monica Segal (Toronto: Doggie Diner Inc., 2002). To order, visit *www.doggiediets.com.*

Mine! A Practical Guide to Resource Guarding in Dogs, by Jean Donaldson (San Francisco, CA: San Francisco SPCA, 2002).

Natural Nutrition for Dogs and Cats; The Ultimate Diet, by Kymythy Schultze (Carlsbad, CA: Hay House, Inc., 1998).

The Nature of Animal Healing, by Martin Goldstein (New York, NY: Ballantine Books, 1999).

The New Knowledge of Dog Behavior, by Clarence Pfaffenberger (Hungry Minds, Inc., 1988).

Peak Performance: Coaching the Canine Athlete, by Christine M. Zink (New York, NY: Howell Book House, 1992).

The Power of Positive Dog Training, by Pat Miller (New York, NY: Howell Book House, 2001).

Training Retrievers for the Marshes and Meadows, by James B. Spencer (Fairfax, VA: Denlinger Publishers, 1990).

Understanding Puppy Testing, by Suzanne Clothier (Stanton, NJ: Flying Dog Press, 1996).

The World of the Golden Retriever: A Dog for All Seasons, by Nona Kilgore-Bauer (Neptune, NJ: TFH Publications Inc., 1994).

Periodicals

The Whole Dog Journal
    ✆ 800-829-9165; e-mail: wholedogjl@palmcoastd.com

Videos

Fields of Gold (Durham, U.K.: John G. White,1998).
    To order, visit *www.johngwhite.co.uk*

The Golden Retriever (Berthoud, Colorado: Golden Retriever Club of America, 1984).
    To order, visit *www.grca.org*

Grooming Your Golden (Sinking Spring, Pennsylvania: Delaware Valley Golden Retriever Rescue, 1996).

Puppy Puzzle (Aloha, Oregon: Dogfolk Enterprises, 1998).
    To order, visit *www.dogfolk.com*

APPENDIX B

Resources

Magazines and Newspapers

Dog World (weekly newspaper)
Somerfield House, Wottan Road, Ashford, Kent TN23 6LW
Tel: 01233 621877
www.dogworld.co.uk
editorial@dogworld.co.uk

Dogs Today (magazine)
Town Mill, Bagshot Road, Chobham, Surrey GU24 8BZ
Tel: 01276 858860
dogstoday@dial.pipex.com

Dogs Monthly (magazine)
Ascot House, High Street, Ascot, Berkshire SL5 7UG
www.dogsmonthly.co.uk

K9 Magazine
i-Business Centre
Oakham Business Park, Mansfield , Nottinghamshire NG18 5BR
www.k9magazine.com

Useful Addresses

The Kennel Club
1–5 Clarges Street, London W1Y 8AB
Tel: 0870 606 6750
www.the-kennel-club.org.uk

The Irish Kennel Club
Unit 36, Greenmount Office Park, Harolds Cross Bridge, Dublin 6W
Republic of Ireland
www.ikc.ie

National Dog Tattoo Register
PO Box 572, Harwich CO12 3SY
Tel: 01255 552455
www.dog-register.co.uk
info@dog-register.co.uk

Pro-Dogs and Pets as Therapy
Rocky Bank, 4 New Road, Ditton, Kent ME20 6AD
Tel: 01732 848499
www.prodog.org.uk

British Veterinary Association
7 Mansfield Street, London W6 9NQ
Tel: 020 7636 6541
www.bva.co.uk

Dogs Trust
17 Wakley Street, London EC1V 7RQ
Tel: 020 7837 0006
www.dogstrust.org.uk

RSPCA
Wilberforce Way, Southwater, Horsham, West Sussex RH13 9RS
www.rspca.org.uk

Breed Clubs and Societies

Golden Retriever Club
Tel: 01270 763849

Berkshire Downs & Chilterns Golden Retriever Club
Tel: 01635 31685

Eastern Counties Golden Retriever Club
Tel: 01255 886326

Golden Retriever Club of Northumbria
Tel: 01207 544367

Golden Retriever Club of Scotland
Tel: 01655 760394

Golden Retriever Club of Wales
Tel: 01685 371761

Midland Golden Retriever Club
Tel: 01663 734159

North West Golden Retriever Club
Tel: 0161 3680310

Northern Golden Retriever Association
Tel: 01522 811859

South Western Golden Retriever Society
Tel: 01425 653146

Southern Golden Retriever Society
Tel: 01276 473320

Ulster Golden Retriever Club
Tel: 01247 455513

Yorkshire Golden Retriever Club
Tel: 01430 861994

Dogs' Homes and Charities

Dogs Home, Battersea, London
Tel: 020 7622 3626

Dogs' Home, Birmingham
Tel: 0121 643 5211

Dogs' Home, Wood Green, Essex
Tel: 0176 383 8329

Dogs' Home, Lothian, Scotland
Tel: 0131 660 5842

Blue Cross
Tel: 0171 835 4224

National Boarding Kennel Federation
Tel: 020 8995 8331

Dogs' Trust
Tel: 020 7837 0006

PDSA
Tel: 01952 290999

RSPCA
Tel: 08705 555999

Shopping

C&V Pet Supplies
32 Kelburne Road, Cowley, Oxford OX4 3SJ
www.petsupplies.co.uk

Champion Pet Supplies
8 Horeston Grange Shopping Centre, Camborne Drive, Nuneaton,
Warwickshire CV11 6GU
www.championpetsonline.co.uk

dogstuff
Ty Cerrig, Tylwch Road, Llanidloes, Powys, Wales SY18 6JJ
Tel: 01686 412736
www.dogstuff.co.uk

Pet Company
974-976 Abbeydale Road, Sheffield S7 2QF
www.petcompany.co.uk

Pet Supermarket
Unit 54A Aidan Court, Bede Industrial Estate, Jarrow, Tyne & Wear
NE32 3EF
www. pet–supermarket.co.uk

PetPlanet
www.petplanet.co.uk

Pets24
www.pets24.co.uk

Petfoodnstuff
www.petfoodnstuff.com

Pets at Home
Epsom Avenue, Stanley Green Trading Estate, Handforth
Cheshire SK9 3RS
Tel: 0870 194 3600
www.petsathome.com

Seapets
Tel: 0845 230 4777
www.seapets.co.uk

Zoo Plus
www.zooplus.co.uk

The General Pet Store
10-13 The Cloisters, Friars Square, Aylesbury HP20 2PU
Tel: 01296 615 553
www.gpsdirect.biz/

The Pet Memorial Company
Odlings Limited, 59 New Cleveland Street, Hull, East Yorkshire HU8 7HB
Tel: 01482 324332
www.petmemorialcompany.co.uk

Index

A

Accidents, cleaning up, 31–32
Activities. *See* Sports
Acupuncture, 189–91
  finding practitioners, 191
  mechanics of, 190–91
Adoptions. *See* Adult adoption;
  Puppy adoption
Adult adoption, 41–52
  bonding and, 47–49
  feeding basics, 49–50
  first night at home, 42–43
  housebreaking and, 43, 46–47
  play time and, 48
  quiet time and, 49
  rescue groups for, 41–42, 272
  schedule development and, 45
  socialization skills and, 50–52
  training and, 47–48
  visitors and, 52, 57–58
Agility competition, 205–8
  AKC classes, 207–8
  health considerations, 206
  titles, 208
AKC breed standard. *See* Breed
Alone time, 85–87. *See also*
  Freedom, controlling
Alternative (holistic) medicine,
  185–97
  acupuncture, 189–91
  advantages of, 188
  Bach flower essences, 196–97
  chiropractic therapy, 191–94
  conventional vs., 185, 186, 187
  finding practitioners, 189, 191,
    194
  homeopathy, 194–95
  tools of, 186–87
  view of, 185–87
Assistance dogs, 263–65
  for disabled people, 264–65
  foster families for, 263
  guide dogs, 265
  hearing dogs, 264–65
  service dogs, 264
  temperament of, 263–64

B

Bach flower essences, 196–97
Back-chaining, 141–42
"Bang" (playing dead), 235–36
Bathing Goldens, 250–51
Behavior problems, 109–20
  attitude toward, 112–14
  correcting, 113–14
  digging, 114–15
  head collar for, 117–18
  jumping on people, 115–17
  leadership and, 8–9, 109–12

preventing, 8–9, 36, 56
pulling on leash, 79–82, 119
Behavior problems
 punishment and, 113
 snooping, scavenging, stealing,
  119–20
Bibliography, 267–69
Birds, retrieving, 139–40
Bite inhibition, 7, 62–63
Blind-person assistance, 265
Bones, giving up, 59–60
Bones and raw food diet (BARF),
 153–54
"Bow" trick, 230–31
Box shaping project, 130–32
Breed
 AKC standard, v, 3–4
 characteristics, 2–7
 information resources, 271–72
 origins, 1–2
 as perfect family pet, 5–6
Breeders
 contracts with, 21–22
 finding, 15–17
 good, qualities of, 16–17
 health screening, 20, 174–75,
  179–80
 housebreaking habits and,
  25–26
 responsibilities of, 18–20
 selecting your puppy, 19
 socialization skills and, 24–25,
  56–57
Breeding
 importance of, 16
 living conditions, 19
Burrs, 249–50

C

Cancer, 183–84
Cars, fear of riding in, 104–5
Cataracts, 177

CD (Companion Dog), 203
CDX (Companion Dog Excellent),
 204
Chewing instinct, controlling, 35,
 60–62
Children
 age of, for puppies, 24
 Goldens and, 6–7
Chiropractic therapy, 191–94
 adjustments, 193
 defined, 191–92
 finding practitioners, 194
 treatable problems, 192–93
Classical conditioning, 100–101
Clicker training, 69–74
 basics, 71–74
 food rewards and, 70
 labeling behavior and, 71–72,
  132–33
 overview, 10, 69–70
 shaping behaviors and. *See*
  Shaping
 using lures and, 72–73
 weaning off of, 73–74
Coat characteristics, v, 3
Come command, 77–78
Commands. *See specific
 commands*; Training objectives
Companion Dog (CD), 203
Companion Dog Excellent (CDX),
 204
Competitive obedience, 202–5
 Companion Dog (CD), 203
 Companion Dog Excellent
  (CDX), 204
 elite level, 204–5
 novice level, 203
 Obedience Trial Champion
  (OTCH), 205
 open obedience level, 204
 overview, 202–3
 Utility Dog (UD), 204–5
 Utility Dog Excellent (UDX), 205

Consistency/organization, 124–25
Contracts, with breeders, 21–22
Corn, 149
Crate training
   adult dogs, 43–45
   curbing barking during, 85
   humaneness of, 86
   puppies, 32–33
Creative thinking skills, 126

D

Diet. *See* Food
Dietary supplements, 155–56
Digestive problems, 173–74
Digging problems, 114–15
Disability assistance. *See*
   Assistance dogs
Doggie day care, 34, 63–64
Dogs, fear of other, 103–4
Dog-to-dog socialization, 62–64
Dog walkers, 12, 34
Down command, 76–77

E

Ears
   characteristics of, v, 3
   cleaning, 247–48
   infections in, 163, 247–48
   touch training, 90
Education (owner-to-be), 23–24
Elbow dysplasia, 180–81
Entropion, 176–77
Epilepsy, 181–82
Equipment, 242–44, 276–77
Exercise
   dog walkers and, 12, 34
   as energy outlet, 12, 112
   fitness and, 199–200
   goal of, 12
   low-impact, 157–58
   for obese dogs, 157–58

options, 12–13
requirements, 4
See also Sports
Eye care, 164
Eye problems, 175–78
   cataracts, 177
   entropion, 176–77
   overview, 175–76
   progressive retinal atrophy,
      177–78
   retinal dysplasia, 178

F

amily pets, 5–7
Fear period, 64–65
Fears/phobias, 97–107
   causes of, 97–99
   classical conditioning for,
      100–101
   helping relieve, 99–101
   inhibiting learning, 99
   negotiating scary situations,
      101–2
   of new people, places, 51,
      102–3
   of other dogs, 103–4
   professional help for, 106–7
   of riding in car, 104–5
   of thunderstorms, 105–6
Feet
   characteristics of, v, 3
   hair, trimming, 245
   pads, caring for, 164–65, 246–47
   touch training, 90–91
"Find my keys" trick, 143–44
Flea-and-tick products, 172, 184
Flea-related problems, 171–72
Floors, slippery, 92–94
Flyball, 200–202
Food
   allergies, 149, 155
   to avoid, 151–52

Food (continued)
  bones and raw food diet
    (BARF), 153–54
  commercial, 145–46
  corn problems, 149
  dietary supplements, 155–56
  etiquette, 59
  homemade diets, 154–55
  ingredients, 147–49, 151–52
  as lures, 72–73
  meat quality, 148–49
  natural diets, 152–55
  for overweight dogs, 156,
    157–58
  price of, 146
  for puppies, 39–40
  quality, 145–46, 147–49, 150–51
  quantities, 49–50, 156–58
  as reward, 70
Foot. See Feet
Foster families, 263
Freedom, controlling, 36, 85–86,
  112

G

Genetic screening, 20, 174–75,
  179–80
Gentle Leader, 117–18
"Go get the phone" trick, 142–43
"Go Get Your Leash" trick, 142
Golden Retriever Club of America,
  16
Grooming, 239–52
  bathing and, 250–51
  brushing basics, 248–50
  cleaning ears, 247–48
  cleaning teeth, 163, 247
  equipment, 242–44, 276–77
  mats, burrs, tangles and, 249–50
  by professionals, 87, 251–52
  regularity of, 13, 87
  restraint tolerance for, 240–41

shedding and, 249
Stand command for, 241–42
table manners, 243–44
for therapy dogs, 221–22
training, 13, 239–42
trimming nails, 245
Guarding problems. See Resource
  guarding
Guide dogs, 265

H

Head characteristics, v, 3
Head collar (halter)
  for behavior problems, 117–18
  for teaching to walk without
    pulling, 80, 81
  teaching to wear, 117–18
Health
  agility and, 206
  breeder quality and, 16, 20
  ear care, 163, 247–48
  early weeks and, 37
  eye care, 164
  grooming and. See Grooming
  maintaining, basics, 162–65
  neutering and, 165–66
  paw pads, 164–65, 246–47
  problems. See Health problems
  resources, 273–74
  screening puppies, 20, 174–75,
    179–80
  spaying and, 165–66
  tooth care, 163, 247
  vaccination schedules and, 37,
    166–69
  vaccine titers and, 167–68
  See also Alternative (holistic)
    medicine; Veterinarians
Health problems, 171–84
  cancer, 183–84
  digestive system, 173–74
  ear infections, 163, 247–48

elbow dysplasia, 180–81
epilepsy, 181–82
eyes, 175–78
fleas, ticks and, 171–72
genetic screening for, 174–75, 179–80
heart murmurs, 182
hip dysplasia, 178–80
hypothyroidism, 183
skin, 171–72
subvalvular aortic stenosis (SAS), 182
Hearing dogs, 264–65
Heart murmurs, 182
Height, v, 3
Hip dysplasia, 178–80
History, of breed, 1–2
Holistic medicine. *See* Alternative (holistic) medicine
Homeopathy, 194–95
Housebreaking
adult dogs, 43, 46–47
puppies, 25–26, 28–32
Human socialization, 56–58
Hunting, 11, 256–60
field trials, 256–57
retriever tests, 258
working certificates, 259–60
See also Retrieval training
Hypothyroidism, 183

I–L

nternational Veterinary Acupuncture Society (IVCS), 191
Intestinal blockages, 173–74

Jobs. *See* Working dogs
Jumping on people, 115–17

Kids. *See* Children
Kong toys, 85, 86
Kramer, Charles "Bud", 210

Labeling behavior, 71–72, 132–33
Leadership
basics, 109–12
controlling resources and, 110–11
elements of, 8–9, 109–10
management and, 111–12
rules, boundaries and, 8–9
Leash
retrieving trick, 142
walking without pulling on, 79–82, 119
Leave It command, 79, 119–20
Life skills, 83–95
alone time, 85–87
groomer visits, 87
stair climbing, 94–95
targeting tool for, 83–85
touch enjoyment, 89–92
veterinarian visits, 87–89
walking on slippery floors, 92–94
Lures, using, 72–73

M–O

Management tips, 111–12
Mats, 249–50
Meat quality, 148–49
Mouth handling, 91–92
Movement characteristics, v, 3
Nature vs. nurture, 55–56
Neutering, 165–66
Nighttime potty trips, 31
North American Flyball Association (NAFA), 200, 201

Obedience competition. *See* Competitive obedience; Rally obedience
Obedience Trial Champion (OTCH), 205
Opportunity, removing, 112
Orthopedic Foundation for Animals (OFA), 179, 180

OTCH (Obedience Trial Champion), 205
Other dogs
  fear of, 103–4
  play time with, 63–64
Overweight dogs, 156, 157–58, 200
Owner-to-be education, 23–24

P

Pancreatitis, 174
Paw pad care, 164–65, 246–47
Personality. *See* Temperament
Pet sitters, 34
Phobias. *See* Fears/phobias
Phone, retrieving, 142–43
Playing dead, 235–36
Play time
  adult adoptions and, 48
  with other dogs, 63–64
Progressive retinal atrophy, 177–78
"Pull off my socks" trick, 144
Punishment, 113
Puppy, at home, 27–40
  crate training, 32–33
  destructive chewing and, 35,
    60–62
  doggie day care and, 34
  dog walkers and, 34
  first night, 27–28
  food for, 39–40
  gates, barriers for, 35
  housebreaking and, 25–26, 28–32
  pet sitters and, 34
  socializing. *See* Socialization
Puppy adoption, 15–26
  children age and, 24
  early socialization, 24–25
  finding right puppy, 19
  health screening, 20, 174–75,
    179–80
  housebreaking and, 25–26
  preparation for, 23–24

rescue/shelter groups, 22–23,
  41–42, 272
  See also Breeders; Puppy
    adoption
Puppy kindergarten, 38–39

Q, R

Quiet time, 49

Rally obedience, 210–12
  judging, 211–12
  overview, 210–11
  sample exercises, 211
Rescue groups, 22–23, 41–42, 272
Rescue Remedy, 197
Resource guarding
  defined, 58–59
  food-bowl etiquette and, 59
  giving up bone and, 59–60
  preventing, 58–60
Resources, 271–77
Restraint tolerance, 240–41
Retinal dysplasia, 178
Retrieval training, 135–44
  without force, 137–39
  hunt tests and, 258
  natural abilities for, 135–36
  with positive reinforcement,
    137–39
  retrieving birds, 139–40
  shaping, 136–37
  tricks involving, 140–44
  working certificates and, 259–60
"Roll over" trick, 233–35
Rules, boundaries, 8–11, 36. *See
  also* Life skills; Socialization;
  Training; Training objectives

S

"Say you're sorry" trick, 236–37
Scary situations, negotiating, 101–2

Scavenging, 119–20
Schedule development, 45
Search-and-rescue dogs, 260–62
  handlers for, 262
  qualities of, 261
  training, 262
Seizures, 181–82
Service dogs, 264
Shaping, 127–33
  back-chaining and, 141–42
  behavior on cue, 132–33
  building relationship for, 123
  clicker training for, 69–74
  defined, 127
  with defined goal, 132
  without defined goal, 130–31
  free shaping, 227
  mechanics of, 127–28
  project, 130–32
  retrieves, 136–37
  retrieving tricks, 140–42
  rules of, 128–30
  super learners and, 121–22
Shedding, 249
Shelter groups, 22–23
Sit command, 74–75
"Sit Up" (and beg) trick, 232–33
Skin problems, 171–72
Slippery floors, walking on, 92–94
Snooping, 119–20
Socialization, 4–5, 36–39, 53–65
  of adult dogs, 50–52
  bite inhibition and, 7, 62–63
  breeders and, 24–25, 56–57
  chewing habits and, 35, 60–62
  doggie day care and, 34, 63–64
  dog-to-dog, 62–64
  family life and, 5–7
  fear period and, 64–65
  fun teaching approaches, 37–38
  goals, 5–6
  human, 52, 56–58
  importance of, 4, 7–8, 53–54

  lack of, results, 56
  nature vs. nurture and, 55–56
  preventing resource guarding, 58–60
  puppy kindergarten for, 38–39
  rescue/shelter dogs and, 23
  rules, boundaries and, 8–11, 36
  for therapy dogs, 220–21
  visitors and, 52, 57–58
  window of opportunity, 36, 54–55
Socks, pulling off (trick), 144
Space, controlling, 111–12
Spaying, 165–66
"Spin" trick, 228–30
Sports, 11, 12, 199–212
  activity resources, 274–76
  competitive obedience, 202–5
  dog agility, 205–8
  fitness and, 199–200
  flyball, 200–202
  Rally obedience, 210–12
  tracking, 209–10
Stairs, mastering, 94–95
Stand command, 241–42
Stay command, 75–76
Stealing, 119–20
Subvalvular aortic stenosis (SAS), 182
Super learners
  building training relationship
    for, 123
  consistency/organization for,
    124–25
  creative thinking skills and, 126
  defined, 121–22
  shaping behaviors and. *See*
    Shaping
Supplements, dietary, 155–56
Supplies, 276–77

T

Tail characteristics, v, 3
Tangles, 249–50
Targeting tool, 83–85, 227

Teeth. *See* Tooth care
Temperament
    of assistance dogs, 263–64
    family life and, 5–7
    personality and, 4–5
    specifications, v, 3, 4–5
    testing, 56
    of therapy dogs, 214–15
Therapy dogs, 5, 12, 213–23
    certification programs for,
        215–17
    facility policies on, 222–23
    functions of, 213–14
    grooming/appearance of, 221–22
    handler role, 223
    obedience skills for, 218–20
    requirements for, 216, 217–20
    social skills for, 220–21
    temperament of, 214–15
    training, 217–18
    visiting experience, 222–23
Thunderstorm phobias, 105–6
Tick repellants, 172
Tooth care, 163, 247
Topline characteristics, v, 3
Touch enjoyment, 89–92
Toys, 85, 86
Tracking tests/levels, 209–10
Training
    adding distractions during, 120
    adult adoptions and, 47–48
    alone time and, 85–87
    breaking tasks down for, 124–25
    classes, 68–69
    clicker method, 10, 69–74
    consistency/organization for,
        124–25
    crates for, 32–33, 43–45
    creative thinking skills, 126
    effective methods, 10–11
    fear inhibiting, 99
    Golden disposition for, 255
    grooming, 13, 239–42

head collar for. *See* Head collar
    (halter)
housebreaking, 25–26, 28–32
importance of, 4, 8
leadership in, 8–9, 109–12
positive reinforcement for,
    67–69, 137–39
preventing behavior problems,
    8–9
relationship, building, 123
resources, 276
retrieving. *See* Retrieval training
rules, boundaries and, 8–9, 36
search-and-rescue
    dogs/handlers, 262
shaping behaviors and. *See*
    Shaping
targeting tool for, 83–85, 227
therapy dogs, 217–18
touch enjoyment, 89–92
for tricks. *See* Tricks
See also Behavior problems;
    Life skills; Socialization
Training objectives
    behavior on cue, 132–33
    Come command, 77–78
    Down command, 76–77
    Leave It command, 79, 119–20
    restraint tolerance, 240–41
    Sit command, 74–75
    Stand command, 241–42
    Stay command, 75–76
    walk without pulling, 79–82, 119
Tricks, 225–37
    back-chaining for, 141–42
    "Bang" (playing dead), 235–36
    "bow", 230–31
    elements of, 226
    "Find my keys", 143–44
    first-grade, 231–35
    general principles, 225–26
    "Go get the phone", 142–43
    "Go Get Your Leash", 142

involving retrieving, 140–44
junior-high level, 235–37
kindergarten level, 228–31
mapping steps for, 140–41
"Pull off my socks", 144
"roll over", 233–35
"Say you're sorry", 236–37
"Sit Up" (and beg), 232–33
"spin", 228–30
training skills, 227
Trimming
    feet hair, 246
    nails, 245

U, V

Utility Dog (UD), 204–5
Utility Dog Excellent (UDX), 205

Vaccination schedules, 37, 166–69
Vaccine titers, 167–68
Veterinarians
    finding, 159–61
    first-visit expectations, 160–61
    holistic. See Alternative
        (holistic) medicine
homeopathic, 194–95
positive experiences with,
    88–89, 161–62
visiting, 87–89
See also Health; Health
    problems
Visitors, 52, 57–58
Visually impaired assistance, 265

W

Walk without pulling, 79–82, 119
Weight, v, 3
Working Certificate Excellent
    (WCX), 260
Working certificates, 259–60
Working dogs, 253–66
    assistance/service jobs, 263–65
    hunting and, 11, 256–60
    natural disposition as, 253–54,
        265–66
    range of jobs, 4, 11–12
    search-and-rescue jobs, 260–62
    sociability for, 254–55
    trainability for, 255
See also Therapy dogs

Other titles in the series

EVERYTHING
YOU NEED TO KNOW ABOUT...

£9.99 ISBN: 0 7153 2060 2   **£9.99** ISBN: 0 7153 2062 9

THE
EVERYTHING
Dog Breed Guides

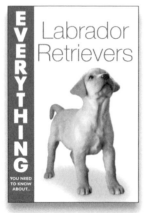

£7.99 ISBN: 0 7153 2331 8

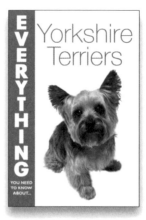

£7.99 ISBN: 0 7153 2332 6

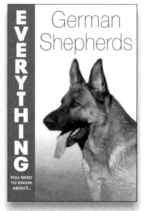

£7.99 ISBN-13: 978 0 7153 2493 6
ISBN-10: 0 7153 2493 4

Available through all good bookshops, and through
D&C Direct, Freepost EX2 110, Newton Abbot, TQ12 4ZZ.
Telephone 0870 9908222.